ANN MILLER MORIN

HER EXCELLENCY

An Oral History of
American Women Ambassadors

TWAYNE PUBLISHERS   NEW YORK
Maxwell Macmillan Canada   Toronto
Maxwell Macmillan International   New York   Oxford   Singapore   Sydney

Twayne's Oral History Series No. 14

Her Excellency: An Oral History of American Women Ambassadors
Ann Miller Morin

Twayne Publishers   Maxwell Macmillan Canada, Inc.
Macmillan Publishing Company   1200 Eglinton Avenue East
866 Third Avenue   Suite 200
New York, New York 10022   Don Mills, Ontario M3C 3N1

Library of Congress Cataloging-in-Publication Data
        Her excellency : an oral history of American women ambassadors /
    Ann Miller Morin.
        p.   cm.—(Twayne's oral history series ; no. 14)
        Includes bibliographical references and index.
        ISBN 0-8057-9118-3 (alk. paper).—ISBN 0-8057-9142-6 (pbk. :
    alk. paper)
        1. Women ambassadors—United States.   2. United States—Foreign
    relations—1945–1989.   I. Title.   II. Series.
    E747.M73   1994
    327.2'092'2—dc20   94-27833
                                                              CIP

The paper used in this publication meets the minimum requirements of American
National Standard for Information Sciences—Permanence of Paper for Printed Library materials ANSI Z3948–1984.∞™

10 9 8 7 6 5 4 3 2 1 (hc)
10 9 8 7 6 5 4 3 2 1 (pb)

Printed in the United States of America

HER EXCELLENCY

An Oral History of American Women Ambassadors

TWAYNE'S
ORAL HISTORY SERIES

Donald A. Ritchie, Series Editor

For Lonnie
and for all the young people
who wanted to know more about women ambassadors

Contents

Illustrations

Foreword

International diplomacy long stood as a male bastion, barring women as relentlessly as did any private gentlemen's club. In the United States, no woman served as chief of a diplomatic mission until 1933; none achieved the rank of ambassador until 1949; and only a token number received ambassadorial appointments until the late 1960s. Even after overcoming the initial resistance to their entry into the diplomatic corps, women faced being slighted, undercut, and marginalized by the "old boy network." Sometimes resented by their own staffs, looked upon suspiciously by their host countries, and rarely enjoying the confidence of the secretary of state, women ambassadors had to struggle constantly to establish their authority and to prove themselves as tough and as competent as the men with whom they worked— if not more so.

Through oral history, Ann Miller Morin has captured the reminiscences of the first women ambassadors. They include Democrats and Republicans, liberals and conservatives, wealthy political donors and career civil servants; each overcame gender biases to establish herself as a diplomat. Regardless of their social, economic, and educational backgrounds, their political affiliations and ideologies, these women ambassadors faced common hurdles, shared common experiences, and preserved a common memory. Their interviews offer candid insights about presidents, the Department of State, the advice and consent of the Senate, and the role of women in international affairs, filling in a critical piece of the puzzle of twentieth-century American foreign policy.

Oral history may well be the twentieth century's substitute for the written memoir. In exchange for the immediacy of diaries or correspondence, the retrospective interview offers a dialogue between the participant and the informed interviewer. Having prepared sufficient preliminary research, interviewers can direct the discussion into areas long since "forgotten," or no longer considered of consequence. "I haven't thought about that in years" is a common response, uttered just before an interviewee commences with a surprisingly detailed description of some past incident. The quality of the interview, its candidness and depth, generally will depend as much on the interviewer as the interviewee, and the confidence and rapport between the two adds a special dimension to the spoken memoir.

Interviewers represent a variety of disciplines and work either as part of a collective effort or individually. Regardless of their different interests or the variety of their subjects, all interviewers share a common imperative: to collect memories while they are still available. Most oral historians feel an additional responsibility to make their interviews accessible for use beyond their own research needs. Still, important collections of vital, vibrant interviews lie scattered in archives throughout every state, undiscovered or simply not used.

Twayne's Oral History Series seeks to identify those resources and to publish selections of the best materials. The series lets people speak for themselves, from their own unique perspectives on people, places, and events. But to be more than a babble of voices, each volume organizes its interviews around particular situations and events and ties them together with interpretative essays that place individuals into the larger historical context. The styles and format of individual volumes vary with the material from which they are drawn, demonstrating again the diversity of oral history and its methodology.

Whenever oral historians gather in conference, they enjoy retelling experiences about inspiring individuals they met, unexpected information they elicited, and unforgettable reminiscences that would otherwise have never been recorded. The result invariably reminds listeners of others who deserve to be interviewed, provides them with models of interviewing techniques, and inspires them to make their own contribution to the field. I trust that the oral historians in this series, as interviewers, editors, and interpreters, will have a similar effect on their readers.

DONALD A. RITCHIE
Series Editor, Senate Historical Office

Acknowledgments

From its inception, this book has owed much to many people. Initial credit belongs to two individuals: Jean Wilkowski, who first conceived the idea of a study of women ambassadors, helped determine the scope of investigation, generously donated her collection of background materials, and opened doors at the highest levels of the State Department for me; and Anne Jones, formerly with Twayne Publishers, who suggested doing a book of oral histories.

Central, of course, were the women ambassadors who shared their recollections and willingly answered dozens of questions. Without their outstanding cooperation, the undertaking would have foundered. All of their stories merited inclusion, but only 14 of their oral histories are to be found in this book. The other interviewees are Eugenie Anderson, Shirley Temple Black, Patricia Byrne, Joan Clark, Sally Shelton-Colby, Frances Cook, Betty Dillon, Eileen Donovan, Millicent Fenwick, Jean Gerard, Rosemary Ginn, Theresa Healy, Marilyn Johnson, Geri Joseph, Anne Martindell, Barbara Newell, Virginia Schafer, Helene von Damm, Faith Whittlesey, and Jean Wilkowski. Sharon Ahmed, whose health precluded her fulfilling her appointment, and Elinor Constable and April Glaspie, two women who became ambassadors after their interviews with me, should also be included in this list. These stories will appear in future publications.

Oral historians Maurice Mattloff and Martha Ross provided expert advice on the techniques of conducting successful oral histories and on the ethical and legal considerations that pertain to the interviewing process. Marc Pachter and the Washington biography group discussed issues related to writing biography and provided moral support.

Advisers during the planning stages were historians Carol Becker, Perry Blatz, Joan Challinor, Samuel Gammon, Joan Hoff-Wilson, Edith Mayo, Anna Nelson, William Slany, and Barbara Miller Solomon. Madeleine Albright, Betty Atherton, Viron Vaky, and especially Robert Gordon, were among the practitioners of diplomacy who shared their expertise. Frances Burwell and Diana Cohen provided insight into the special problems confronting young professional women. Stephen Low, then director of the Foreign Service Institute, kindly made it possible for me to attend the weeklong ambassadors' seminar at the Department of State. Sen. Nancy Kassebaum described the confirmation process from the point of view of the Senate Foreign Relations Committee; the late India Edwards, who worked for Presidents Truman and Johnson, explained the White House focus; and Amedou Ould Abdallah provided a look into the way envoys from other countries at the United Nations regard American diplomats. I thank them all.

Allyson Collins and Linda Zackin, both graduate students at American University, volunteered to research and prepare background papers for several countries to which the subjects were accredited, which proved to be very helpful in preparing for interviews.

I want to express my gratitude to Lucinda Conger of the Department of State Library; to Patricia King and Ruth Hill of the Schlesinger Library at Radcliffe College; to Janet Damon of the Bureau of Drugs, Tobacco, and Firearms Library; and to the staff of the Goodhue County Library, Red Wing, Minnesota. The staffs at the National Archives and the presidential libraries have all been helpful and patient. I wish to cite these individuals: Erwin Mueller of the Truman Library; Kathy Struss of the Eisenhower Library; David Humphrey of the Johnson Library; David Horrocks of the Ford Library; Martin Elzy of the Carter Library. Several persons at the Roosevelt Library and at the Nixon Presidential Materials Project were also a great help. Senate staff member Jane Reynolds Toelkes very kindly tracked down several hard-to-find volumes at the Library of Congress, for which I was most grateful.

Colleagues who were interviewed include Edwin Adams, James Akins, Kathleen Anderson, William Blue, John Bovey, Elizabeth Brown, Pamela Burdick, Findlay Burns, Eugene Champagne, John Clingerman, Carleton Coon, David Cox, Joseph Cunningham, Robert Dalton, Willard Devlin, Milner Dunn, Thomas Dunnigan, Elbridge Durbrow, Mark Easton, John Eaves, Millan Egert, Eric Fleisher, Charles Floweree, Harry Geisel, Katherine Gerardi, Jean German, Judy Harbough, Llewellyn Hedgbeth, John Hollingsworth, Hume Horan, Betty Jane Jones, Joseph Jova, Edward Keller, Stephanie Smith Kinney, Brian Kirkpatrick, Robert Kott, Gerald Lamberty, Leo LeClair, John Linehan, Peter Lord, Peter Lydon, Leonard Marks, Jean McCoubrey, Ruth Meehan, Roy Melbourne, Richard Moose, Harvey Nelson, David Newsom, Arthur Olson, Richard Parker, Roger Provencher, Gerald Reiser, Lewis Revey, Donald Roberts, Dorothy Robins-Mowry, Fernando Rondon, Walt Rostow, Edward Rowell, Mary Ryan, Charles Salmon, Dorothy Sampas, Irene Sanders, Theodore Sellin, William Sherman, Ronald Spiers, Wells Stabler, Perry Stieglitz, Sharon Stilke, Charles Tanguy, Peter Tarnoff, Elkins Taylor, Timothy Towell, George Vest, Paul Wackerbarth, Raymond Wanner, Keith Wauchope, Linda Wauchope, Robert Wenzel, Donald Wetherbee, Mickey Wetherbee, Brooks Wramplemeier, and

Owen Zurhellen. I am greatly indebted to them all, as I am to those who asked that their names not be listed.

Relatives of women ambassadors whose testimony was invaluable were John Anderson, Jean Chesley, Phyllis Darling, Allister Farkas, Elizabeth Hedin, Rodney Hinton, Persis Johnson, Margot Pomeroy, Eugene Rawls, Vivian Rawls, Marian Sanger, and Grace Watson. Friends included Frances Adams, Pamela Burdick, Liz Carpenter, Ethel Chipowski, George Gorman, Maryann Guyol, Rodney Hinton, Margaret Hutcheson, Demetrious Jelatis, Vivienne Jelatis, Patricia Johnson, Ellen Ann LeClair, Esther Maurer, Helen Meyner, Arthur Naftalin, Jean Newsom, Anne Revey, Charles Richardson, Elspeth Rostow, Catherine Filene Shouse, and Catherine Ullrich.

Donald Dawson, Douglas Henderson, Lady Bird Johnson, Elaine Mannon, Sylvia Jukes Morris, Charles O'Donnell, and Elliott Roosevelt answered questions by mail, and Joe L. Todd procured a rare oral history tape for me. My thanks to them and to those who were interviewed by telephone: Richard Bogosian, William Canup, William Crawford, Fred Galanto, Frances Doolittle Loesser, Marquita Maytag, Marian Rondon, and Dorothy Williams.

Many of the persons listed above lent or gave me documents, photographs, or other materials for the study, as did Marion Baskin, Sara Collins, Margaret Colvin, Stephen Dujack, and Dee Hahn-Rollins. These were much appreciated.

For help in obtaining photographs, I am indebted to Sybil Cooper, Pauline Myers, Philip Scott and Robert Tissing of the Johnson Library, to Gordon Hoxie of the Center for the Study of the Presidency, and to Department of State personnel, including Kim Banks of *State* magazine and Lore Mika of Foreign Buildings Operation.

Deborah Reid of Techni-Type prepared transcripts of the women ambassadors' oral histories, and Ann Levine transcribed the interviews of friends and colleagues. Both women produced accurate and literate records, and their enthusiasm for the project provided encouragement over the months and years. Cynthia Koren restored order to the files and bookshelves following two office moves. Danielle Levine and Lee Morin read an early draft of the manuscript and made a number of thoughtful suggestions that helped shape the final product.

Donald Ritchie provided professional help throughout the many stages of the manuscript. Editors Mark Zadrozny and Cindy Buck of Twayne Publishers accomplished the difficult task of shortening the manuscript to the publisher's requirements while retaining all 15 testimonies. On a basic—and crucial—level, Ken Kraushaar and Clay Villanueva of Uni-Sol Inc. kept our computers updated and operational.

The greater part of project expenses were self-financed, although assistance has come in a number of ways. The American Association of University Women (AAUW) Educational Foundation awarded a Research and Projects

Public Service grant. Thanks to advice and information from Howard Green, the New Jersey Historical Commission awarded a grant to fund the transcriptions of oral histories by two ambassadors from New Jersey. The Minnesota Historical Society transcribed testimonies of two ambassadors from that state; Bonnie Wilson coordinated that work, and working with her has been a pleasure. The Carol Laise interview was commissioned by the Schlesinger Library, Radcliffe College, for their Women in the Federal Government Series and is used with its permission.

The Association for Diplomatic Studies and Training (ADST) endorsed the Women Ambassadors Project and generously allowed me to receive tax-free contributions through them with no service charges. These included a grant from the Anne Cox Chambers Foundation as well as gifts from individuals, including one from J. M. Bennett, Texas Historical Commission. ADST also paid travel and transcription costs for the Constance Harvey oral history. Eugene Bovis, executive director of ADST, was especially helpful. Jewell Fenzi and Foreign Service Spouse Oral History Inc. graciously processed other donations to me from individuals.

Transcripts of the oral histories will be available to the public as a separate collection in the Foreign Affairs Oral History Program at the Lauinger Library, Georgetown University, Washington, D.C., and in the ADST division at the National Foreign Affairs Training Center, Arlington, Virginia. Copies will also be available at the Schlesinger Library at Radcliffe College, Cambridge, Massachusetts.

I welcome this opportunity to thank once more Frederick Laise and Samuel Bunker, trustees for the estate of Carol C. Laise, and the trustees for the estate of Clare Boothe Luce, especially Paul Czarnowski, for granting permission to use the Laise and Luce oral histories.

Holsey Handyside, a Foreign Service colleague and family friend, deserves special acknowledgment. He has, from the beginning, supported this work with ideas, encouragement, and financial help. As a former ambassador himself, and with an encyclopedic knowledge of the State Department and the Foreign Service, he has been a superb guide and mentor all the way.

Finally, I thank my husband, Laurent (Lonnie) Morin. While it is customary to thank a spouse for patience and encouragement, in this case it is mandatory. He has continued to work part-time at the Department of State since he retired as a Foreign Service officer, but he has always made the time to do, with unflagging enthusiasm, whatever task needed to be done. Too numerous to list, these have included everything from researching to checking drafts to handling virtually all the word processing. Moreover, his patience and equable disposition have remained intact throughout. As much as mine, this is his book.

I

PRESENTING HER CREDENTIALS

For the first 155 years in the history of the United States, no woman represented this country overseas. U.S. diplomacy began officially in 1778, when the Continental Congress elected Benjamin Franklin to be minister plenipotentiary and its sole representative at the French court. Not until 1933 did President Franklin D. Roosevelt send the first U.S. woman, Ruth Bryan Owen, to be chief of a diplomatic mission, as minister to Denmark. The first woman ambassador, appointed by President Harry Truman in 1949, was Eugenie Anderson, and she, too, went to Denmark. Both women were "noncareer." The first "career" woman, Frances Willis, was sent in 1953 by President Dwight Eisenhower to be ambassador to Switzerland.

Except for token appointments—only two per president from FDR through JFK—the picture remained bleak until the social upheavals of the late 1960s made the odds slightly better for women in the ambassadorial lottery. When I began this study of women ambassadors in 1984, the list provided by the Department of State's Office of Equal Employment Opportunity contained 44 women's names, covering the 51 years since Mrs. Owen was appointed—an average of less than one appointment per year.

This book derives from that project, suggested by Ambassador Jean Wilkowski, who, while diplomat-in-residence at an American university, discovered there was a dearth of printed matter available for students curious about women in diplomacy and women ambassadors. Knowing I had once done a study about children in the Foreign Service based on interviews and questionnaires, she suggested that I write a book about women ambassadors using their firsthand accounts. She pointed out that these women were pioneers, and that by studying the first 50 years of their inclusion as envoys, I would encounter the first woman ever to serve in Africa, the first at a Muslim country, the first at the U.N. and so on. Of the names given to me in 1984, I was fortunate to be able over the years to interview 34.

Besides the full-length oral histories I compiled with the woman ambassadors, I also conducted more than 150 shorter interviews with persons familiar

1

The date 10 August 1953 marked a very important "first" for career women: Frances Willis was sworn in as ambassador to Switzerland by Chief of Protocol John Simmons. Willis was not only the first career woman to become an ambassador but also the first ambassador sent to Switzerland by the United States. Up to that time, the two countries had exchanged ministers. *Photograph by H. J. Meyle. Courtesy of U.S. Department of State.*

with them. These proved invaluable. History will eventually pass judgment on the success or failure of an ambassador. In the meantime, colleagues form opinions and pass them along over lunch tables or in office corridors, and these "corridor" reputations offered many points worth following up in the oral histories.

With the help of several diplomats, I prepared topics of discussion along four general lines of investigation. First, I wanted to find out if these women ambassadors had character or personality traits in common, explore whether these were the same for careerists and noncareerists, and look for similar early influences. Second, how successful were they? Were there reasons other than luck why some succeeded and others did not? The third consideration was to find out what effect being a female played on an each one's performance as an ambassador. What were the positive or negative effects of operating in such a male-dominated world, including interactions with people from other cultures? Finally, I wanted to know if any of these women had influenced U.S. foreign policy.

For facts about the ambassadors' careers, I combed the presidential libraries, beginning with the Franklin Roosevelt Library at Hyde Park, New York. The Lexus-Nexus computer data files at the State Department library provided a treasure of newsclips, and State's freedom-of-information service provided copies of reports from embassies at the time my subjects were in charge. My extensive readings in foreign policy and diplomacy, women's studies, and general history—including pertinent periodical literature—were augmented by information from the diplomatic files of the National Archives.

My own background provided two benefits—entrée to the principals and their colleagues, and some knowledge of the profession. As the wife of a Foreign Service officer, I experienced diplomatic life in its many forms—at a consulate, two consulates-general, and several embassies around the world. I understood an ambassador's preeminent position in the community and authority over every U.S. citizen in the country other than those in military units. I knew how the different sections of an embassy function, as well as representation and diplomatic protocol. My status as spouse allowed me to attend the weeklong ambassador's course as an observer, to take notes, and to read through the briefing book. One of the ambassadors taking the course graciously permitted me to follow her through the entire confirmation process, including her swearing-in at State. These special favors considerably broadened my understanding and were deeply appreciated.

From the transcribed oral histories, the editors and I have selected 15 that, taken together, should cover the many facets of the story, enabling the reader, as one editor said, to "know what it's like to be a woman and an ambassador." It bears saying early on, however, that the majority considered themselves ambassadors who happened to be women, not women who happened to become ambassadors. The distinction is, I think, crucial.

Selecting whom to include was difficult. Each of the 34 stories was different and fascinating, but space limitations meant choices had to be made. We decided to include larger selections of fewer testimonies rather than bits and pieces of a great many, believing this would make for a richer, more interesting book.

We wanted to offer testimonies of experiences at posts of different sizes, with different climates, cultures, and stages of economic development, located on different continents. We also wanted to select persons who would reflect the diversity of ethnic backgrounds, cultures, and religions that are our country's strength. Another consideration was to select a balance of career (eight) and noncareer (seven) appointees, from a range of professions and life-styles. Lastly, we needed careerists with experience in the four main branches of embassy work (called cones).

The selections were made from much longer documents transcribed from taped interviews. All transcriptions were done by professionals, checked against the tapes and edited for accuracy by me, then returned to the ambassador in question for review and approval. A few chose at that time to delete a sentence or two, generally any reference to living persons that might appear indiscreet, but most only corrected the spelling of names. None made any substantive changes.

The testimonies are presented here in the women's actual words. There has been some rearranging of the order in which things were said to consolidate discussion on a topic or to present events in chronological order. Much has had to be left out, but there has been no tampering with context. The ambassadors' words have not been paraphrased, and any additions made by me are bracketed.

A word about the terms *career* and *noncareer*—they are used to distinguish between Foreign Service officers and persons appointed from outside the service. Neither word is intended to be pejorative, nor is the use of *political*, which is sometimes used interchangeably with *noncareer* in this context. I discovered that many of those to whom the latter is applied take umbrage because they equate the word with political patronage. Women whose careers were in academia or with government agencies other than State were quick to deny they were "political appointees," pointing out that success at another career was why they received appointments. They believed they should be listed with the careerists. Those whose careers were actually in politics had no quarrel with either *political* or *noncareer*. All three terms are used here within the narrow definitions of diplomatic custom.

Before this study began, I agreed with most Foreign Service officers that it is a pernicious practice for presidents to name a high proportion of ambassadors from outside the service. (Since World War II noncareerists have comprised from one-quarter to one-third of all ambassadorial appointments.) Obviously, whenever political appointments are made, the number of posts available for careerists who have spent their lives working toward a top slot is reduced, and if it happens on too wide a scale, morale within the service suffers. I did not, however, appreciate the advantages that a political appointee with access to the president can bring to the execution of U.S. policy. As the testimonies of Clare Boothe Luce and Anne Cox Chambers exemplify, she can often get things done expeditiously by taking problems directly to the most powerful person in the world: the president of the United States.

Political or noncareer ambassadors fall into several groups, three of which are represented in these pages. The first category is those who were themselves politicians, such as Anne Armstrong and Clare Boothe Luce. The second group, and the one that causes raised eyebrows, is made up of those who were given embassies after contributing money to a campaign. The fortunate timing of Anne Cox Chambers's donation to Jimmy Carter will be discussed in these pages, as well as the much less opportune timing of Ruth Farkas's contribution to the 1972 presidential campaign of Richard Nixon. The irony was that Farkas, in fact, had excellent personal credentials as an academician—the third group. Others in this category are Mabel Smythe Haith, Mari-Luci Jaramillo, and Jeane Kirkpatrick.

The career diplomats came from the four Foreign Service cones: political, economic, consular, and administrative, the central sections of an embassy. Traditionally, political and economic work has been more highly regarded than consular, with administrative least valued hierarchically. (The various attachés and representatives of other agencies such as AID [Agency for International Development] and USIA [United States Information Agency] are not part of this discussion, except for the observation that the agency you represented determined your standing within the embassy.) Additionally, *how* persons entered the service could affect the way others regarded them: those who entered by passing the old three-day written tests plus oral examination felt superior to those who had risen from staff or secretarial positions or were brought in laterally from other agencies.

These perceptions reflected the prevailing American social climate in the bad old days. As times have changed, so have the terms of reference among embassy personnel. It would have been unthinkable in 1930 for an ambassador to come from the ranks of the administrative branch, and it would have been considered foolhardy ambition for a consular officer to aspire to the top. Or an African-American. Or a Hispanic. Or a woman.

Deep roots nourished the elitism of the diplomatic personnel of the United States and some other countries, particularly those on the European circuit. From the beginning, our ministers and ambassadors were selected from among the leading U.S. citizens, and for the most part they were members of the East Coast upper classes, products of private schools and often graduates of Yale, Harvard, and Princeton. They spoke foreign languages and were knowledgeable about art, literature, and music. They had the leisure and the money to live abroad and expected to underwrite their expenses and pay for the privilege of wining and dining official guests. However, education and social class, not money, were the main considerations, because Europeans put a high premium on these elements, and, to quote from Sir Harold Nicholson, a noted British diplomatist, "when foreign affairs were a class specialty, the social element was assuredly important."[1] Consuls, a breed apart, earned their living selling consular services. They were usually found at seaports and had virtually no contact with the diplomatic establishment in the capital city. The class distinctions laid down so long ago died hard, and long affected attitudes among embassy personnel.

The size of the Foreign Service has played a large part in perpetuating elitism. When Constance Harvey entered, there were still only 700 officers (there are now 4700), and it was indeed an exclusive club. There were many fewer posts, the most sought after being in Europe, the center of world power. Foreign Service officers' paths crossed and recrossed. Moreover, personnel stayed overseas for virtually all of their careers and went directly from country to country, spending little or no time in Washington. Lacking a home base, they gave their allegiance instead to the institution of the Foreign Service. To an extent, that camaraderie has continued to this day, at least within a geographic area, and it is certainly true that at the senior levels everybody knows everybody else. If it is less like a family than in Constance Harvey's day, when colleagues from all over Europe called to wish her a happy birthday, nevertheless, loyalties still run deep.

The process of making an ambassador usually begins with a list of names suggested by the relevant geographic bureau at State, members of Congress, private citizens, governors, mayors, ethnic and religious groups, friends of the president, and so on. The exception is when a president has his own choice for a particular country, in which case no other name is considered. Otherwise, the names are winnowed down to a "short list," and after a lot of jockeying between the White House and State, a final selection is made.

At that point the nominee is formally asked if she wants the job, usually by a phone call from the secretary of state, a high-ranking State official, or the president. She is told not to mention her nomination to anyone other than close family members, because secrecy is essential until the country to which she is to be accredited has agreed to take her, a process known as *agrément*, or official acceptance. (Countries rarely refuse to take an individual, but it can happen, especially if a name is made public prematurely.) Once agrément is granted, the White House announces the name of the nominee in a press release and sends the nomination to the Senate, where it goes first to the Committee on Foreign Relations. Since the United States now staffs around 165 embassies, confirmation hearings crowd the committee's calendar; usually three to six names at a time are called to be interrogated and scrutinized for their suitability. Any committee member, present or not, has the right to delay the proceedings, enabling some senators to use the confirmation process either to try to force foreign policy changes or as a bargaining chip to gain something they want for a constituent or for their state. This political game-playing can be devastating for a career diplomat, who must remain in a diplomatic no-man's-land with no place to hang her hat until a vote is taken. But in most cases the name is quickly voted out of committee and goes before the entire Senate for pro forma confirmation.

Once the majority of the Senate approves the nominee, she becomes "ambassador designate," which she remains until taking the oath of office at her swearing-in.[2] The last step in the making of an ambassador is the presentation of her credentials to the head of state of the host country. This ceremony, like the swearing-in, may be elaborate or simple in the extreme. Examples of both are found in these accounts. Nowadays, as a rule, the new ambassador withdraws her predecessor's credentials, presents her own, and then delivers a verbal or written message from her president.

There were two reasons this country, despite widespread misgivings about the murky business of diplomacy, established diplomatic missions: to advance American interests and to protect American citizens. To the founding fathers and mothers, diplomacy smacked of lies and deceit and kings and skullduggery, of which they had had quite enough with the British, but the struggling nation needed money and allies and had to have relations with other countries in order to protect its seamen, who were being captured and imprisoned.

The diplomatic protocol codified at the Congress of Vienna in 1815 has been observed ever since. The most exalted representative from a country was the ambassador, who represented a king. If he had a special mission and full powers to negotiate, he was called "ambassador extraordinary and plenipotentiary" (AE/P), and ranked first in order of precedence. Often, however, more than one ambassador plenipotentiary was present at a court. Who among them went first? The solution, which still holds, was to rank them according to when they arrived, with the earliest arrival called the *doyen*, or dean of the diplomatic corps. A minister with full power was called "envoy extraordinary and minister plenipotentiary" (EE/MP) and held lower rank.

Following the war of independence, Americans, in addition to being suspicious of "diplomatists," wanted no part of anything connected to royalty, including the title "ambassador." The men sent out by the United States represented not a person but the state (by which is meant the nation), and they therefore went by the lesser title of "minister."

Our practice of sending ministers led eventually to national embarrassment, because no matter how important the United States became, its envoys ranked below *all* ambassadors, however insignificant the country they came from. There was an irony in the situation since it could have been avoided, the Constitution in 1787 having given the president the right to appoint, with the advice and consent of the Senate, "ambassadors, other public ministers and consuls" (article II, section 3).

By 1893 the situation had become serious. Not only did our ministers sit below the salt at social functions, but their efficiency was greatly reduced by having to wait for appointments everywhere they went. That year Congress passed an act that the president could raise the rank of his envoy whenever he learned a foreign country was prepared to send an ambassador to the United States. Following passage of this act, Great Britain, France, Italy, and Germany conferred the title of ambassador on their envoys in Washington, and President Grover Cleveland returned the compliment. The shift to ambassadors, he said, "fittingly comports to the position the United States holds in the family of nations."[3] In the years since 1893, diplomatic titles have suffered from inflation, and today all our representatives are AE/P, no matter how tiny the host country or how unimportant it is to the United States.

We had no profession of diplomacy until 1915, when the diplomatic and consular functions were organized into two areas of competence with separate entrance examinations. Women's entry into either of these was unthinkable before passage of the Nineteenth Amendment in 1920, granting women the right to vote. In 1922 Lucille Atcherson applied to take the diplomatic entry exam and passed it. Next she applied to go overseas. This set off alarms at the State Department, where officials stalled, unwilling to permit such a dangerous precedent.[4] Then, in 1924, the Rogers Act amalgamated the two services. One exam was to be given to all applicants, and successful candidates were to be equally available for diplomatic or consular duties. The first combined examination was announced for January 1925, and several women applied to take it.

One can only imagine the consternation among the men at the Department of State. Its 600 Foreign Service officers, a veritable gentlemen's club, had no intention of accepting women, and they came up with a battery of reasons to support their position. One was that overseas posts with difficult climates posed "physical considerations" (which somehow did not apply to the American women clerks and secretaries working there). Then there were "adverse customs and social restrictions" that would preclude women from serving in public positions. Above all, there was the impossibility of women handling consular work involving seamen because they couldn't inspect ships or associate with rough sailors. (How this worked out in practice for Jane Coon provides one of the lighter moments of this story.) For these reasons and more, women could not serve at the majority of posts and therefore could not meet the requisite of "worldwide availability." Some of the men wanted an executive order by the president making women, blacks, and naturalized citizens ineligible to take the examinations, but Secretary of State Charles Evans Hughes overruled the opposition, saying that these would-be applicants were "entitled to fair and impartial treatment." He added the shocking rider that "it would be only a question of time before women would take their place in diplomacy and consular work just as in other professions."[5]

In 1924, in a last-ditch effort to keep out any more women, members of the Board of Foreign Service Personnel had proposed creating a combined examination that would be too difficult for women to pass. (The record of these deliberations by top State officials seems incredible today.)[6] But despite the hurdles of a three-day written test plus an oral before a board of examiners, by 1929 four women had been successful candidates. That year Constance Harvey also passed both sections, and in 1930 she became the sixth woman to be a Foreign Service officer.

Although in subsequent years more women passed the written examinations, all were disqualified by male examiners in the more subjective oral examination. (One question asked well into the 1960s was, "Do you expect to marry someday?" An affirmative answer could fail a woman.) From 1930 to 1945 no women entered the service by examination. Indeed, from 1930 to 1937, Harvey and Frances Willis were the only two remaining U.S. women Foreign Service officers, the other four having resigned. (In the late 1930s, seven other women were brought in laterally from State under special arrangements.) While Harvey never became an ambassador, she was the first U.S. woman consul general, and she deserves a place in this book because her story illuminates the pre–World War II service and is a benchmark for the stories that follow.

It cannot be overstated how important a watershed World War II was for the nation and its institutions, including the Foreign Service. By the time the war ended, world power had shifted to the United States, bringing with it a concomitant increase in responsibilities. Suddenly the United States was shouldering responsibility for rebuilding Europe and Japan, processing whole populations of refugees, and mounting a bulwark against communism. The formation of multilateral entities required more and more personnel. The Foreign Service had to transform itself. It needed more officers than could be supplied from the traditional Ivy League sources. In 1946 the Foreign Service Act was passed; along with the Manpower Act of the same year, it greatly expanded the institution. The postwar years saw an influx of persons from land-grant colleges and other public universities, few of whom enjoyed personal wealth. The net result of the personnel expansion was a partial democratization of the Foreign Service that rendered it somewhat more representative of the national demography. With movement on so many fronts, women who had manned the desks during the war were among those who moved into more responsible positions.

Secretary of State John Foster Dulles, in 1954, established a commission headed by Henry M. Wriston (president of Brown University) to combine the Foreign Service and the Department of State. As part of this, Foreign Service staff officers (FSS) were given the opportunity to became career officers (FSO) by examination (which under the Wriston program had shrunk from the traditional three days to the one-day examination used today). Some at higher grade levels, like Nancy Ostrander and Carol Laise, were required only to pass an oral and a language examination.

This was a very, very difficult time for all personnel. Shortly before the unsettling "Wristonization," the Eisenhower administration had carried out a deep reduction in force (RIF) program, and Sen. Joseph McCarthy (R-Wis.) had launched his scurrilous attack against the Foreign Service and the State Department, accusing them of being riddled with Communists. Margaret Tibbetts and Nancy Ostrander, who lived through this period, described its effects on them and the lasting damage that McCarthy's campaign did to the service.

The question of marriage has from the beginning vexed women career diplomats. A man's career was always considered more important than a woman's, and when a woman married, she followed where her husband's job led. Therefore, she could not be available to go where her country needed her and had to leave the service. No directive ever spelled out this policy, but custom was so strong that most women believed such an edict existed. Whenever a woman officer announced she was to be married, regardless of circumstances, her superior invariably asked, "When will you hand in your resignation?" The practice stopped in the 1970s, and several of those who had been forced out were readmitted. Of these, many have done very well. Jane Abell Coon is an outstanding example.

For a time, husbands of women ambassadors created a problem for both the United States and the host countries. Questions arose as to what were suitable activities for a husband to pursue at the post, but perhaps the biggest problem was where to seat him at formal dinners. (Wives of ambassadors were automatically given the status of their husbands and were no problem.) Clare Boothe Luce's husband Henry, one of the most powerful men of his time, did not cause hostesses to blench since his own achievements entitled him to a place of honor equivalent to his wife's. But it was customary after dinner for women to withdraw while the men talked to each other, and it was then that Henry Luce set protocol on its ear by joining the ladies, thereby freeing Clare to talk shop with the men. Another, and wrenching, example of role reversal happened not long ago to careerist Melissa Wells, former ambassador to Zaire, when she was forced to evacuate dependents from that violence-racked country. Among the evacuees was her husband, Alfred Wells, who was sent to safe haven while she stayed behind. The men who protested the entry of women into the service could never, in their worst-case scenarios, have imagined such an eventuality.

How to address a woman chief of mission has worried people from the beginning. In many countries it is still customary to call a chief of mission "Your Excellency," but to Americans the term sounds old-fashioned. Unfortunately, there is no female equivalent for the preferred "Mr. Ambassador," and each woman must therefore decide for herself. Many have chosen to be "Madam Ambassador," although many married women have preferred "Mrs. Ambassador." Today some opt simply for "Ambassador."

An ambassador has three basic duties: representation, reporting, and negotiating. Too often representation is taken to mean party giving, an activity that leaves diplomats open to being called "cookie pushers." While it is true that dinners, receptions, and other such events are a significant part of an ambassador's duties, they are but one tool used to convey a positive image of a country. An ambassador puts forward the national best foot in many other ways, by cutting ribbons, making speeches, traveling around the country, meeting businesspeople. When a flood devastated Salerno and Clare Boothe Luce immediately went to the Italian city, talked to survivors, and saw to the distribution of relief packages (clearly marked "USA"), that was representation. When Mari-Luci Jaramillo went into the Honduran country-side and talked to the poorest citizens about their needs and discussed democ-racy, that was representation. It can be a backbreaking job, and the U.S. ambassador has a very high profile, being constantly under public scrutiny. Women have generally handled this pressure very well, and with a gracious touch that goes far in overcoming the resentment that have-nots in many countries feel toward the haves in ours. Anne Armstrong was so outstanding at representing the United States in Great Britain that she was credited with a marked increase of positive feeling toward this country during her year there.

To do the job of reporting correctly, an ambassador must be an analyst and forecaster. She is the woman on the spot who, with her team, gathers the economic, political, and social straws and weaves them into reports. Much of this information is gleaned from local politicians, government officials, influential private citizens, and members of the diplomatic corps at those same maligned receptions and dinners. An American ambassador to France once remarked, not entirely in jest, that he had sacrificed his liver for the good of his country.

The embassy is where the ambassador resides, while the chancery is the mission's office quarters. In modern usage, however, the ambassador's home is called the "residence" and the office the "embassy." Embassies or legations are set up only in capital cities. A large subordinate office in another city is a consulate general, while a small one is a consulate. The consul general or the consul in charge reports to the embassy.

If an embassy is to run smoothly, an ambassador should either be a good manager or able to delegate responsibility. Not only must she oversee the four central sections of the embassy, but she must ensure that the representatives (attachés) of other U.S. government agencies (there may be as many as 20) are able to carry out their activities within the guidelines set for achieving the mission's larger goals. She has help and guidance in the person of the deputy chief of mission (DCM), usually a careerist, who is ready to assume any responsibility and is able to run the mission in her absence.

Regardless of how good the deputy is, the ambassador must be the leader. She sets the tone for the embassy, and it is to her that everyone will instinct-ively turn in times of crisis. She must be able to handle herself well in public. Whatever the situation, she must face the glare of publicity and explain events to the media.

Considering the complexity of the job, it is a miracle anyone succeeds, and certainly understandable that an ambassador's performance can be spotty. Did an ambassador enhance or detract from the image of the United States? Did he or she further or hinder U.S. interests? These are the important questions, whatever the sex of the president's representative.

2

THE PAST AS PROLOGUE
Constance Ray Harvey (1904–   )
First Woman Consul General 1959–1964

Constance Harvey was born in 1904 into a decorous, protected upper-middle-class world where young women were chaperoned by their mothers and protected by their menfolks. They were taught early on that their options would be limited and their ideas, except in matters domestic, would not count for much. They were turned out as proper young ladies well-prepared to produce and nurture the next generation of Ivy League men. Constance Harvey, however, had other ideas. She wanted to experience life herself, not vicariously through a husband.[1]

Her father, of English ancestry, was a lawyer who believed in classical education. Her mother, a homemaker with French roots, wanted her only child to be thoroughly conversant with French language and culture. Consequently, when Constance was seven the family moved from the country to Buffalo, New York, so that she could attend a private school. French lessons began when she was ten, then Latin, then Greek when she turned thirteen. She read constantly and "dipped into my father's big, fat books."

Her name was inscribed for a place at a woman's college when she was eight years old, although the method of choosing the school was somewhat less orthodox. The family was in New England, having attended Mr. Harvey's twenty-fifth class reunion at Harvard.

At that time they thought, "Well, we're in New England, we must try to find a college for little Constance. We'll go through by train. We'll go to Smith and we'll go to Vassar and whatever is on the way home." So we started out for Smith, but we never got to any other college because—although I did not tell my parents why—I chose Smith right away. It was because in that lovely June weather, when school was closed, we went all around that town in a wonderful streetcar which was open without a center aisle, where the conductor came along the platform outside to collect tickets, and where you could hang onto the bars with your feet and go up and down as if you were on a roller coaster. I thought, "This is where I want to go to college."

After high school, her mother took her to France where she attended the Lycée des jeunes filles in Beauvais and later the Sorbonne.

[At the lycée] we had to be in bed at a certain hour, of course, with the lights out. We slept in cubicles, not dormitories. There was never any toilet paper in the johnnies; you carried it in your pocket. And we had a washbasin in each cubicle, but I never had time to wash more than one foot before the lights went out—and my face. I'd do right foot one night, and left the next. We were allowed showers every two weeks and a bath every month, I think. I was learning—of course, I did know French—but I took a lot of work in French, translating.

The next autumn she and her mother went to Italy, where her father joined them.

This is in 1923—I saw [Premier Benito] Mussolini enter Florence for the first time. I remember him distinctly, standing up in an open automobile. The streets were lined with people, not enthusiastically. They were afraid of him.

In 1924 Harvey began at Smith and in three years earned a B.A. degree, majoring in Italian, and a Phi Beta Kappa key. Although she had no particular goal, the idea of doing something in international relations began to take hold. She turned to her Episcopal bishop for advice, and he recommended that she go to a summer school he knew of in Geneva. There she lived in a pension for international students where she met Nelle Stogsdahl, who was to become the fifth woman Foreign Service officer and "almost a sister" to Harvey.

When we left the summer school, in 1927, we decided we'd better do something to prepare ourselves more than we were already. I decided I wanted to go to Columbia Law School; that's where my father had gone. Nelle said she did, too. She wanted to live in New York. One day, when we got back to the United States, we went to see the head of the law department. It was a Friday afternoon, late. There were two gentlemen. They said, "Oh, we don't take women in the Columbia Law School." I said, "Oh, I wanted to come here so badly. My father went here." "No, we don't take women."

I looked at them, and I said, "You know, Nelle, it's too bad. We'll just have to go to Yale. We know Yale takes women." These men looked at each other and said, "Come back and see us on Monday." They must have had an emergency meeting, because on Monday they took us!

Columbia was really fascinating, and I had two wonderful professors. One really did help me, I'm sure, to get into the Foreign Service. He had been the legal adviser to the State Department for years before. I was two years at Columbia, and Nelle was only one. She took the [Foreign Service] exams the year before I did. Then, of course, she was sent to Beirut, where she met her fate and married an English Foreign Service officer.[2]

Even after earning an M.A. degree in constitutional and international law at Columbia, Harvey was still wary of the challenging three-day Foreign Service examination and so enrolled in a cram school in Washington.

I went to Crawford's Cram School. It went out of existence long ago. Angus McDonald Crawford ran it in Georgetown, in his front parlor and dining room. In those days that was *the* place to go to get really prepared for the examinations. Nelle had gone there and gotten in, and I went there in the fall of '29. Crawford didn't think I was going to get in. He had several girls there, and he didn't think any of us were going to get in. I was quite sure I was. So I did!

My father died when I had been about a month at Crawford's. My father was very supportive of my going into the Foreign Service. He had always, from my really young days, said, "I want you to marry, but I do not want you to marry for the worst of all reasons, that is, economic reasons. I want you to be absolutely able to support yourself, because you must be free to choose *not* to do it for that reason." He was terrified that I might marry one of the sons of one of his very wealthy friends. His death was a shock. I felt, "I'll never again really have someone to protect me. I've got to make it somehow."

I remember taking the exams. It was freezing cold weather, and it was very icy. I remember one of my fellow students holding me up so both of us didn't fall flat on our faces. The examinations lasted three days. We had 17 examinations, I think, all together, and then there was the oral. I didn't do so very wonderfully on the written, but I got through it. I did *very* well on the oral. I remember sitting with a couple of people in the outer room waiting to be called in. There were five examiners. The young man who was sitting next to me said something marvelous just before the door opened and I was beckoned in. He said, "Miss Harvey, walk in very slowly." And I did. I just sort of strolled into the room and sat down. I heard later that the next man that had gone in to take the exam had fallen over the rug—flat down on his face. And they flunked him! So I was very grateful to my neighbor for his good advice.

These five men were sitting with their backs to the light. I think it was sort of towards sunset, so I couldn't see their faces very well. I don't remember many of the questions they asked me, but one was—and this was in 1930— "What do you think, Miss Harvey, about the advisability of the United States recognizing Russia?" I remember I answered, "Well, I know that you gentlemen have a lot more information than I have." They looked with real pussycat grins across their faces at that. "I believe that we should. We should be very careful that there is a complete understanding that they do not try to impose their system on us." Well, they gave me a pretty good rank.

Then I took orals in languages, and a young FSO gave me my exam in oral German. Imagine! I remember he said to me in German, "Speak a little German." So I said back to him in German, "What do you want me to say?" And he laughed and gave me 100! That was about it. Oh, I remember someone who became my immediate chief years later gave my exam in oral French. I got him talking to me in French about the beautiful Romanian women. He'd been stationed in Romania. I did not take an exam in Spanish. I'd gone to Spanish summer school at Cornell, and I'd carefully concealed the fact I knew any Spanish. I did *not* want to go in that direction. I did take one in Italian. The examiner was one of the interpreters. My Italian was pretty good.

You had to know one [language], and you had to take a written in it as well as an oral. Then you were given oral exams in the others.

When Harvey entered the Foreign Service in 1930, four other women were in the service. By the next year only she and Frances Willis were left.[3] Willis went on to become the first woman to have three posts as chief of mission, and the first (and to date, the only) woman to reach the rank of career ambassador (CA). There are many reasons why Harvey did not achieve Willis's distinction.

Two are probably important: Willis had as her mentor the very influential Under Secretary of State Joseph Grew, and she was much more of an establishment player who went by the book. Harvey had no mentor and was more of a risk taker.

I think it was the fifteenth of April that I set out for my first post. Everyone in Buffalo laughed because I was just going to Canada; I was going to Ottawa. I had a little new Ford, a little yellow convertible. Our family physician, our dear friend, said, "I think you should have somebody go up with you. I'll have my chauffeur drive you up in your car, and then he can come back on the train."

So we set out. His chauffeur was a very young boy, very young. All of his belongings were tied up in a great big handkerchief that he was taking for overnight. We had a nice trip to Ottawa and arrived slightly late in the evening. I stayed at that magnificent hotel, the Château Laurier. I went in under this great cathedral entrance that it has, feeling so proud of my "coming out" as a Foreign Service officer, with my chauffeur. Then I looked at him with his little parcel, and I thought about myself, and I felt very small all over again. I wasn't a very great person after all!

I was in the consular branch of the legation.[4] It was a legation, remember, not an embassy. Only Japan and France had embassies then in Ottawa. At the frontier they asked the new minister what he was going to Canada for and he said, "I'm the new American minister to Canada." They bowed and said, "We hope you enjoy your congregation." He loved telling this, especially to reporters.

I was in Canada a bit less than a year. It was 40 below in Ottawa all winter, and everything was white. Even the animals turned white to match the snow.

It was a small group [at the legation]. We had the minister, the commercial attaché, and the first secretary and a second secretary.[5]

Harvey, although an officer, might have had clerical work fobbed off on her, but this never became an issue because "I never did learn to type." She still remembers "something terrible" she did early on.

Almost at once I lost the keys to the office, at the circus, down in the sawdust. I was horrified. I thought, "My goodness, think of all those documents." I told him [her chief] the next morning, and he said, "Oh, Constance,

I don't think anybody will ever know what that key belongs to in the sawdust." He didn't think anything of it.

About security, I remember when I was in Bern, a wonderful young American woman there as a secretary went out and walked on the street and found one of her papers floating down the street in front of her. She picked it up, and it was indeed a secret document. You see, we burned papers at that time, and we didn't have shredders. This was just before the war broke out. The Germans were burning their documents, and so we thought we'd better burn ours, too. This was a carbon; it didn't burn well.

After Canada, Harvey was sent to the Foreign Service School.

They would send us to nearby countries for a very short period before they took us into the school, because then, they said, we [the officers] would know what a passport is when we start talking about it. It was a very practical way of doing things. You got your feet wet a little bit before you went to [school].

I remember one thing very clearly, and it should be told to every class. There was some high official whose message to us was this: "You're sitting behind a desk, and the whole power of the United States government is behind you. On the other side of the desk is somebody who is wanting assistance or information or help. You must try to make things equal between you, because it isn't fair not to do so." I've never forgotten that.

In August 1931 Harvey was assigned, as a vice-consul, to Milan, where her mother joined her. About her limited social life there she expressed one particular regret.

This is one of the things I repent, that I did not look after the young women who were living abroad. They were the ones who felt lonely, and I didn't do very much. I was very class-conscious. I'm ashamed to say I really was. It always struck me as amusing that the secretaries didn't have to put their birthdays down in the book [the *Biographic Register*, which lists information about FSOs], and, of course, I did. My colleagues would call me up

18

across Europe and say, "Hello, Constance, happy birthday." I think in the beginning I felt a little pompous, being an officer.

At my first post the Japanese ambassador gave an enormous New Year's Eve party, to which I received an invitation. Well, I didn't get anybody who offered to go with me. I decided I would go alone. I had a very beautiful dress, and I went with my own car, and I had a very pleasant evening. I'm glad I did that early enough. I was often asked to dinner parties and this, that, and the other. I practically always went to these things on my own. The men would go on their own, and I would go on my own. I just got used to it, and it didn't bother me after a while.

Occasionally, Harvey discovered that a male colleague liked her "a little bit too much."

It didn't worry me very much. They weren't obstreperous. Only you could tell the difference a bit—when somebody's a little smitten, they can't completely hide it. I never had any serious problems from any colleagues. There were people who were great gentlemen in our service.

Even on her limited salary, Harvey felt fortunate in her living arrangements.

Especially when my mother became such an invalid, I had the most wonderful servants during all that time. Our salaries were cut, and I couldn't afford to pay my houseboy and a cook and a maid, so I asked them if they could take a cut too, and they said no. The houseboy came back to me, occasionally, when I needed him. Then I got others who were delighted to have a smaller wage, and I had no problem. I had a rent allowance, and it was adequate to cover the rent.

We were for a year in one very nice apartment, very high up. We had to leave there because the building was sold. We went to another one then, which was nearer the office and was a bit bigger. With two beautiful terraces outside on the fifth floor, with great balconies with roses growing over. I was there six years.

I must say, under fascism there was no funny business. I would walk home from my office—if I had something I really had to stay over for—at one or two o'clock in the morning with no thought of it whatsoever, no problem. No crime because there was a policeman in his great big black cloak on practically every street corner.

I didn't feel oppressed [by fascism] exactly. In the beginning people all said, "Oh, he [Mussolini] is doing a great deal for the country," and in some respects this seemed to be true for a while. I saw fascism come up, you see, come up and then all go to pieces, like a deck of cards.

They [Italians] began to think that Americans were rather suspicious people. At all the cocktail parties in the last year I was there, young Italian women of the high society were used as spies. They were supposed to come back and report what the foreigners were saying. This was all announced as a natural thing. It was patriotic. They couldn't do it for money; that wouldn't be proper. The government had to do something to show it was grateful for the services, so they started giving them leopard coats, which came from the leopards caught in Ethiopia. Every girl in Rome and Milan who had a spotted coat—you knew exactly who she was. It was like a uniform! Incredibly stupid. There was a lot of tension. I left in November of '38. It was just after Munich I was transferred to Basel.

I had gone to Basel unclassified. I was a vice consul when I went back to Zurich after the war. I protested against that, and the head of personnel said, "Oh, that's good enough, vice consul. You go ahead and do it." Then I became consul. That was awfully late in my career, though, really, compared to anybody else. [Harvey was a vice consul for 17 years, an unusually long time compared with the careers of her male colleagues.]

Oh, I loved Basel. Basel is a fascinating city. I want to say at this time, for the record: to be an American consul general in a European city was no great shakes. It didn't get you into the high society. But [Consul General Clarence] Spiker had come from China with one letter of introduction from an English friend of his in China to a Baseler. He was immediately surrounded by all the finest people—the great elite of Basel—and I went right in on his coattails. We literally, over and over again, went to dinners with white tie. That was the old Basel.[6] It's a very funny city, but it's also a very attractive city. It has a wonderful museum. The greatest Holbeins [paintings] in the world are there. Magnificent. We wrapped them all up in blankets and got them on a truck to get them [away from] the frontier. Most of the pictures were taken away and stored somewhere, probably in the mountains. Everybody I knew had either a machine gun on top of his house or he had everything ready to *faire sauter les ponts*, blow up the bridges. All that sort of thing was ready. German Switzerland was ready for the Germans, I can tell you that, far more than French Switzerland. They were right next to it and they were going to have none of it.

The beginning of December I went up to Bern from Basel. My mother came soon afterwards. They wanted to get me and my mother away from the frontier, I think. My mother died in Bern on the tenth of May, just a few days after Holland had been occupied. I never told her that Holland was being occupied.

She was to be cremated, and it takes three days in the canton of Bern for a permit for cremation to be issued because they want to be sure. A very good friend, who was the military attaché, said, "You can't wait three days. You've got to get a special permit to have it done immediately. We may be invaded from one hour to the next." The German army was all lined up in the Black Forest to come right down the Schaffhausen Valley through the Belfort Gap. They expected it to happen. So she was cremated immediately.

Most of the people had sent their wives and children away from the city, way down to the south of Switzerland. Then the line broke in the west, in the Ardennes. The Germans knew the Swiss were going to be a tough nut to crack; it wasn't going to be so easy. I knew about the *reduits* [fortified caves] in the mountains, where they had all of this ammunition. In the case of invasion, they were going to abandon the cities and retire to the mountains and fight from there. I remember saying to a Swiss officer, "Are you leaving your wives and children behind?" "Oh, yes," he said, "of course." That's why they were not an easy nut to crack. But the whole thing went the other way. Then France fell. All these people were on the roads in France. I thought, "My God, I'm so glad my mother's gone and safe." I didn't miss her till the war was over. No, at that time I just felt awful.

I left Bern on New Year's Day of '41. I was transferred to Lyon. The real reason was I had asked the department for a transfer. I said I felt a little lonely without my mother and didn't seem to have that much to do, and I would be glad to be sent to London or anywhere where the action was. One of my old chiefs was then in Lyon and asked for me. One of the noncareer vice consuls, also from Milan, came to Lyon, too, so that was sort of like old times for a while. You see, we were not yet at war, and we were neutral. Then I began my nefarious life. Our military attaché, General [Barnwell R.] Legge, and his wife were very, very close friends of mine in Bern. Soon after I got down to Lyon, [he] asked me if I would help him about some things that he needed help about, so I said, "You bet I will. No problem." And so I did. I got into a whole lot of business for our military attaché in Bern which did not go through the embassy at Vichy.[7]

After the war I was given the Medal of Freedom by General Legge. Quite a few people were who had been up to some monkey business just to help out. The citation had to be changed in the War Department, because at first it had been written that I'd been of great assistance, etc., etc., since my arrival in *January* of '41 in France. They changed it to *December* '41.

"Miss Constance R. Harvey, American civilian, performed meritorious service in France from December 1941 to November 1942. She maintained important

Constance Ray Harvey in Zurich, Switzerland, probably in 1945, upon receiving the Medal of Freedom, the nation's highest civilian award, for her undercover wartime work at Lyon, France. Gen. Barney Legge is at left. *Courtesy of Constance Harvey.*

liaison with French contacts, gaining valuable information on the situation in and around Lyon until the German army moved into southern France. Despite close surveillance by Gestapo agents and the French Vichy Militia, Miss Harvey continued her work with the contacts, without which much valuable information would have been delayed and important missions would have been impossible."

The citation cuts out eleven months of the time Harvey was assisting General Legge, eleven months when "we were supposed to be neutral."

I've always been glad that I could do it. I learned in Washington after I got back that the War Department had the very best information from any source on what was going on on the Russian front from Barney Legge.

When I got to Lyon I was immediately put in charge of Belgian interests. Their office was closed; everything was done in my office. I helped General

Legge in various ways. I got lots of information from the northern part of France from various quarters and by various people. That went to Legge as fast as we could get it to him, with the [diplomatic] pouch going immediately—like that! Right from Lyon, not through Vichy.

I went back and forth quite a bit to Switzerland. Sometimes Barney would come down and meet me in a field near Geneva. Once I took him a plan of all of the German antiaircraft stations in and around Paris. He turned kind of pale and said, "I'll remember this!" I thought it was pretty good, too. And I didn't have any problems. There was always a Gestapo at the border. They were always right with the French official as you left and entered France. This was not occupied France, either, but nevertheless he was there. Quite often you could spot them, because they were all over the place. The Gestapo came right into our office all the time. I always went up to Switzerland in my Ford. Fortunately, the key to the glove compartment was completely different from any other key to the car, so when I got out to show my papers to the *douanier* [customs officer], I would leave my keys conspicuously dangling in the ignition. The other key was down here around my neck under my dress. I probably turned off the engine, but I left everything open and soared right through. I learned all the tricks.

Harvey found that she was both too busy and too fascinated by her work to be frightened.

I was *determined* to do it. Of course, I've been frightened in my life, but not doing that sort of thing, not a bit. I wasn't myself involved in any routes, but, for instance, what we did do was to get out practically the whole Belgian government in exile. We got out the man who had been the Belgian attaché at Vichy with a nice Belgian passport with a picture on it that was his but with the name of somebody completely different, with a whole different life story, all signed by C. R. Harvey, in charge of Belgian interests.

I didn't make up these passports. The Belgian employee made them up, and he knew all about everything. I just signed what he brought for me to sign.

Then I was ordered back to Bern, because they were desperate to get people into Bern, for they were sure that the Germans were going to occupy southern France and Franco was going to join Hitler. I knew better, because I had a good source for knowing that that never would happen. But in any case, I and the consul—who was a very young man—were ordered to go to Bern. We all rushed back.

I finally made it with my Persian cat, with barely enough gasoline to roll into Geneva Christmas Eve of 1941, and I was glad that the head of the Swiss government had said this was the one night of the whole year when there wouldn't be a blackout, because the blackout in Switzerland was blacker than it was anywhere else—it was black! But this year there was a great big Christmas tree all full of lights. I spent the night there, and then, having left my car behind because I couldn't get any more gasoline, with the cat in a basket, we went up on the train to Bern, where we were supposed to report the day after Christmas.

I wasn't very pleased to be there. I didn't want to be there at all. I said pretty soon to the deputy, "I think I'd better go back. The consul general down there hasn't got anybody with him. He needs people back there. I think I should go back. There's not going to be this business of Switzerland being shut off." They didn't believe that. They said, "Now you people are all keyed up. You've got to relax. This is now a quiet country, and we've got plenty of interesting work to do here. You can be doing review of newspapers." So I did that for a few days, then I went back and talked to the deputy. He was a nice man. He said, "No, no." I pounded on his table and broke his inkwell, and then he said, "I'll telegraph." He telegraphed to the department, and they said, "Yes, send her back." So I was sent back, and therefore, a year later, I got interned, but I never regretted it.

[Working for General Legge] was my own independent enterprise until we got into the war, and then the consul general, who had come out fairly recently, called me and [another vice-consul] into his office, and he said, "I know all about you kids, what you've been up to. You can take me aboard now. We can share it together."

I got anything I wanted into [the diplomatic] pouch. Industrial diamonds traveled up to Switzerland quite frequently. Once, at least, I got a whole great box of gold sovereigns which was to pay part of the British Secret Service. The embassy didn't know anything about that either. These things had to be done, that was all there was to it. I knew that any kind of information would go right straight to the War Department, who, of course, would pass it right on to the Department of State, so they did know before long that I was up to shenanigans, but Vichy didn't know.

I'll tell you about one thing at the very end. We already knew that we were going to be interned by the Vichy government on the Wednesday after our landings in North Africa. On the Monday before we were to leave for internment, this Belgian, who worked so hard for Belgian interests with me, we heard that he had been taken from the military hospital where he was under military arrest, probably on orders from the Gestapo, and that he was on a train to be taken to a concentration camp.

I said to my chief, "I've got to go and see the police. I'm going at once." He said, "You can't do anything. How can you?" I said, "I've got to go. I *must* go." So I went, and I spent an hour and a half or two hours in the police chief's office and refused to leave. I said, "Look here, I went to school in France. France is a second country to me. If you don't get this man back to the hospital so that he can have the operation which he's scheduled to have, I'll spend the rest of my life working against France." Well, I cried. I didn't have to act very much, I felt absolutely inflamed with fury. I said, "I will not go to a comfortable, diplomatic internment and let that man go to a concentration camp." Finally he said, "I'll telephone." So ten minutes before the train left they got him off, and he was taken in a police ambulance back to the hospital. I followed in my car with his wife. We got in and sat down on his bed and laughed and laughed and laughed.

We were all interned, and we were sent to Lourdes. We spent about two and a half months in Lourdes. We were interned in three different hotels, and the French were kind about it. They let us go have meals in each other's hotels, provided we had a guard to take us around. The guard almost always had to be Monsieur Dupont, a very low-ranking officer in the French Foreign Service.

I went with about three other people from my hotel to another hotel one night in January of 1943. At the dinner table we began to talk about something most of us hadn't thought about yet. Instead of being exchanged, as we had expected, the Germans might think they wanted us. We talked about what would happen if they did, and whether they'd come and get us. Monsieur Dupont looked pretty troubled at this. During the blackout, as we walked home, he walked with me, supposedly taking my arm in the darkness. Well, I practically had to carry the poor little man, he was trembling like an aspen leaf. If you've really felt physical fear yourself, you'll never forget it. He was really a little Mr. Milquetoast and scared to death.

It was less than a week later the German army [took us] to Baden-Baden, where we were to spend 13 months. Monsieur Dupont went with us as the representative of the neutral government of Vichy. Then one Sunday somebody came up and said, "Monsieur Dupont is locked into his room with a German armed guard standing outside. And in another room, a bit down the corridor, Tom Cassidy, who was the attaché at the embassy in Vichy and really OSS [Office of Strategic Services, precursor to CIA], had been locked into his room, with an armed guard standing outside. "Nobody can see them. They are incommunicado." About a day later we were able to see Cassidy, but Monsieur Dupont had disappeared and we never saw him again. When we were on walks, in a long crocodile tail with the Gestapo before and behind, it was about the only time that we really could speak freely. Cassidy told a couple of us, "I've sent that man to his death. He was getting out information I was able to cook up about the results of British bombings. He was afraid to do it. He didn't want to do it, but he did it." And poor Cassidy just had to live with this.

Well, there's a sequel to this story, and it's a thrilling sequel. After the war, in the embassy in Paris, one day in walked Monsieur Dupont. And he was a changed character. What had happened was, he had been taken under sentence to be executed and put in solitary confinement in the Alexander Platz Prison in Berlin, where he was apparently forgotten for a year and a half, until he was liberated. And instead of breaking him, he had become a man!

The correspondent of the *Baltimore Sun* [Phil Whitcomb] got interned with us. He started what he called the "College of the Internees." Inside of 24 hours he had a bulletin written, and everybody was supposed to sign up for various classes to teach and classes to learn. We laughed and laughed, and we signed up just to please Phil. It was our godsend. Everybody did do things; that was very nice. I had a class in American literature, for which I had one Bret Harte book and a very small anthology, and I had four elementary school kids to teach who were Americans. I also taught Italian to adults. And, of course, I took many other interesting courses. We had practically no books, and everybody had to remember what they could. Books came later.

Harvey and her compatriots were eventually exchanged for German diplomats who had been interned in America.

You see, they wanted the military commission from North Africa captured at the time of our landings. That's what they were holding us for, but the War Department didn't let them go. Finally, the Germans said they would exchange us for the diplomats who were at the Greenbriar.

Embarking on the *Gripsholm* was incredible, marvelous. We went with blazing lights at night. These great arms came out from the ship and cast light on the ship itself, so it was clearly visible what it was.[8]

She was released in early February 1944, and by fall she was back in Europe, this time at Zurich. The war was winding down, and already the emerging super status of the United States was apparent.

I was telling you about the elegant dinners in Basel, when we were all dressed up, and the consul general had all these friends of the elite. After the war, that was very different. Instead of being looked upon as just sort of an ordinary, common, American official, people just practically fawned in front of us. They could have sent monkeys to be consul general and they would have done the same thing. The power that we had suddenly acquired just went to the heads of them, and of us.

Harvey was in Greece after the war, at the time President Truman was going all out to rebuild that ravaged country through the auspices of the Marshall Plan, which evolved into the U.S. AID program. By the time Harvey went to Bonn in the early 1950s, the United States was firmly established at the head of the Western alliance. The power of the country was naturally reflected in the authority of the diplomats assigned to carry out policy.

I was made the head of a group of Americans which dealt only with the representatives of other Allied embassies in Bonn. What happened was that once or twice a month we met with the Allies who were not in the military government, the others like the Belgians, the Spaniards, and Dutch. It seems to me we did have a Frenchman in there. We told them what we thought they ought to know. We had a meeting ahead of time to decide what we should *not* tell our friends and allies about what was going on in Germany. I did that for several months, prepared what we had decided to do, and reported on what we had done. They just left us to make these decisions. It was really quite remarkable when I think of it now—the people sort of respectfully receiving the crumbs from my table.

Constance Harvey, except for very brief periods, had been out of the United States since 1930. In 1955 she was obliged, for statutory reasons, to return for assignment to the department. Like most Foreign Service careerists, she did not look forward to it.

I didn't know what I was going to do. I had to go shopping around to get a job. To my great relief [a friend in the Office of Western European affairs] said, "I'll take you."

To my surprise, I rather enjoyed my time at the department. You know there are kennel dogs and field dogs, and I was a field dog. I did not want to go back to the department, but when I did I was quite happy there during those four years.

One of the prominent Italian cabinet members was coming and I was to host a lunch for him. My chief said, "You can use my privileges at the Metropolitan Club." Then just the morning of the lunch—a couple hours before—somebody came in and said, "Don't you realize that no woman can go into the club until after five o'clock?" So they had to get another younger officer to take the lunch. Some months later, when I was faced with another big lunch, I gave it at Blair House, where they couldn't turn me down and didn't want to turn me down.

[Clare Boothe Luce] used to come for meetings in Washington, and I always sat in on those. [Harvey was in charge of Italian and Austrian affairs.] I think it's one of those meetings where I realized she seemed to me like a very bright, brilliant child who just couldn't wait to speak her piece. A precocious child. She had a difficult gift, a gift which is also a great handicap at the same time. She couldn't resist a *bon mot*. But she was brilliant, she was really a brilliant person. She was usually late for everything, but I didn't point this out. Once the man who later became the Italian ambassador to Washington did. John Foster [Dulles] trotted right along behind her and picked up her things off the floor. Oh, yes, he did.

[Frances Willis] was regarded with the greatest admiration by her colleagues, including me. She was, to me, *the* great lady of the Foreign Service so far. She got ahead very fast. She didn't let herself be vice-consul very long. She got herself out of any kind of job that was really menial. I spent the whole of my youth in the Foreign Service doing things that I felt were beneath my abilities, to tell you the truth. That was true for many men also.

Most men, however, also received help and guidance from their male chiefs and coworkers.

It was just natural for them to do it. I didn't feel it was wrong for them to do it, but I thought they ought to have done it with me, too. I don't know why I never suggested it to them. I suppose I hadn't quite put it in words yet, but I realized that this was one of the real problems at my time in the service, which was with my whole career: that I was never really given any guidance—or practically none.

I knew I was discriminated against, but I didn't expect to have anything else.

I knew [before taking the exams] it was not going to be that simple. Do you know what I honestly felt? I very much doubt that if I'd been a man I would have gone into the Foreign Service. Because it wouldn't have been intriguing to me. What I should love to have done—if I had been a man, but I never particularly wanted to be one—I'd have wanted to be an international, private lawyer. I knew if I tried for this as a woman, I'd be writing a brief for a man the rest of my life. I never would have gotten anywhere at all.

But it intrigued me to go into [the Foreign Service] as a woman and see what would happen. I don't know whether it would have made any difference if I'd been a man; it might not have. When I was at Milan one time, the embassy in Rome telephoned up and said they wanted me to go and take charge in Malta, that the officer was going to be away for a few months and they wanted me to go down there. And my chief wouldn't let me go. He said he couldn't spare me, but I'm not sure that was the only reason. I don't think he approved of it, [for me] to go to Malta to take charge. I was sorry not to do that. That would have been interesting, and that was fairly early in my career.

In 1959 Harvey was made consul general to Strasbourg, France, an assignment that meant a great deal to her.

That was my greatest satisfaction—to have my own post. I really felt at home in it, and I enjoyed it. I think they were glad to have me. Everybody in Strasbourg was very kind to me.

3

LA SIGNORA D'AMERICA
Clare Boothe Luce (1903–1987)
Italy 1953–1956

Movie stars aside, it can be argued that Clare Boothe Luce was second only to Eleanor Roosevelt in name recognition among American women in the middle of the twentieth century. Successful as a magazine editor, author, journalist, and playwright, she went on to become a U.S. congresswoman, from Connecticut. She and her second husband, Henry Luce, were friends of the cognoscenti on three continents and moved in the most glittering social firmament, themselves stars of the first magnitude. They were unique as a couple, both being successful as individuals, but her enemies whispered that her later successes came about because she was the wife of the powerful, rich, and influential owner of the Time-Life publishing empire. But, in fact, her vivacity and wit and skill as a hostess played no small part in bringing him into social prominence.[1]

Clare Boothe Luce was gifted lavishly at birth with energy, brains, beauty, and determination, but she was also endowed with a sizzling wit and a caustic tongue. It is true, as Constance Harvey says, that she couldn't resist a bon mot, but one cannot help wondering how much of her need to "show off" was a result of having to cope with the constant barrage of put-downs any high-achieving woman faced in the first half of this century.

In 1952, when Gen. Dwight D. Eisenhower was elected president, he maintained that he owed his victory only to the American people and not to any lobby or interest group. This was, to say the least, disingenuous, because, of course, like all presidents, Eisenhower owed his success in part to others. Prominent among them was Henry Luce, who effectively had used his Time and Life magazines to promote Eisenhower's candidacy over that of Sen. Robert Taft of Ohio before the Republican National Convention, and in the subsequent campaign against the Democratic nominee, Gov. Adlai E. Stevenson of Illinois. Luce's magazines influenced millions to vote Republican. Clare also did her share of campaigning and gave over 40 speeches for Ike. There is no question he was in their debt.

Clare Boothe Luce, former U.S. ambassador to Italy, in her retirement years. Luce was the first woman to represent the United States at a major embassy. *Photograph by Carl Mydans. Courtesy of Clare Boothe Luce.*

There was reason to believe Henry Luce wanted to become ambassador to Great Britain, and Eisenhower, perhaps leery of sending out such an outspoken man as his emissary, may have preferred to pay his debt to the Luces through Clare, by naming her ambassador to Italy. In any case, it was a fortuitous choice. She had the ability, the brains, and the background to succeed, and certainly the timing was right for her, since she had just been defeated in a bid for the U.S. Senate. The appointment of a vocal former congresswoman to an important diplomatic mission caused a sensation on both sides of the Atlantic. When her ship, the Italian liner Andrea Doria, *docked in Naples, the crowd that came to see "La Signora d'America" had to be held back by the police, and she and her husband were spirited off via the tourist-class gangway. She was just over 50 when she became America's fifth woman chief of mission and second woman ambassador, and she faced the daunting task of overcoming hostility not only from male chauvinist Italians but from many members of her own embassy staff as well.*

Although certain writers have disparaged Mrs. Luce's efforts as a diplomat, the evidence shows her mission was successful. Her own people, including her deputy, spoke very highly of her in interviews. Perhaps the most telling argument is that she succeeded in her mandate to help contain communism in Italy.

Being an ambassador was very interesting, very rewarding, very exhausting. As a process, the diplomatic experience is very different from the political experience because, in politics, to use the phrase of one of the founding fathers, the people are the king, and you are getting your orders from the people. [The people] make the decisions, and you are supposed to follow them out. Their decisions are often very close decisions. They're often confused, they're often ignorant, they're often conflicting, so that the poor congressman is driven to guess what it is that his constituents really want. As you can't possibly please everybody, you please yourself. You do what you think is right. So the political experience is one of trying to keep your conscience and your constituencies together.

The diplomatic experience is a good deal more agreeable, because you're taking orders from your commander-in-chief. And while you do have the right, and the duty even, to disagree with the Department of State's policy (and you sometimes can change their minds), nevertheless, you have the comfortable feeling of following orders for the United States and the American people as a whole. And that's a very rewarding feeling after politics. You work like a team—that's another very agreeable thing about diplomacy. Even if the ambassador is no good, they do their best. I'm really very impressed with the way Foreign Service officers shape up those without experience. They're really wonderful.

Also, the diplomat has a great deal of privacy compared to the politician. It is a goldfish bowl as far as you are, so to speak, on parade, but you are not subject to the intrusion, at least in my day, of the press. You didn't have to account for your actions to anybody but the boss man, who was the secretary of state or the president. And your private life, while it had to be aboveboard, which is very important, your privacy, when it was invaded, was invaded by your peers rather than anyone who met you on the street who could come up and say, "I'm your constituent. Will you take me home and give me a cup of tea?" You know? And not always a cup of tea either.

My mission got off on the wrong foot. This was in the McCarthy days and most of the embassies were staffed by people of the Rooseveltian heyday when New Dealers sponsored a very, very mild and very necessary reform. I myself began as a New Dealer. [Ellsworth] Bunker was the ambassador. He had called the entire staff together and told them he would have no more [negative] talk about me becoming the ambassador.

Luce saw several reasons for this initial hostility: her sex, her marriage to a rich and powerful man, her Republican party affiliation, even her profession as a playwright. She confessed, however, to having also made a mistake early on, one that "operated against me."

After I was appointed, an interviewer came. He didn't speak—hardly a word of English—very poor English. I said I wouldn't see him unless he spoke English because my Italian was not, at that point, very good. I'd just begun my Italian lessons. I said I knew [Prime Minister Alcide] De Gasperi. I said to this interviewer, "What kind of hobbies does Mr. De Gasperi have?" There's no word in Italian for *hobby*. I finally said to him, "What does he like to do when he is not working, to amuse himself?" And very gradually got the idea through to him. He replied that he did not know the English word, but he'd say it in Italian. [So he said a word], and I said, "Oh, we have the same word for it in English: *entomology*." And he said, "Si."

Okay, we now found out that Mr. De Gasperi was interested in insects. I said, "Butterflies?" and he just didn't understand "butterflies," and I didn't know the Italian word, but I [took] "Si, si, Signora," as being agreeable. So I reported to my husband that I had made my first interesting discovery in having discussed Italy with an Italian—that De Gasperi collects butterflies. Harry had the *Time* people get a frame and box of beautiful butterflies of North America for the entomologist.

I told the State Department that I'd already picked the gift I'm taking to the [prime] minister, and they asked me what, and I said, "He's an entomologist, and he's a butterfly collector." The next thing I'm told is that I have made a serious mistake. He's not an entomologist, he's an etymologist. He collects books on linguistics, or languages.

Fine, except someone in the department thought it was so funny they [told] the press, and it gets in the press that I am so ignorant I don't know the difference between butterflies and books. But it also gets into the Italian press, where one little writer [who] was the wittiest and the cleverest of all the Italian political commentators, wrote something called "L'histoire des Papillons"; it was *pappilloni* in Italian. He said that it was appropriate that a well-known American butterfly—that was me—should bring butterflies to the man with the butterfly brain. [*Laughs.*]

Stephen Shadegg, one of her biographers, reported that Luce thought published accounts had never given her proper acknowledgment for her part in settling the problem of Trieste, the vexing territorial dispute that nearly led to war between Yugoslavia and Italy.[2]

You've seen many different versions partly because I never wanted to press my own view on anyone. I was content to let everyone figure it out the way they wanted to at the time. But the actual fact was, very soon after I arrived the prime minister ordered the Italian troops to Trieste, to the border. And I had been briefed about the so-called Trieste situation. Faced with what looked like war which was about to come, I remembered that the State Department advice had been, "When it boils up, calm it down; when it calms down, forget it." And that struck me as a recipe for constant conflict.

The Italians were doing, or the Italian leadership was doing, pretty much what leadership does in any country when in a domestic jam: trying to create a diversion with a foreign country with whom you have sufficient disagreement so that the diversion seems logical. So there it was, and I strived to find out from my [deputy] what steps we were taking, what steps I should take to get the question solved. And was told that it was probably insolvable within the present context. You know. So I wrote some letters, and got back equivocal answers, and they all came to the same thing: "As soon as they calm down, they'll forget it. Forget the whole thing."

I knew it was boiling up again, because the situation in Italy was such that the next prime minister, and the next, would all return to Trieste to settle their own political disagreements. (As a matter of fact, De Gasperi said to me, "If I had had this Trieste settled, I would still be prime minister.") So I then said, "Well, how do you get this thing settled?" And somebody in the embassy said, "You have to get [to] the National Security Council; you have to get it on the agenda." So I said, "How do you get it on the agenda?" And he said, "Well, you know the president. He can put it on."

Well, I did know the president. And this was one thing where it goes to show that it's important to *know*, and by *know*, I don't mean just shake his hand. I knew that Ike, President Eisenhower, was the kind of military man who never had the time to read more than a page on any question, so I sat down at my own typewriter and tried very hard to put the complicated Trieste question—it was terribly complicated—and the reasons for solving it on one sheet of paper. I said to myself, "My goodness! This guy is a soldier. If there's anything that he is familiar with, it's that famous little childhood poem, 'For the want of a nail the shoe was lost; for the want of a shoe . . .,' and so on." So I paraphrased it.

I wrote at the bottom of this letter, "Dear Mr. President, Please let us try to solve this. Put it on the agenda," or whatever. And the word came over, "Go ahead. Try to solve it." Well, cheers! And then [*laughs*], it was impossible, of course, to solve it without the British, because the occupying powers were the British and ourselves in Trieste then.

When it was all right to try to do this, and [since] it was not only all right, it was most agreeable with the British ambassador, the news was that we could put it on the agenda. [This] permitted my opposite number in Yugoslavia [James Riddleberger] to tell Tito to "lay off because we're going to get this solved." Obviously, Riddleberger was in favor of his client. I was in favor of the Italians. Anyway, everybody fell back, and the arguments began.

At what point the French latched onto it, I don't know, except to say that the French always latched onto everything *pour la gloire*, and they don't give up. [*Laughs.*] I never will forget that French ambassador who insisted that he sit in on the meetings at the American embassy and insisted that every word of everything should be translated into French and the final document should be in French. That wasn't bad enough, but we [all] had to go to the [Italian] Foreign Office, and there we finally became like a musical comedy, with the English ambassador and the American ambassador and the French ambassador marching three abreast. There would be reporters as we went in and reporters as we left. I think that went on for some time.

Trying to conduct these diplomatic negotiations in public—that's when I first realized that modern communications had absolutely ruined the diplomatic technique of getting things solved. It's really a very serious problem. So I said, "How do we get this thing where it belongs? Where it isn't in the headlines with the dope story, or whatever?" I told my husband what I had in mind, and he said, "It's worth a shot."

I made a trip back to Washington, and I went to see the secretary, whom also I knew very well, Foster Dulles, and said, "Foster, if I can get them to agree, and I'll do my best, and you tell Riddleberger to go ahead on his end, and we'll persuade the Italians to appoint a team and the Yugoslavs to appoint a team to negotiate this thing in a place where they will both agree, not in Italy and not in Yugoslavia. And then you pick a diplomat, and the British pick one to chair it, and see if they cannot decide."

Our man, Tommy [Llewellyn] Thompson, chaired the Trieste proceedings. In the end, when they began discussing the ownership of Trieste, the whole city and everything it encompassed, they hit a roadblock. It had a certain similarity to the difficulties the Israelis are having with Golan Heights. What they were arguing about was the crest of a hill, 14 acres—the size of a golf course. That's all there was: a golf course. But it was on the crest of the hill, and the Yugoslavs didn't want the Italians looking down on them, and vice versa, and there it was, absolutely, hopelessly, stuck.

Now, I was dressing to go to a dinner when a telephone rang, and I was told it was very urgent. I remember my husband was there. It was someone who'd worked for my husband, and my husband said to me, "Doesn't want to talk to me. He wants to talk to you." I got on the phone, and he said, "May I come and see you? It is really very urgent, and your husband will tell you I'm a serious man."

I was going out to dinner, but I put aside the time, and he came to see me. I'll never forget it as long as I live. He laid down a map and that's how I remember his pointing. He said, "This is all that it's about. These few little acres. Now I'll tell you what the real argument is about. The *real* argument." Even today I'll be in trouble if I tell you what real troubles it was about. All I can tell you is, there was a way in Tito's own interest, and there was a way that certain very important people in Italy would be satisfied on the question of the debt they thought was owed to them. I said to him, "Why are you telling me these things instead of the CIA?" "Well," he said, "I'm going to tell them tomorrow, but I thought you should have the first crack at it because you have worked so hard, and you're the only person that has."

So there I had the secret, but I did not have the means at my disposal of twisting Tito's arm, and there were reasons why it couldn't be twisted, even on the cables. So I was very unhappy about it and said, "I will go back to Washington." I got back to Washington, and the day before I was going to see the president there was a big dinner given at the Pan American Union, a big diplomatic dinner, enormous. And the man I sat next to was an old friend, Bob Murphy, and Bob said to me, "How's the Trieste affair going?" I said, "Bob, it's hung up because we have a little problem that I can't solve. I can take care of the Italian end, but I can't take care of the Yugoslav end because our ambassador there has gotten us painted into a corner, because he insists that there is no possible way of changing Tito's mind." (That was also part of my information.) I said—and I remember using that phrase, because it always stuck in my mind—"What we need is someone who knows Tito well enough to twist his arm." And he said, "You're talking to the man."

It always reminds me of Churchill, when we were talking about what makes a great man, and he said, "I've told you all these things, and you've forgotten the most important thing." I said, "What's that?" He said, "Luck."

Well, anyway, there I was, lucky enough to sit next to Bob Murphy, who had been in the OSS during the war and who had had OSS contacts with the partisans in Vis [Vis, Yugoslavia, Tito's headquarters]. He was on a first-name basis with Tito.

We were then giving wheat to Tito under our Marshall aid. Now, one of the unbreakable rules in the State Department was, you were not permitted linkage. Our government would not be able to marry two separate problems. Kissinger got all over that by coming right out and saying, "We're going to proceed on a quid pro quo basis." But in my day you weren't supposed to link things. So I said, "Now, if you will go over and tell Tito that unless he gives in on those 14 acres, no wheat. He won't know, because he's a totalitarian and he thinks that the State Department, the president, and everybody would act the way he would act in those circumstances. Could you go?" He said, "I can't go like that unless the president sends me."

So the next day I went to see the president. I said, "Mr. President, I only have one favor to ask, and we've almost gotten this Trieste thing solved. If Bob will stop in Rome and then go on to Belgrade, and be briefed in both places, and make his call on Tito, we can settle this thing." I think if you looked this up, you will see that he wasn't gone but three days or four days. A few days later, with great sighs of relief, Tito and the Yugoslavs signed the treaty.[3]

I haven't sought to make any great capital out of this because what is Trieste to the average American? But . . . the Italians knew I did it, and everybody in the embassy knew.

This is very funny: after I left Rome, I think the first public service job that I took was with the Carnegie Peace Foundation. They had put an awful lot of money up for articles on how nations deal with conscience. So the executive secretary came forth with a document called "La Problème de Trieste." And so help me, I took it home and read it, and I was really enchanted to discover that the French had settled it. [Laughs.]

There were various interpretations, and generally Bob Murphy was given the credit, which was due him. His visits, "surprisingly," unblocked everything. And I was perfectly happy he should have that credit.[4]

When I left, [the Italian foreign office] gave me a huge dinner at the Villa Madama. I said to [Vittorio] Zoppi, who was the head of the foreign office— that's the kind of name you don't forget—I said to Signor Zoppi, "You have all made these wonderful toasts and said these marvelous things about me. Would you privately tell me the truth why you say you're all so sad that I'm leaving?" He gave me a most unexpected answer. He said, "Because you've always told us the truth."

Now I don't mean to imply by that that other ambassadors didn't tell the truth, but I'll say this is where my congressional experience came in very useful. Knowing how Congress will vote and what the mood of the American people is, is politically of great value. Most of the things that happen in your foreign countries are comparable. It wouldn't matter so much in a country that was very rich, but it matters that we're on the giving rather than the receiving end. Most countries in the fifties were on the receiving end.

The other triumph I had, which did not make me so popular with the Italians, was what was called offshore procurement. Dr. [Vittorio] Valletta was the head of Fiat, and there were two labor unions there: one was the Christian labor union, I think that was called CHISLU, and then there was the Communist labor union. The name of the game at the American embassy was lessening the Communist vote and the Communist influence, and where it was most important was in the labor unions. The fellow who was the shop steward was the Communist who was going to put in other Communists.

Now, what kind of arm-twisting could we do which was legitimate, which wouldn't be called interference? Well, I found the recipe for that. There, again, the Congress really was very useful. The Congress had passed a bill called the offshore procurement bill. This was part of a plan to restore the industries of the French and the Germans and everybody by buying in their countries the matériel that would then be assigned to NATO [North Atlantic Treaty Organization], the hardware of various sorts for the NATO forces. This was terribly important to the Italians and even more important—most important—to the largest industrial complex of all, which was Fiat, owned by Gianni [Giovanni] Agnelli's family. Then the other important industry was the shipyards. The congressional law had a clause in it that none of these funds should be used in any way that would increase the Communist influence in any country where the funds were going. Italy was one of those countries, and it was almost on the verge [of going Communist].

This was something I had to do, and it finally came down to the point where I would either make good on what I was saying or not. You see, we can't interfere. I can't say, "You know my heart bleeds for you." My story was the same to all of them, whatever the industry, be it shipowners, automobiles, whatever it was. I always told them the same thing, which was, "Yes, I did understand that if we canceled the order it would mean unemployment, and I couldn't feel more badly about the whole thing, but the Congress would send for me and I would be fired. The next ambassador would be fired, too, if we allow any Communist-dominated factory." Which was true—true in the sense that the Congress had written the legislation. It was not quite true that if push came to shove they would have penalized the poor Italians, but I had to act as though the Congress meant what it said. And they didn't believe me. Not at the beginning.

If you could see the Italian newspapers! You cannot imagine the press I got when I canceled a very large ship order. They were building a new ship, but I canceled the contract. I said, "It's invalid. The United States will not honor or allow this contract to be signed because you just had an election and your shipyards have gone Communist." Which they had, to test me, you see. I'm sure they did it to test me. They still didn't believe it; they thought publicity would get to me. And then I canceled the second order, and then things began to happen. Very quickly.

I would have these endless conversations with Valletta, and he would send me after every one of these conversations enormous boxes of red roses. My little secretary, that I loved so dearly, used to say to me, "You know, I always know how the questions are going by the length of the stems [*laughs*], and the number of the roses that come." That was her barometer about how things were going. The nut of this was that the day came when Gianni Agnelli himself, together with Valletta, came in on a very big contract. And I said no.

This was the one that I had to say no to. Everybody else sort of zipped up and got in line, but Fiat was the biggest one of them all, and I just said, "No. No way." Gianni Agnelli pled, and Valletta begged me to do it, and I said no. Agnelli left first, and Valletta stood at the door, talking to me for a minute. Then Gianni Agnelli yelled at him and he went along out.

That night, I got the biggest bunch of roses that were ever sent, awfully nice roses. I thought, "My God, I know what happened: he ordered them before this conversation." I ran into him three or four days later, and I said, "Well, Dr. Valletta, I was embarrassed by your wonderful flowers. I know you were very unhappy when you left." And I said, "Even if you did put in the order ahead of time. . . ." He said, "No, I sent them afterward." Then he said, "You did make it difficult for us. We'll have to use our own money to buy up those shop stewards!" [*Laughs.*]

But I'll always remember one thing he said, and one thing I said to him. He said, "Don't you realize if you close us down that you are going to throw hundreds of people out of work?" I said, "No, I don't think that will happen. Every one of your papers has given wide publicity now to why I cancel orders. You know what's going to happen? Joe Boni is coming home to sit down for dinner and his wife's going to say to him, 'You vote for the Christian Democrats. We have to put the meat on the table.' I'm counting on that little Italian wife and mother to notice where [the meat is coming from]."

The archives in Congress are full of the cartoons that they wrote about me. And incidentally, my name, which has always been a misery here—you know, "loose woman," "loose talk," all that kind of thing—in Italy it was just wonderful. "Clara Lou-chay" meant "clear light." There were a lot of cartoons, many of them puns on my name, during the Trieste thing. "The light at last," you see. I remember one Trieste cartoon with two characters, one was saying to the other, "It's a strange thing. In Italy the only man is a woman." I was always shown smacking along. The Communist papers made me look like a hag. I was made to look like an awful witch, with shrunken bosom, and the papers that were for me would have me going along with bosoms pointed out—it really was very funny.

Anyway, I have this to say, I found nothing but courtesy from my colleagues. I mean *mes colleagues diplomatiques.* I had a lot of good friendships with many of them. I had a good feeling about Italy and the Italians and made many lasting friends, and in many ways, it is the heart of my life in Washington. That and congressional life is why I like to live here.

Mention of friendships led to a recollection about Frances Willis, the distinguished career diplomat.

The first woman I ever met in the Foreign Service I met under the most extraordinary circumstances, and that was on May 10, 1941. I was coming from Amsterdam and spent the night at Ambassador [John] Cudahy's [in Brussels], that was the morning the phoney war ended. I think she was the consul; I don't know what she was. At any rate, this remarkable woman became an ambassador. I think she probably was the first ambassador to Switzerland. She was a regular Foreign Service officer, a wonderful woman. I thought she was *une femme serieuse* [a reliable woman]. She was straight and very effective. I'd always thought that the women undergo the same hazard in this occupation—I mean, the ambassadorial career—as they do in federal office.

You may have noticed that whereas there are a great many women mayors and aldermen and even a number of governors, there's still very few senators or even congressmen. There were 17 women in Congress, when I was in Congress. And there are now only about 25. The problem for women is that once they have to leave their husbands, the husband must either give up his business or there's a divorce ahead of them. I mean, I refused to take the post when Ike offered it to me unless Harry would promise to spend six months with me. In those days you got three months off for the summer, so that was nine months of the year. I said, "If you'll do it, that would be only three months apart."

And the same thing is true now. Therefore, ambassadors almost by definition are going to be widow ladies or divorcées, now that [divorce] is permitted, or spinsters. And Willis was a spinster. I don't think it's a career for young women to embark on unless they are prepared, and some women are, to make real sacrifices.

We're seeing more and more women ambassadors. It doesn't distress me at all. It's a funny thing for a woman to say—that I should even suggest I might be distressed—but I've always thought, myself, that getting the job done as well as possible was a good deal more important than whether you put in a black or a woman or an ethnic of some sort, or someone who had a certain religious bent. Oddly enough, women are well qualified as diplomats, I think much better than these politicians. I mean, by nature. Not by where they went to school or anything of that sort, but by nature. Women like to strive for agreement. I don't want to sound like a member of NOW [National Organization of Women], and I never have been one either, but I think women are better negotiators.

She left Italy in 1956, and three years later, Eisenhower nominated Luce to be ambassador to Brazil. Democratic senators, led by Wayne Morse of Oregon, opposed the nomination, but she was approved in the full Senate by a vote of 79 to 11. The continued attacks on Luce became venomous and included Morse's calling her personal physician to ask if she had been under the care of a psychiatrist. (She had not.) The day after Sen. Stephen Young (D-Ohio) read into the Congressional Record *a poem entitled "The Woman with a Serpent's Tongue," Luce gave a statement to the press in which she blamed her difficulty on Wayne Morse's having been kicked in the head by a horse. Next day she sent her resignation to Eisenhower.*[5]

I've taken many a blow, especially in Congress—especially in Congress. Anyone who's been attacked by *Time* magazine took it out on me.[6]

We sent John Cabot [to Brazil]. Jack Kennedy said to me, "Clare, you've only made one mistake in your life. You've made a terrible mistake, because if you had not resigned, I would have kept you. You know that." He was a good friend of mine. I said, "Jack, you would have kept me? How would you have done that? John M. Cabot was *the* expert ambassador in the field of Latin American affairs, and the Brazilians asked him to leave four months after he got there."[7] So anyone who got there was in trouble. But do you know, I have Brazilians who say that they still want me. They still remember I didn't come.

I'll tell you a story that was never printed; or I don't think it was ever printed. [Winthrop] Aldrich, our ambassador [to the United Kingdom 1953–57], for some reason or other was not altogether a success. Somebody—it was toward the end of my stay in Rome—put it in the paper that I was going to replace Aldrich. This piece of news, which was instantly printed in Italy, not only startled me and my husband, it embarrassed us, because we had just accepted an invitation from Aldrich for a dinner that he was giving for the queen. What to do? Nothing to do but go. So we got there, and I was sitting in earshot of my husband—it was not difficult to do because he had a very loud voice—and on this occasion I couldn't be more pleased because he was sitting next to Harriet Aldrich. There was a little silence, and Harry's voice was heard to say, "Harriet, there's something I want you to know, and that is that I'm not trying to get your job. I assure you there's nothing in the rumor." Everybody laughed, and it broke the tension.

From the time I came back, [rumors] started about where I would go next. But it was too much of a strain on my marriage. The only reason that Harry consented—found it easy in Rome—was because he had an office in Rome. *Time* had an office in Paris and London and Berlin, so he was overnight away from any of his offices, and he enjoyed it. He loved to travel, and he loved parties, and altogether he was happier when he was my "spouse."

Henry Luce's willingness to be a "spouse" did not, however, extend to all of his wife's activities, namely, when she was a "very successful playwright, making a half a million dollars a year." She thought the reason was simple.

I could write my plays entirely alone. I couldn't have done the embassy thing without him, not in that [era]. I could do it now if I were younger, if I were a young woman. Today I wouldn't feel the lack, but even a male ambassador is ten times [more] effective if he has a good wife. You've got to have a wife.

Now, in one sense, [Harry] was not a "wife," in that he paid no attention to the embassy. My embassy "wife" was Tish Baldridge. And Matilde St. Clair was a marvelous woman. She was the daughter of an American and an Italian, and she spoke aristocratic Italian. She knew everybody in Italy. She had been the social secretary to the embassy since the end of the war, and she was a superb character, a very close friend of mine. I had Matilde and I had Tish. But where Harry was wonderful is that he knew inside and out what I was not very good at, the actual talk of business. Harry was great from the start on the publishing, and he was a man who understood success and how to get from the bottom to the top. All the businessmen were just as eager as possible to lunch alone, man-style, with him. So I was very fortunate.

From what I have seen of ambassadors in any given capital, the hardest-working ambassador is certain to be the American ambassador. In Rome I was always so amused by some of my [foreign diplomatic] colleagues who would play golf and tennis, and most often they'd be off on trips. I never had time to do anything but work, work, work.

By the time she left, Luce had changed the atmosphere at the embassy from hostility to one of mutual admiration and respect. It is clear that her staff appreciated her for her human qualities, especially for her sense of humor and ability to laugh at herself.

When I left, much of the original staff was still there. They gave me a decoration—wasn't a real decoration—but it had on it: "*Pazienza, Sforzo, Coraggio,*" [Patience, Effort, Courage]. So we all did very well, and it was really a great bunch of men and women.

But the most telling moment came just before Luce left Rome for good. Then, her career diplomats, who in their professional lives were the epitome of reserve and decorum, serenaded their ambassador.

They assembled outside the residence, and led by one of the political officers at the embassy, they sang "I've Grown Accustomed to Her Face."

4

TRAIL BLAZER
Margaret Joy Tibbetts (1919–   )
Norway 1964–1969

On a cool, damp day in late April 1964, a limousine with three women seated in the back pulled into the White House driveway. They were there at the invitation of President Lyndon Johnson to meet and be photographed with him as public evidence of his "interest in full utilization of the talents of women." All three had just been promoted from class 2 to class 1 in the career Foreign Service; for the Department of State, this constituted a "historically unique event." Never before had three women reached class 1 on the same list. Even for one to make it was unusual.[1]

Later, Johnson signed one of the photographs taken that day, "To Miss Margaret Joy Tibbetts, with high regard." Not long after his meeting with the women, President Johnson called a surprise press conference to announce Tibbetts was to become an ambassador.[2]

Tibbetts's career was full of milestones. She was born in Bethel, Maine, on 26 August 1919, exactly one year before passage of the women's suffrage amendment, and she stayed ahead of the pack from then on. At Wheaton College she was a Phi Beta Kappa student and graduated summa cum laude (in history). At Bryn Mawr, where she went on scholarship, she earned an M.A. and a Ph.D., again in history. She came over to the Foreign Service from State's Office of British Commonwealth Affairs, and from her first days she worked in the prestigious Bureau of European and Canadian Affairs (EUR). Except for the Congo, her posts were all in Europe. Her assignments ranged from drafting St. Lawrence Seaway legislation to serving as officer-in-charge of the consulate general at Leopoldville, Belgian Congo, to negotiating military base and atomic weapons agreements and other military matters relating to NATO, to accompanying Martin Luther King, Jr., when he received the Nobel Peace Prize in Oslo.

Duty, honor, and integrity were the yardsticks by which her parents, thirteenth-generation Mainers, lived. Her doctor father spent his life caring for the

Margaret Joy Tibbetts, U.S. ambassador to Norway, 1964. *Courtesy of U.S. Department of State.*

sick, and her mother, a trained nurse, had a special ability to "make life an adventure" for her two daughters and one son.

That son was killed in World War II, and Tibbetts, who would probably otherwise have become a university professor when she completed her Ph.D., felt a duty to aid the war effort and so entered OSS, where she became a research analyst on Great Britain and the Commonwealth. The rest of her career flowed from that appointment. Luck, of course, played a part in her success, particularly the luck of being mentored by the highly successful Frances Willis, the first career woman to be an ambassador. She was also lucky in reaching higher rank just when Lyndon Johnson sent out scouts to beat the bushes for suitable women to place in high positions.

But she was well prepared to take advantage of her breaks. George Vest, himself one of the highest achieving Foreign Service officers, says of her: "She was a brilliant person, as well as one of the most charming personalities in the Foreign Service. She was wonderfully incisive and witty, and she was a great person, one of the best Foreign Service officers I ever worked with in my 40 years in the Foreign Service. Her guidance was impeccable. Her constant courtesy and encouragement to a younger officer was always ever-present."[3]

In at least one respect, however, the customs of the times limited her. After her return from Norway, when she was a deputy assistant secretary of EUR, she felt obliged to return to Bethel to care for her elderly mother. Subsequently, she became a college professor. Had she been a man with such high rank—she was a career minister—she probably would have been given a leave of absence without pay. Instead, her resignation was accepted. Even 15 years later more than one senior man declared it regrettable that Tibbetts's talents had been lost to State when she was only 52 and at the height of her abilities. If the service had accorded her the consideration her reputation merited, she might well have outdistanced the redoubtable Frances Willis. Both women held doctorates and were very able, with comparable qualifications, although it was said Tibbetts brought "more steel" to the job.

I had a fairly good knowledge of my own position in my class, and I knew that if all went well and I stayed out of trouble, someday I'd be an ambassador. But I've always said and believed that the women's movement pressure and President Johnson's initiative of naming all these people at that point moved it up by six or seven years.

Why was I the choice of the establishment? I think that I had more experience in political work than most people. I had more political experience than most women. That's always an accident, but it had happened. When I was in the Congo, I had been in charge quite a lot by one of those quirks of fate. The man who was the consul general had a tendency to be restless, and he traveled, perhaps more than he knew. Anyway, when the inspectors came, they discovered that I'd been in charge approximately three or four of the preceding eight months. That's the sort of thing with inspectors, they must write something, you know. They made a big deal of it, so there was perhaps the feeling, "Well, she can, if necessary, operate a post."

Also, I think the last ambassador for whom I'd served, Douglas MacArthur II, than whom there is no one tougher, had given a grudging seal of approval.

I prepared myself carefully for the Senate hearings. I went through the usual things one does, and the atmosphere couldn't have been more friendly. Sen. [George D.] Aiken [D-Vt.], of course, was pleased that [the nominee was] someone from northern New England, and Sen. [J. William] Fulbright [D-Ark.] was pleased that I had a good academic background. They asked me only the mildest of questions. They asked me why I'd studied Norwegian, and I said, "Because the people in Norway spoke Norwegian." [*Laughs.*] They seemed to think that was very satisfactory.

Tibbetts was much taken by the king and his easy manner of receiving her credentials.

I became very fond of King Olav of Norway, because he was very relaxed. His system was quite simple. You went on up and handed a document to him, and I think he said, "I'm supposed to listen to a speech and to make one, but let's forget about it," so I said, "Thank you very much, sir." The president had given me a letter, and I handed it to him, and he put it on the desk, which was very large and very cluttered. I wonder if they ever found it.

Tibbetts did not inherit any particular problems aside from the "longstanding shipping problems." A "continuing issue" was the Vietnam War and its impact on Norwegian opinion. She was able to select her own DCM when the one at the post left shortly after her arrival.

He went on home leave at the end of November. During the course of the home leave, the department decided—which pleased me, although I didn't have anything to do with the decision—that they were to change, and then I was able to pick my choice. The department offered me a list of names.

President Johnson greeting (left to right) Margaret Tibbetts, Katherine Bracken, and Carol Laise in the White House Oval Office, 28 April 1964. Johnson made determined efforts to advance qualified women to positions of power and invited the three career Foreign Service officers to publicize the fact that for the first time in U.S. history, three women had been simultaneously promoted to class 1. Two of the three subsequently became ambassadors. *Photograph by Cecil Stoughton. Courtesy of LBJ Library Collection.*

I wrote them a note and said, "Don't kid me. I've been in the business. These are the longstanding, well-known dogs. [*Laughs.*] Why not give me someone from the list of good ones?" And they wrote and sent me a second list from which I picked John Bovey.

We knew each other quite well. We talked back and forth with considerable candor, of course. That's the beauty of having an old friend. You can shut the door and you speak as friends. And that's very important, because there's always so many people running around who do everything you tell them to whether it's right or not.

Her ties with the local government were congenial.

I had a very close relationship with the two foreign ministers with whom I worked. An American ambassador who doesn't have a good relationship with Norwegians is out of his mind. I mean, the American ambassador in a country like that is so important because the United States is important. I had a good enough relationship with the prime ministers, but neither one of them spoke English at that point, so that was less productive until I got so I could get along in Norwegian.

In discussing diplomatic nuances, Tibbetts described her relationship with the Soviet ambassador.

I think he's now the ambassador to London. He was learning English when I was there, and he was always very eager to practice. He wasn't a bad fellow; he was sort of a mechanical little person. You have no idea what these people are really like. He told me one day when he was practicing his English on me at the diplomatic lunch that he had a son at Moscow University, and he was very worried because the boy wouldn't obey his grandmother. I said, "You know, you don't sound a bit like somebody from another world to me." He said, "Well, I think we all have the same problems." We came and we went on official (duties), but it depended on the state of relations as to [how friendly we were]. But personally, there was no problem. We danced very gaily together at one of the diplomatic parties—he's an excellent dancer.

At that time the United States had no diplomatic relations with China. A minor diplomatic incident occurred when the Finnish ambassador invited both Tibbetts and the Chinese Communist ambassador to the same formal dinner party. There was great embarrassment on all sides, Chinese, American, and Norwegian. Asked by a Norwegian what she thought she was doing, the Finnish ambassador replied, "I thought I would make peace by bringing them together." [4] *Another form of diplomatic discourse was initiated by the Norwegian foreign office.*

There was a Norwegian contact for a long time that attempted contact with a government with which we wished to talk.[5] When the foreign minister sent for me, he said that [it] had to be just me. I had to do the Norwegian translations, because they would give me things that this man sent in Norwegian, and if I'd waited for them to translate into English, it would take forever. Eventually, one point after about eight or nine months, it looked as though it might develop into something good. With the department's permission, I got Roz Ridgway, who was then a second secretary in the political section, and we brought her in to do this, simply because it's never wise to have something which is important in just one person's hands.

Tibbetts found that her young officers were "a very mixed bag" and so followed their training closely ("I am a nut on training officers").

Some of them, like Roz Ridgway, you didn't have to train. You know, it was her first political job, but you had no problem. Just give her a subject, and she'd watch me and watch John and then she'd do it. Some of the others, if I didn't like a despatch he'd written, I'd get him in myself. Or sometimes, after I'd talked with his section chief, we'd go through it.

If you're in a country, you must remember that it is *their* country and not try to be too aggressive. I used to tell the boys at the embassy, "Remember, we're seeking information. When you want something from the foreign office, don't make a long visit. Don't come in and sit down and clear up all your points, because this man is busy and working. If you make it a short visit, you can get in anytime you want to. Remember, he's doing you a favor by sitting there, if you're seeking information."

If it's a point of negotiation, it's different. But always be pleasant and be easy. You know, a great deal of diplomatic reporting—the political reporting—it's the indirect question. You don't say, "Why are you people acting so stubbornly on this question?" You say, "Well, isn't it possible that some of your people are being a little bit obdurate on such and such?" This is the way you go into it. Subtle and indirect.

I must admit, I didn't pay much attention to the young people in the consular section, because that's the one area of Foreign Service work in which I never did anything. The administrative work I know quite a lot about, unfortunately. I'm a good executive, but not an administrator. John and I worked on [the paperwork], and we would decide privately which officer is good and which one less so. I tried to have them at the house at dinner parties and not just cocktail parties, which are a nuisance, but dinner parties, and particularly those who had some language capability. And that, again, is great training for them if they're any good at all.

Tibbetts has said elsewhere that her three major successes were in London drafting political messages, at NATO with the agreements, and being an ambassador.[6] She felt that her sex had had no great impact on these particular successes.

I don't think that many things have ever been more difficult for me being a woman, and maybe it's because I was fortunate enough to land in the heart of the department. When I went to London, I went from EUR to the political section in London. And I was always helped by the fact Frances Willis, who had been the great establishment woman, was a very good, close friend of mine when I hit London. She was very wary at first, but when she saw that I wasn't going to do the sort of thing that she didn't think was right, she let me go pretty much on my own.

There are obvious things when you are a woman that you have to compromise and adjust on. I think I've told this anecdote a million times, but when I was in the Congo, I was doing economic work, and the consul general was not much interested in it, fortunately for me. There was a fancy men's business club known as the Cercle, and the consul general said to me, "I don't know how you'll do economic work. You can't get into the Cercle to talk to people." I said, "Well, I'll do it." What's the point of making a remark like that?

Anyway, we had this report on how to establish a business in the Congo, and I was working on it. I sent the report in, and about six months after it had been in, the Department of Commerce sent me a long commendation. The consul general was very surprised, and he said, "How did you do that? You couldn't go to the Cercle or the Rotary. How could you talk to these businessmen?" I said, "Mr. ——, I've got to put you out of your misery sometime. I couldn't go to the Cercle, and I couldn't go to the Rotary, but I went to see the men in their offices." And he just sort of looked at me.

I never found anyone [who] didn't like to deal with a woman. You see, you're representing the United States; the country is so important. They don't care about *you*, but they feel about the United States. Maybe they grumbled to themselves, but they're going to grumble to themselves one way or the other.

Ninety-nine times out of a hundred, when I'd be interviewed by some women's page thing . . . they'd say, "What do you need to be a woman ambassador?" And I [would say], "Well, you need to be fairly intelligent, and you need a good digestion and a strong constitution."

The question of a woman ambassador is not, "Is she a good woman ambassador?" but, "Is she a good ambassador?" And that's the only point that matters. And it's going to matter. It's the only way, basically, in which they should be judged.

I think women have a different type of intuition. I was always helped as a political reporter because men aren't terribly observant, as every woman knows, and women are more observant. Well, this is an anecdote I've told before. When I was in Brussels, the constant argument in Belgium is the question of the language, and it's of importance to us only because it is a governing factor in Belgian politics. Ambassador MacArthur said to me, "Do we fuss about this too much?" I said, "If your friend, [Paul-Henri] Spaak [the Belgian foreign minister], is out on his ear next week because of a vote on the language issue, you'll be interested." He said, "Well, that's true."

One of the areas which was of most concern was the Waterloo district. There was a large supermarket in that district, and one Monday morning I said to the young men who worked for me (there were three of them), "Did you all go to the Libre Service Supermarket?" And they said, "Yes." I said, "What language were they talking?" Because that was the issue in the paper night and day—the election was coming up—what was the language in Waterloo? And they all looked at me. Not one of them knew.

I said, "Well, when the people were telling the children not to get in the candy, or buying meat?" No, they'd been thinking of themselves, which is what young men tend to do. And I said, "Well, just for an experiment . . ." And I called up their wives, and every one of their wives could tell me what the majority of the people were speaking. They said immediately that they were all speaking French. Some of them were Flemish people speaking French.

If you're dealing with a foreign man and you want to know what he is thinking, you apply your woman's intuition to what sort of a person he is, but don't forget what the *optique* [aspect] is from which he is looking. So you can't overdo it. I mean, you can't read things into it which aren't there.

On the other hand, Tibbetts said her sex had nothing to do with her successful analysis of the Congo and the great problems that would arise there "if things weren't done."

That [success] wasn't because I was a woman. That was because I was one of the better trained officers that had been sent to the Congo. Thirty years ago, the people they were sending to Africa were not always the outstanding officers in the Foreign Service, by any means. Also I'm articulate, so when I was debriefed, I wasn't afraid to say what I thought.

I had a lot of friends in the Congo that the consul general didn't have, because I made friends with the professors at the university. The consul general, and this is inevitable in his position—I mean, you can't criticize anyone—was strictly in the Rotary, upper-businessman class and the governor general and so forth. What the governor general tells you is what he thinks the United States government is interested in hearing.

One day a young man came in the office, and he said he'd written an article about some sociological researches he'd made in the eastern Congo and he wanted it translated. It had been accepted by a journal in Great Britain, and they had told him he had to have an English translation. Like many people, he could speak English well, but he couldn't write it. He'd gone to the British consulate, and they had said, "Don't waste our time." He wanted to know if I'd recommend a translator. Well, I was interested in the nature of the article, and I said, "I'll do it myself." He said, "You're not professionally trained." I said, "Try me," and I made the translation, and from then on we were friends. He was a professor at the university, and one thing leads to another, so I think I had much better contacts.

When I first went to London and Frances Willis invited me out to tea, she asked me if I was much interested in the women's issue, which, in 1949, was not very burning. I said no. I'd never paid much attention to it, because I'd always been too interested in getting ahead on what I was doing, and when I was in college at Bryn Mawr, everyone was a woman. I mean, the question never would arise. She said it had been her experience that you did most for women by becoming a competent officer. Well, that's what I was interested in anyway.

When I first went to Brussels, I was replacing a very old friend of mine. It was as head of the political section, and [he] said to me, "Your problem is not going to come from any of the men at the embassy. You're an old EUR hand, and that's what they like, but one of the women in one of the other sections has been agitating for two or three years on the grounds that she's not a section chief because she's a woman, and to have a woman come in as section chief, that's going to give you problems." Although [she and I] personally got along well, she was always completely convinced that what had worked for me had not worked for her. She would have liked to use the women's issue very hard. I've never been sympathetic with it, because I think a woman has to be competent to get there. When I was named ambassador and I went over to the White House to see the president, I was waiting in the anteroom and an aide to Esther Peterson, who was the consumers' adviser, came in. This aide said to me, "You know, when you were named, the huge outcry came from all these women's groups—BPW [Business and Professional Women], AAUW [American Association of University Women], Democratic Women, all of these outfits—because you had nothing to do with them." Their argument had been that since I, Margaret Joy Tibbetts, hadn't paid my dues by working in the feminist movements and the Democratic National Women's Committee, I didn't deserve to be named.

Since I'm a beneficiary, I shouldn't be critical, but it was the same way when they used to have that Federal Woman's Award. I always felt that was an insult. You shouldn't nominate someone for being a good woman; you should nominate someone for being a good officer. The terrible thing is that most of the women who won the Federal Woman's Award were *outstanding*. They shouldn't have been given the Woman's Award; they should have been given the Medal of Freedom. I don't mean people like me. They discontinued it about six or seven years ago because it is not consistent with the pattern of the times.

Tibbetts discussed the highs and lows of being an ambassador.

I started as a working officer, and I liked the working part of the job. I like the political work; I enjoyed the fact there was enough substantive work in Norway to keep me interested and seeing people. At the same time, I must admit that I sometimes felt envious when I looked at my younger colleagues and I was sitting there next to the lord mayor, absolutely trapped, and they were out circulating and talking with the interesting people.

There's a great deal of the social life that is terribly dull. [But] it's important to the people. That's what I'm paid for, but I personally was not as interested in some of the social life. I wasn't as interested in the Norwegian-American Women's Club as I might have been. I wasn't as interested in the chamber of commerce luncheons, but you have to do it, and I have to be interested.

Perhaps the hardest thing is that you have to be turned on all the time, whether or not the function is worth it. You have to be just as enthusiastic about going through the sixteenth kindergarten school as you do about the first. I know enough to do that. The other thing, when you're out traveling around—which is very valuable, you must do it—you must make things move along, otherwise you can spend days and days and days going through, but you must do it in such a way that they don't think you're hurrying. It's something you have to learn to do, and you have to learn that your own staff will sometimes overschedule you or underschedule you, but you work it out.

Norwegians who were against the Vietnam War often demonstrated outside the U.S. embassy, but there was no real terrorism at that time or place.

Terrorism in Norway is if anybody throws a rock through the window. It's headlines for months. I can't imagine that Scandinavia will ever become a very fertile field for it. What you had was constant agitation and editorializing and people buttonholing you at parties and a great many people whom you respect very much telling you, sadly, that they thought the United States was on the wrong track. But the only thing to do [was] to grit your teeth and ride it out and keep cool.

I always insisted, "Don't make too much about it." If somebody breaks a window, as they did from time to time, get the glaziers right in and repair it, and don't talk about it.

Not all three areas of ambassadorial work—representation, reporting, and negotiating—appealed to her. She enjoyed reporting and negotiation, but "representation I did as a pro forma thing."

I did what I had to do and what I thought was wise, but I certainly didn't do any more than I had to do, and I always left promptly. That's one good thing about me—you could count upon the fact that at eleven o'clock I was up like a shot and out. I entertained enough to try to meet all of my obligations. I split up the money. Of course, I had the bulk of the money. You certainly don't get as much as you spend. There's always a certain amount that you can't collect for, but you have to do it anyway.

In April 1952 Roy Cohn, a member of the staff of Sen. Joseph McCarthy (R-Wisc.), and David Schine, an unpaid consultant, toured Europe looking for "communistically-inclined" officers in the American embassies and for "communist books" in the United States Information Service (USIS) libraries.[7] Tibbetts was in London at the time of their disruptive visits.

I didn't see them. They hit very hard at others. They really hit in the political section. I [had] a good friend [who worked in Far Eastern affairs], and he, I think, spent 13 years in London simply because the department didn't dare transfer him somewhere else. He was the one most affected. But I think our minister dealt with them fairly sharply, to the extent that he could. [He] did a great deal to protect the people in the embassy. He was very, very good at that. I don't mean shielding us from being asked questions or anything like that, but his attitude was, "If your conscience is clear, you can go anywhere in the world. This group has a clear conscience." And that gives you a great deal of morale booster.

I think the McCarthy period some 30-odd years ago was very, very damaging. [It] left [State] very damaged.[8] It's like a car that's been in an accident: you repair it, but somehow it's never quite the same. Because certainly the people who were in the Foreign Service, some of our most able people, were so badly hurt. Then for years and years and years, you had a lot of able people who were sounding off, mouthing policies in which they didn't really necessarily believe, simply because it was fatal not to say the right thing, and I think that was very bad.

Tibbetts described some of the challenges of an ambassador's private life.

What you have to watch if you're an ambassador is if you have personal friends—for example, I liked the air attaché and his wife very much, but I had to be careful not to see more of them than I did of the army attaché and his wife, because the military get terribly childish about this sort of thing, incredibly so. I did have a private life, and I had Norwegian friends, but I'm by nature a loner. I like to do things by myself, and I'm an intense reader. If I had an evening at home alone, all I wanted to do was sit, just sit. I'm a bird watcher and a skier. All these things I like to do by myself. I have to get out and restore my tissues.

Margaret Tibbetts was the third woman to head the U.S. mission in Norway.

Mrs. [Florence] Harriman, of course, had been a novelty. She was back in the dark ages. Frances Willis had been extremely good, and this was a great asset to me, because when I arrived, Trygve Lie [cabinet minister, formerly secretary-general of the UN] said to me, "You know, it came up in the cabinet, another woman," and Lie said, "Look, the last one was better than most of the men." And that was absolutely true. But they all liked the fact I was a professional.

When I was back in the department after I came home from Norway, one day somebody came in from Mrs. [Katie] Louchheim's office,[9] and she said, "Oh, they've just had the world's brightest idea. Wouldn't it be nice if we could get certain posts reserved for women?" I said, "That's the worst idea in the world," and she said, "Why?" I said, "Well, first of all, it would do irreversible damage to our relations with any country if they discovered that we were making them a convenience for placing women, and secondly, frankly, as one of the people who'd be considered, why should women be consigned to a particular post? Anything to do with quotas is just hopeless, and the men would laugh themselves sick. They'd be delighted if you could lock women out of certain or difficult posts."

So this is what you have to watch. I think that some posts have gotten sort of reconciled—these places [to which several women were sent] like Scandinavia, Luxembourg, and so forth. But they have discovered that if they get a professional, it doesn't [matter]. Before I went to Norway, when I was sort of in limbo—Johnson had just said I was going to be an ambassador—one of the Dutch informally asked at the department if there was a chance they would get me because, he said, they'd had a number of nonprofessional ambassadors. They knew I was a professional. The fact that you're a woman doesn't matter if you're a professional. This flattered me greatly.

This doesn't mean that a nonprofessional cannot be good; Katherine White was excellent. She was really very good, and she was very popular with the Danes, which is what counts. She kept it strictly a business, and she knew exactly what she was doing.

Roz Ridgway told me, "You know, you turned me down at one point earlier." And then I remembered dimly, and I said, "No, you can't have too many women; you've got to look at the balance of your post and relations." Then when Roz came up as a good officer, George Vest told me she was excellent, and I grabbed her. But I think that at the first stage I believed that I mustn't let personnel get the idea that all women are going to go to one post. You know, people in personnel can be very single-minded. They can think that just because *X* is a woman, you automatically want all the women

there. You have to apply the same rules. I certainly never favored women—
that would be fatal. You've got to be fair with everybody, and if you're
working with the men, they must feel that you're absolutely fair.

*In Tibbetts's opinion, the State Department guided her career. But with each
new assignment, "I landed on my feet."*

I came into [the Bureau of] European [and Canadian] Affairs. I had no
more idea that European Affairs was any more important than anything else;
it was just where I happened to land. I landed with people who trained me
very thoroughly. I got along well with them and was quick to learn. I could
see, as I got older, why I had done so well, in a way, because you never had
to tell me anything more than a certain amount of times. It was then, after
a while, that they decided to use me. I was there to be used; I was a good
instrument, so to speak. The fact that I was a woman was very helpful. Again,
Frances Willis had been right there in EUR, and it had been very useful to
EUR to be able to produce a woman political officer. They had met every
obligation laid upon them in advance with relatively little pain to themselves.

*After Norway, Tibbetts was assigned to the department as the first woman
deputy assistant secretary (DAS) and spent two years in EUR. Going into such
an active position in Washington, she did not miss the ambassadorial life.*

I didn't feel deflated. I didn't miss the attention. Some people do miss the
attention; some people do miss the social life. I didn't miss that at all, because
I was very happy to resume work.

*Two years into the assignment, circumstances obliged her to retire to Maine.
Had her career continued, she probably would have been offered another embassy,
but she would not have accepted just any post.*

If it had been a good enough embassy, yes. It had to be an interesting job, because I couldn't have taken an eating job, one of these things where you just eat around. There are enough dull aspects of being an ambassador; you've got to have some interesting ones.

5

DEDICATED PUBLIC SERVANT
Caroline Clendening Laise (1917–1991)
Nepal 1966–1973

Carol Laise prided herself on playing by the book, which toward the end of her career, she ended by rewriting. She performed the duties of positions never before entrusted to a woman, and in doing them earned respect for her sex from the institution she served. For a decade she was the most highly visible woman role model in the Foreign Service, and her success was a crucial factor in the advancement and acceptance of other women at State.[1]

Her record was unusual in many respects. Unlike the career women who had come before her, she did not come up through the Foreign Service ranks but entered at a senior level; she served as a Foreign Service officer at only one overseas post prior to her elevation to an ambassadorship. She remained more than six years at her post, under two presidents, and enjoyed the use of a government plane to visit her husband. She was the first woman assistant secretary, and the first woman director general of the Foreign Service, where she headed a task force to restructure the entire institution. Laise's recommendations were later incorporated into the Foreign Service Act of 1980.

While there is no doubt her achievements were due in large measure to her own integrity and competence—"her strength was that State felt they could trust her"[2]—two other factors were also at work: her marriage to Ellsworth Bunker, who faithfully served seven presidents, giving her entry into the highest circles of government, including the White House; and the pressure on State, brought on by the discrimination lawsuits in the 1970s, to showcase its few women with sufficient experience and seniority to be assigned to high-visibility positions.

Both her parents were college graduates and had been teachers. Laise and her older brother were raised in Washington, D.C., according to the Protestant work ethic of self-discipline and service to others. Her mother's family, of German and English extraction, came from New England, while her father's Scotch-Irish

61

and German ancestors had settled in Virginia's Shenandoah Valley. The children were both high achievers and, indeed, eventually earned adjoining entries in Who's Who in America. *Laise was an excellent student at American University in Washington. A member of an earlier class remembers her for another reason: "Carol was a major contributor to community building in the entire student body at American University in the thirties."*[3] *After earning her bachelor's degree in government in 1938, she continued on at the graduate school, earning expenses by working as a research assistant at the Department of Agriculture.*

I took, when I was in graduate school, one of the early professional examinations for admission to government service and passed it. In those days, you didn't get into government except by being on competitive registers and by competitive examination. I think I took it in 1938 or '39, but for a year at least, the registers did not move as far as women were concerned. But then the defense buildup started. I got an offer to join a new service in the Civil Service Commission. It was an interdepartmental placement service, a totally new concept where all of the qualifications and records of government employees were put on IBM cards to develop a proper placement system. We were all hired to do the coding and to develop the systems for this concept to work. Through this, I got introduced into the organization and management type of work here. The whole enterprise floundered in the end because it proved to be very difficult and expensive.

It's never been tried since, but it did serve one important purpose that perhaps justified the investment in it. It had gotten all of the records on code and on IBM machines of all government employees across the country, so that when Pearl Harbor happened and it was necessary to have people who had the engineering backgrounds to undertake the fast reconstruction job there, we were able to locate all those people who had the skills that were needed.

[During the war] women were in demand because there was no danger of their being drafted, and women who had background in public administration were new and rare. I spent three years in the Washington office developing plans and policies. Then, in order to broaden my experience, I requested and went to one of the field offices that was very active on the West Coast where there were Navy yards, air stations, and all kinds of civilian-manned facilities. I spent two years in Seattle, Washington.

[Then a call] came to help out in the London office of UNRRA [United Nations Relief and Rehabilitation Administration] in the personnel division, to help wind up the UNRRA operation. That was 1946. The appointment to UNRRA was one that was arranged with the knowledge of what I could contribute and what the situation was there. It was not intended to be one of those misfits that often happen in international organizations, but because it was done at a fairly high level, somehow sex did not enter in, and as a result, when I got to London, there was considerable shock that I turned out to be a woman, the reason being, Washington used my shortened name, "Carol." [The Americans] thought one *r* and one *l* spelled female, and in Europe that's not the case at all. *They* thought they were getting a man. Initially, there was no disposition to giving me the job which I was sent for because they saw this as a problem. My response was a perfectly genuine one—I had come to help out in a situation and I would have to be prepared to do anything they wanted me to do. So they sort of tried to see if there was some other place that they could use me that would create less of a problem, because the acting head was a demobilized [British] major, and I don't think [he] took very kindly to this development. But the chief of personnel felt it was important that I work for them, and in the end they went ahead with it. And certainly, from my perception, it worked out very happily. That's the only time that I'm aware of where sex was a problem.

Laise was in London from 1946 to 1948. Toward the end, she was sent to Geneva to help in the transition between the UNRRA and the International Refugee Organization (IRO) and other successor organizations to UNRRA.

Then I was asked to come back to the department, to continue what amounted to looking after the organization and management programs that the U.S. had in all the international organizations which we immediately joined. I clearly took to it and stayed in the Bureau [of International Organization Affairs (IO)] for seven years. My service was an extraordinary range of exposure and training on the appropriations committees of all of these international organizations.

It was during the McCarthy period, and obviously, one of the really great targets was UNESCO [United Nations Educational, Scientific, and Cultural Organization]. Dean Rusk was the assistant secretary. He had been preceded by Alger Hiss,[4] so everybody in that bureau was suspect. We were required to develop a procedure of clearance of American personnel for international organizations which, given the fact that it was supposed to be an international secretariat, not subject to the pressures of international governments, was a very, very difficult thing to negotiate.

Laise entered the Foreign Service through the Wriston program, which combined the service with the State Department. She was "very keen" to get involved in bilateral diplomacy.

I felt that Asia was important to the future of the United States, and I was interested in going to Asia. I also found on the basis of my negotiating experience that where the traditions were shaped by British administration, it was easier to relate and function as a woman. And equally, I felt that in India there was a goal of hospitality to the notion of a woman. So that everything conspired to make a bid for a post in Delhi. That came about, I'm glad to say, and that is how it happened that I went as first secretary [in the political section] in the embassy.

Laise had no special training at the Foreign Service Institute before coming on board.

It certainly was in those days very much learning on the job. It was just being thrown into the water to sink or swim. But I must say that in the embassy in Delhi, my colleagues were extremely helpful and kind. Because it is a collegial relationships system, I got tremendous support from them in what was expected of me in the reporting assignments. I got very good training there.

A great advantage for Laise in her new assignment was that she already had Indian colleagues from her UN days, not only in education but also in politics and journalism.

I was there for four years. The first two years were primarily covering internal matters in India. So that essentially I was in the position [of following] the fortunes of the Congress party and the evolution of the parliamentary system. This meant getting to know all the members of Parliament and Indian leadership, seeing them in their own environment, trying to understand the dynamics of their political system, and reporting it.

Then the last two years that I was there, I focused more on the international matters. That involved more representation for the government in Delhi and less travel into the countryside. It was in that context that I got to know Mrs. [Indira] Gandhi [future prime minister]. I moved into handling some of the international issues of India and the West, the most notable one being the [fleeing] of the Dalai Lama to India in 1959, and all the Tibetan refugees with which the United States played a considerable role.

The only problem that I ran into in India was—and it wasn't a problem, it was just a nuisance—the tendency in political circles to assume that women in political sections were spies. I sometimes hit the Communist press, or the Communist-supported press, as being Mata Hari in the U.S. embassy at Delhi. And it still goes on. It comes back again and again. In fact, whenever there is a big CIA plot, they go back to their files, they dig up stuff that then gets repeated and repeated and repeated, [that] because of my activities in financing the election of one of Mrs. Gandhi's opponents, I was thrown out of India!

Well, the first really major story on this erupted after I had left India. As far as I recall, a European woman (and they include [Americans] in that same category) was seen to be campaigning for Ashok Mehta, a member of the opposition in the state of [Uttar Pradesh]. Then they go through the list of the embassies to see where there is a woman and find on an old embassy list my name as "first secretary, political." So they then produce that as the story. An opposition newspaper dug out the story of what really happened: a member of the same party as this gentleman in the opposition, an Indian, was married to an Austrian, and they were campaigning for him.

But it didn't die there. No, it was raised then as a question in Parliament, and Mr. [Jawaharlal] Nehru [the prime minister] responded and dismissed the whole thing and said what an irresponsible paper this was anyway. And that ended that, but you see, that ended it as far as the substance was concerned, but then the custom is for it to repeat itself in various versions until it just becomes a legend. So it still gets regurgitated. I got a copy of it from somebody in India only within the last year.

India, adopting a nonaligned policy, was feeling very lonesome at that stage, given the incursions the Chinese had made on its borders in 1959. The familiar support and prop that India had always looked to in Great Britain had become a diminishing value as a result of the decline in British fortunes after World War II and the attempt of Britain and France in regard to the Suez Canal. [This] caused them to turn more attention toward the United States.

Those two factors meant that when the president of the United States [Eisenhower] paid his first visit to India, the outpouring of enthusiasm was absolutely overwhelming. It was very difficult for us to get to the airport even to meet him because of the blockage of the road with the crowds and the traffic. And indeed, nobody of importance would have been there on time if he had not been delayed in his arrival by a holdup in Afghanistan. He rode in with the prime minister and the president of India to the center of Delhi at Connaught Place. The crowds were just so great that the entourage could not move—our security people were wild. Mr. Nehru got out of the car and used his stick in a good-humored way to push the crowd away so the car could get through.

The other memorable visit was the visit of Vice President Johnson in 1961. He had been on a mission at the instance of the president [Kennedy] in Southeast Asia, and on his way back to the United States he stopped in India. It was a very brief stop, but it was a very memorable stop.

My most vivid recollection was more social than substantive. A reception was given for him at the embassy residence. The ambassador was then [John Kenneth] Galbraith. Since at that stage I was the member of the embassy staff who had been longest in place and had the widest acquaintance, the ambassador laid on me the responsibility to introduce the vice president to everybody important in Delhi, because there was not a receiving line. He came late and he came into the garden, and all of the guests were collected in the garden. It was a very difficult job because it seems to be the custom that when an important entourage comes into a party, everybody falls away, so they're not within reach to introduce. It was a very difficult experience of darting into the crowd and trying to pull people into the circle to introduce them to Vice President and Mrs. Johnson. It was, I think, on the whole, a thoroughly satisfactory experience all around, but it was a little nerve-racking at the time.

The meeting with Lyndon Johnson was Laise's first encounter with the man who, as president, would influence the course of her career. Laise's work in New Delhi won her a promotion to class 2 and a year at the Senior Seminar.[5] It should also be mentioned that Ellsworth Bunker had been her first ambassador in India, and during his tenure Laise had become a good friend of Mrs. Harriet Bunker, who subsequently died. Bunker therefore often saw Laise socially as well as professionally.

With the new Kennedy administration, a number of personnel changes were made. Laise was appointed deputy director of South Asian affairs.

It seems to me every administration coming in wants to rediscover the wheel and shake things up because they think the department is fairly stuffy, a fudge factory, a bowl of jelly, you name it. All it indicates to me is that on the whole, they simply don't understand the requirements laid on the department. The department is, in a sense, a staff arm to the president. Their product is advice to the president, [which] has to be coordinated with a great many other branches of the government, particularly Defense, Agriculture, Commerce, Labor, Treasury, and sometimes Justice. And as a consequence, it's a slow business. I'm sure, sitting in the White House, when you want to get things done, it seems incredibly protean. But diplomacy is protean. I'm afraid presidents just don't like to accept the fact.

At that time, South Asian Affairs comprised the "PANIC" countries: Pakistan, Afghanistan, Nepal, India, and Ceylon. It was very active and exciting because the Chinese made even deeper incursions into India than they had in 1959. In 1962 the Chinese invaded and penetrated rather deeply into Northeast India. It happened at exactly the same time as the Cuban Missile Crisis. I remember it was on a weekend, and I was the duty officer for the weekend. The assistant secretary was there, and we were trying to deal with the problems that our ambassadors were raising. The garage of the State Department was filled with limousines. We knew that something was happening, and it wasn't our area. But the fact of the Chinese action radically affected our relationship with India and Pakistan because India, [which] had already appealed to America for assistance in the military field, now made its appeal even more extensive. And in fact, a military mission did go out to India.

The ambassador requested my return to India because with the turnover of personnel that had taken place there were very few [who] had the extensive contacts that I had had, so I went back for three months to help out during that period.

Following that, the department was engaged in a certain amount of high-level negotiations with the British to try to meet the Chinese problem. So during that time, not only was I on a special assignment in Delhi, but I went to London for talks. I then joined in the [Averell] Harriman mission and went on to Delhi to assist the embassy in developing programs. It was a fairly active period. During that period also, Governor Harriman and Duncan Sandys from the United Kingdom sought to reactivate negotiations on the Kashmir problem. I was part of those talks. This was between Mr. Nehru of India and President [Mohammad] Ayub [Khan] of Pakistan.

The evolving relationship with India was rudely and traumatically affected by the assassination of President Kennedy in November 1963 and the subsequent death of Mr. Nehru in 1964. The arrangements for the funeral preoccupied the Department of State for a very intense and emotional period of time, because a great many countries sent very high-level delegations to the funeral, and it was the responsibility of the department to look after those delegations and see that they were properly recognized and that arrangements were made for them to pay their respects and to participate in the ceremonies. Each of us looked after our own particular country.

Laise was promoted again in 1964 and in 1965 won the Federal Woman's Award, not only for her work as director of the Office of South Asian Affairs but for an entire career.

I have a picture of that promotion, because on the occasion of the promotion to class 1, it was with Kay Bracken and Margaret Tibbetts. Tibby preceded me in her appointment as ambassador. The three of us, though, were promoted to class 1 at the same time, and we were invited by President Johnson to come over and visit with him in the White House.

Following Mrs. Gandhi's visit in the spring of 1966, I began to get indications from the White House that they thought that since the President was interested in appointing more women ambassadors, I ought to be considered for one such post.

A flurry of memos between presidential aides provides a blunt assessment of her capabilities.[6] One memo lists "her primary abilities" as being in the fields of political reporting, negotiations, and personnel administration. She was said to be "calm, businesslike, a person of great integrity and a hard worker." But the memo goes on to say, "She tends not to delegate sufficiently and, with her passion for thoroughness, slows down the flow of work." Moreover, while Laise's superiors at State recognized her potential to be a chief of mission in time, they thought she should first be a deputy chief of mission. There was also concern over Nepalese reaction to the appointment of a woman. However, the desk officer, though not enthusiastic, thought the Nepalese "might be able to live with a woman ambassador." He pointed out that the queen of Nepal herself was a very powerful figure.

A memo from another aide describes Laise differently: "48, attractive, bright, very feminine." This source considered Laise to be the outstanding female career Foreign Service officer.

These documents are very revealing of the times and indicate two struggles going on: Johnson's attempt to bring equal opportunities to minorities and women, and the old-line careerists at State fighting changes that threatened their hegemony.

Johnson's people had to be very careful to select strong candidates. Nobody wanted the embarrassment of a weak appointment that would bring shame and ridicule to the administration. Laise was a Wristonee whose major experience prior to entering the Foreign Service had been in administration and personnel, and she had served abroad only in New Delhi. She did not have the broad

Carol Laise addressing guests after taking the oath at her swearing-in as ambassador to Nepal, 18 October 1966. She is flanked by Secretary of State Dean Rusk and Vice President Hubert Humphrey. It is unusual for such high-ranking officials to attend the swearing-in of a career officer. *Courtesy of U.S. Department of State.*

experience of a traditional "generalist" officer like Tibbetts. By 1966 personnel policies had resulted in there being more senior officers than available senior positions, and giving posts to women was not welcomed by men at State. Any woman candidate for ambassador had an uphill climb.

They asked if I had any views on the subject. My response was I thought I was being very well used where I was. It rather placed us all in something of a predicament, because I think my superiors in the department felt about the same way that I did: that in terms of my training and particular responsibilities and the problems in the area, it was more important to remain where I was, and that the post that was being suggested was not of such a priority that I should be transferred into it. However, I made it clear to all concerned that if the president, for whatever reasons, wanted me to go to Nepal, I would be delighted to do so. Naturally, the president's wish prevailed. And I've never regretted it.

Despite misgivings in the department, her sex presented no problem in Nepal.

So long as the representative of the United States is competent, understands their problems, and is able to interpret it with results from Washington, [the Nepalese] will give a cordial reception to that representative regardless of sex. I think the key factor is that they respect authority, and the United States is very important to them.

Laise described her arrival at Kathmandu.

I was flown in on the attaché's plane. We started to land and had to pull out of our descent and circle again because there were cows on the runway and they had to clear them off. I suppose the most significant factor about that day was my having to tell [DCM] Harry Barnes that I planned to be married within a month, in Kathmandu at the residence, to Ellsworth Bunker. I had to get his advice on how to organize it there in a way that it would not become public knowledge until the day of the event.

On Christmas Day [1966], I informed His Majesty that I would be getting married to Ellsworth Bunker on the third of January. He seemed thunderstruck at the idea, and I do not know to this day what his initial reaction was. But in the event, he seemed very pleased, and the Nepalese seemed to take it as a proper acknowledgment of their importance that, in effect, there were two American ambassadors resident in Kathmandu.

The worldwide U.S. diplomatic community was as thunderstruck as the ruler of Nepal. Not only was one ambassador marrying another, but Ellsworth Bunker was among the most illustrious and respected envoys in the history of U.S. diplomacy. Then ambassador-at-large, Bunker had also been ambassador to Argentina, Italy, India and Nepal, mediated the Dutch-Indonesian and the Saudi-Yemeni disputes, been the U.S. representative on the OAS (Organization of American States) council, headed the American Red Cross, and been awarded the presidential Medal of Freedom. He was a man of great integrity who had been entrusted by presidents of both parties with difficult missions requiring tact and a deft touch. His forte was negotiating. It is a measure of Johnson's confidence that Bunker was soon sent as ambassador to Vietnam, since Vietnam was without question the overriding concern of Johnson's administration. Bunker was 72, 23 years older than Laise, and in a letter to President Johnson, dated 2 December 1966, he said, "I am planning to marry again and am extremely happy that I have been able to persuade Carol Laise that it would be a good idea. It was not the easiest of my negotiations."[7] *Keeping their wedding as private an affair as possible involved keeping the news away from the press.*

We didn't say anything about it before I left Washington. Ellsworth had every good reason to come to that part of the world because his son was with the Ford Foundation in India, and so he spent Christmas there, and as a former ambassador to Kathmandu, it was not unnatural that he would pay a visit to Nepal. And so I sent out invitations to a reception honoring him, a former ambassador. The press in Kathmandu is not as inquisitive as the press in Washington. I think, probably, the first inkling that anybody got of something happening was that President Johnson sent his congratulatory message through the international wire service. He sent it a day ahead of time, because originally we had planned to be married on the second of January, but since New Year's Day fell on Sunday, the second turned out to be a holiday, and we didn't want to ruin anybody's holiday. So we postponed it to the third, but the White House didn't know it and the telegram came a bit early.

The Bunkers were married in January 1967. In April, Ellsworth went out as U.S. ambassador to Vietnam. From that time on, the course of the war determined his schedule. A New York Times *article of January 1973, six years after the wedding, reported that Ambassador Bunker was obliged to postpone a scheduled visit to his wife in order to inform South Vietnamese President Nguyen Van Thieu of a bombing halt ordered by Nixon.*

When my husband went to Vietnam, wives were [not] allowed there. The military wives, I think, never did go during the time. The civilian wives returned shortly after '68, I guess. The president had given my husband a plane, with directions to come to Kathmandu and get a rest every month, and some change, recreation. That didn't work out that he came every month, but the plane came and either took me down or brought him up.

I suppose you would have to say that the quality of our time together had to make up for the quantity. I think the arrangement that we had was perhaps one of the things that kept it on an even keel. Because we each had our interests and our occupations to pursue, and when we got together it was when we could give it time.

Our only [verbal] communication was through ham radio, operated in Nepal by an American Jesuit who founded some of the schools there. I had to make the trip out to the edge of the valley where he had his set every Sunday to make the contact. The reason that this all started as our avenue of communication was because Father Moran, the ham radio operator in Nepal, had exchanged messages with [Deputy Ambassador] Bill Porter in Saigon, so they knew that it was a good connection. Subsequently, I think, ham radios were forbidden from sending out of Vietnam, except for this one that operated when Ellsworth spoke to me. But you know, we were speaking to the whole world, and so generally it was just for voice contact and most of our communications were by letter, through unclassified pouch. They would get it to Bangkok, and Bangkok would get it up to Kathmandu by Thai Airlines.

Jane Coon, describing this period, stated that the marines called the airplane the "honeymoon special" and said it carried many Saigon embassy staffers to Kathmandu for R and R (rest and recreation). She continued, "One day I found Carol at the residence poring over cookbooks. She was making out menus for Ellsworth's cook in Saigon, where she had stashed an identical set of cookbooks. She seldom boarded the plane without a huge bowl of pansies, or whatever temperate flower was blooming in her magnificent garden." [8]

While it would have been very nice to be together, I think as long as Ellsworth was in Saigon, it made sense for me to be in Kathmandu. I certainly never got fed up with it. It was probably, under the circumstances that existed in Saigon, the best of solutions.

I've always presumed that the department [was] perfectly prepared to leave me there as long as Ellsworth was in Saigon, because that's the way the president wanted it.

Laise commented on certain advantages of being a woman.

I was discussing this question recently with another woman ambassador to another part of the world, and I think we were both prepared to speculate that where the personal qualities are such as to command respect, then a woman perhaps does have some advantages that certain men would not have. It's not true of all men, and it may not even be true of all women, but I don't believe that a woman is as threatening to a male official in a developing country as perhaps another competitive male would be. The other ambassador recorded, as I experienced, a willingness to be candid and confide in a rather extraordinary degree, and we were trying to figure out what might have led to it, whether it was just a personal chemistry or something more than that. I tend to feel it was not so much a matter of personal chemistry as it was the fact that the presence of a woman simply was easier somehow for them to cope with.

She returned to the United States in 1973 to become assistant secretary for public affairs, the first woman to be an assistant secretary.

[The position] had been vacant for a couple of years. The Watergate events were building up. Kissinger came in as secretary of state. [He] indicated his desire to build a dialogue with the American people about foreign policy. We were recipients of enormous amounts of mail and invitations for him to speak, which were way beyond his capacity to cope with. Therefore, it fell to us not only to answer his mail but also to advise him on what it was important for him to do in terms of his style, of building the dialogue. It was a very extraordinary period, because it was the period of Watergate, when the country was disillusioned with Washington, and the only person who really had any credibility at all was Henry Kissinger. [My job could] be properly characterized as sort of an ambassador to the United States, doing public affairs in the United States.

Laise served next as director general of the Foreign Service, a position she described as "no more, no less than the assistant secretary of state for personnel management."

I think the pressures are much greater in the office of the director general because lives are at stake, and one's career is at stake, and it takes its toll, believe me. I got high blood pressure as a consequence.

At the end of 1977 Laise retired voluntarily.

At the time we were appealing to reestablish a mandatory retirement at 60. Although as a career minister I had the right to continue until 65, I felt that since I was initiating the charge to reestablish 60 as a mandatory retirement age, I needed to reinforce a belief in the cause that I was espousing. We won, by the way.

Laise was only the second woman to become a career minister. She attributed the speed of her rise to the women's movement.

The record of the Foreign Service in having women anywhere in the service, and certainly in the higher ranks, was deplorable. My impression is that the women's movement forced the department to have more visible appointments of women to high places. I think the department has sought, where it had qualified women, to speed up the process. I'm not suggesting that they should set the standards aside, but they gave the opportunity, and I think the progression was faster than normal. The upper ranks are still very thin indeed, largely because not very many women came in through the examination process during the sixties. The evolution of my career has been in new areas of diplomacy, and so I was essentially leaning against an open door. Therefore I've had no particular sense of discrimination, and therefore I don't have any personal sense of suddenly having greater effectiveness because of the women's movement.

I give contributions to assist women to get elected to national office, and purposely I accepted to be on the board of a women's college because it was a women's college. I felt it was important to support the women's colleges in developing the confidence in women to cope in the world.

I've always been in public service, and I viewed it from the standpoint of somehow being in service. I mean, during the war one was certainly imbued with that, and it stayed with me because I moved from wartime service to a relief agency, relieving the suffering and dislocation of war, and then into the Foreign Service, where again it was building new institutions to promote peace and reduce the prospect of another war.

If the Greek definition of happiness is to be occupied in something that enables one to exercise one's talents to the fullest, I think it's fair to say that I've been afforded that opportunity and have thoroughly enjoyed it.

6

ACCIDENTAL WATERGATE VICTIM
Ruth Lewis Farkas (1906–   )
Luxembourg 1973–1976

The years of the Watergate scandals were not a comfortable time for an American to be overseas in the high-profile position of U.S. ambassador. For Ruth Farkas in Luxembourg, the discomfort index was immeasurably higher because of rumors that she had "bought" her position with a 1972 Nixon campaign contribution of $300,000 and was therefore a part of the corruption.[1]

After a lifetime in education and social work, much of it spent in philanthropical endeavors to help those less privileged, she found herself at the age of 65 in an insalubrious climate, deprived of the daily companionship of her husband of 44 years, in the company of a wary diplomatic corps, with an entirely new profession to master, victim of a hostile press, bespattered by the mud of Watergate, and forced to recross the Atlantic to testify before a grand jury. Even after President Richard Nixon was forced from office, scandals kept erupting like a string of firecrackers popping one after another, and each one burned her a little, although she was no longer central to the issue.[2]

Farkas did the best she could to overcome her unfortunate circumstances. Serious in her intent to be a good ambassador, she tackled her job with diligence and integrity, worked closely with her staff, and concentrated on doing those things she knew best, namely, education, philanthropy, business, and banking. She used her own resources to make up shortfalls in government allowances and refurbished the official residence partly at her own expense, decorating its walls with paintings from her collection of French impressionists.

Without complaining, she took responsibility, maintained her dignity, saw to it that post morale was kept up, represented her country appropriately and conscientiously, and, perhaps most important, made no diplomatic blunders.

The irony is that she had not wanted to be there in the first place. Many believed it was her family, particularly her devoted husband, George, who wanted her to crown a lengthy and impressive career with the distinction of being a

U.S. ambassador. As early as 1961, President John F. Kennedy had sent her as a delegate to the Pan-Pacific Southeast Asian Women's Associations Conference. From 1964 on, she was a member of the U.S. National Commission to UNESCO. She had also served as consultant for the State Department in 1963, 1965, and 1968, and was on the Foreign Service Selection Board as well as the President's Special Education Committee for Information on Human Rights. Her special interest was the President's Committee for the Handicapped, which tied in well with her lavish generosity to New York City hospitals. (Later on, her efforts would be largely responsible for the establishment of a special experimental surgical unit at New York University Hospital to repair congenital physical defects in infants and children.) In 1968 Lyndon Johnson had considered her for ambassador to Costa Rica, but then her husband suffered a heart attack and her enthusiasm waned. While she was in Luxembourg, often alone, the state of his health was a constant worry to her.[3]

Did she "buy" her ambassadorship? This was not her perception, nor was it in keeping with her reputation. Documentary evidence in the Nixon Library paints a distasteful picture of White House advisers deliberately setting out to make use of a philanthropic couple who believed in the president. Ruth Farkas did not think of ambassadorships as being "for sale." But the Nixon White House staff, in their zeal to build up secret funds, did. Contributing money to a candidate was not against the law, but selling presidential appointments for cash was, as Nixon's people were well aware.[4]

The amount the Farkases gave, staggering though it seems to most people, was in line with their donations to charitable and cultural institutions. The same year as the $300,000 gift to CRP (or CREEP, Committee to Reelect the President), they had given away a total of nearly $3 million. Both were motivated by the conviction that from those to whom much is given, much is demanded.

Both George and Ruth Farkas were very high achievers. The couple had become engaged while she was in her junior year at New York University and had married immediately upon her graduation in June 1928. They had four sons. He had built up a small family clothing business into the Alexander's department store chain and had invested heavily in real estate. Her interests were very different from his, and in an era when it was unusual for women to have careers outside the home, George saw to it she was able to pursue hers by providing full-time household help. She went on to earn a master's degree at Columbia and later a doctorate in education at NYU, where she had also taught sociology. Her mother had had a special influence on Ruth Farkas.

My parents owned a lot of these houses on the middle East Side, where a lot of people who were early immigrants came and settled or lived with families. A lot of them had very little income, and often, when the breadwinner of the family would die, there was nobody to help them, except the church, or the synagogue, or the mosque, or whatever it was. And so [my mother] had decided in her later life that what she would like to do was set up some kind of a program in which if the church or the synagogue or any other religious group would promise to feed them and help clothe them, she'd give them free rent. And she did that for many years. Eventually she was written up as the "best landlord of the year."

I'll tell you what she used to do. We used to look forward to it. Every other Saturday, we used to go to what we called "the houses." [My youngest brother and I] sat in the janitor's apartment until my mother came down. Or sometimes she'd take us upstairs to an apartment where there were people, and she used to say, "Now you sit quietly and listen." I remember very often her saying to my brother and me, "You know how lucky you are? Do you realize how lucky you are? All the things you enjoy that these children don't?" It made me aware very early in life of the vicissitudes of life, and the needs.

An incident at a cinema when she was young was evidence of an early awakening of a lifelong concern for the elderly.

There was a cinema in Flushing, Saturday afternoon. You could go at three o'clock if you were with an older person in the family, so we'd get my cousin who was 16 and we'd go. We used to look forward to it. But this time there was this picture, *Over the Hill to the Poorhouse*. I'll never forget it. So we all went in and we sat down. And this picture starts about this poor old woman that nobody wanted. I started to cry. I cried so loud, the usher came down and said, "If you don't keep quiet, you're going out." So everybody's pushing me and shoving me, and my brother says, "If you don't stop it, I'll knuckle you." I couldn't help it. So I cried again. They wanted to put me out. We had five other cousins [with us]. And they said, "Well, if she goes, we go." "Well," [the usher] said, "you're all going." So we all had to go out of the movie.

I was very touched. I don't know why, but I always do get touched by the elderly people. When I was in Luxembourg, I became interested in the aging set. Everybody else there thought I was "whacks," you know. I just couldn't help it.

When I graduated from high school, [there] was a school for young ladies on Fifth Avenue, in the eighties. My mother said, "You're not going away to school yet. You're going to stay home." She said, "You need a finishing school anyway. You've been brought up with your brothers; you act more like a boy than a girl." So she sent me to this school for young ladies. I remember coming home one day, and I said, "I'm not learning a darn thing." She said, "You're not?" I said, "No, you're throwing your money out, because I'm not learning anything. They teach you how to be the wife of an ambassador, and they teach you how to present yourself to the queen. I'm not learning anything." She said to me, "Well, you never know. One day you can be the wife of an ambassador, or one yourself." When I did become the ambassador, nobody had to tell me about protocol or anything like that. I was very grateful. In fact, my husband said to me one day, "If your mother were alive, she'd say, 'Well, I told you.' "

Through a serendipitous conversation with President Lyndon Johnson, Farkas was considered for ambassador to Costa Rica.

I was there at the time when the public members were going over the different ambassadorial resumés, and there was a problem with one of the ambassadors. The problem had to do with some kind of beef that Costa Rica was said to have, and also something with hybrid corn. Our government was supposed to buy it, and at this particular time our president decided that we didn't need it. They said that the beef wasn't up to standard—I don't know. All I know was that [the] ambassador was so damn upset. President Johnson asked me, "What do you think?" Because I'd known about it. I knew [the ambassador], and I knew what happened. I told him what I thought, and he said, "That's wise advice and a good decision," and then he said to me, "I wonder what kind of an ambassador you would make?" And I said, "Try me." I never realized that he would designate me. He sent my resumé to Costa Rica, and they accepted me. And I told him I couldn't go because my husband had had a heart attack.[5]

Farkas described how she and her husband came to make a substantial contribution to Richard Nixon's 1972 presidential campaign.

There was a [rule] in our firm [Alexander's] you didn't give money to any presidential campaigns. Ever since Wendell Willkie [the Republican presidential candidate in 1940]. Well, my husband was very fond of Willkie, and it's the first man that he ever stumped for or advocated to be president. The day my husband came out for Willkie, we were picketed. You know there's always this group that's anti: "Don't buy in Alexander's. They're just Republicans." And never mind how much good they do in the community. So that's when my husband said to our top executives, "No more. That settles it. There'll be no more politicking."

My husband thought a great deal of Richard Nixon. He agreed with him very, very much on a lot of things. At Nixon's second campaign he had retired, and he said to me, "You know, I'm free now. I can do as I *damn* please. I don't have to answer to anybody for what I give." So that was when he offered to give, I think it was $350,000 [*sic*], for Nixon's campaign.

I told you about New York University closing down the School of Social Work? This was in early August [1972]. I was in Europe when it happened, and I flew to New York, and the president [of NYU] said, "We need a million-and-something dollars. How are you going to raise it by October?" [I said], "We'll do it, because that school shouldn't be closed down." We got several men together and each decided to put in $325,000.

My husband was in Hawaii at the time. He traveled all over the world, as you know. I got hold of him in Hawaii. I said, "Honey, we need 300-something thousand dollars." "Well, honey," he said, "you know we've promised something to Nixon's campaign, and you know me, I never go back on my word." I said, "I know, but this is more important than anything that's going to happen. The president can live without our money."

He says, "Well, I'll tell you what I'll do. I'll call up Maurice Stans and tell him the problem and tell him, "Look, we'll give you $175,000 before January [1973] and the rest after, because I don't want to lose a lot of income that I get from my bonds." And Stans said, "That's perfectly all right. We're having enough, so don't worry about it." So that's how I gave the money to the school and saved the school. Have a plaque [that] says, "Thank you for saving our lives."

So what happened was, when I gave the first check to Mr. Stans, I went with this Senator [*sic*] Wyman, who was at that time in the House of Representatives. Great guy. He was 20 years in the House of Representatives. He's a very nice man. There was one thing he said, and I'll never forget it. Stans said, "You don't expect anything for this?" And Wyman said, "She expects nothing. She's giving it because her husband wants to do it, and he's not well, so she's giving it. As you realize, she cannot give you the whole check."

When I was designated first to be the ambassador, I really didn't want to go because I had a sister-in-law who was born in Brussels. She said to me, "Ruth, bad climate for George." And so I said [to George], "Honey, I don't want to go." He said, "The president has designated you. You didn't say no to the designation, you can't change your mind now. You accepted, you go. I'll be with you as much as I can." So I said, "All right."

Then I went before the [Senate Foreign Relations] Committee, and as I was answering questions there, a note came in[6] [that] said that my husband gave money to the campaign. Then they asked me the question, "Was that to buy an ambassadorship?" What was it that Senator Ervin said to me?[7] "I guess Alexander's must have had a good Christmas." I said, "They always have a good Christmas." Then Senator Percy said, "I think we have to think about this and take it into consideration."

I said, "While you're at it, Senator Percy, why don't you take into consideration what we gave this year—$1.5 million to one hospital, a couple of hundred thousand dollars to another university, built a hospital for the aging." I said, "That $350,000 [sic], while it's a lot of money, does not compare with what was given to charitable purposes." I was mad.

By that time I really didn't want it, and I couldn't care less. I said to my husband, "Now I'm not going. I'm sure I'm not going." He said, "Look, honey, if you don't go, then you're guilty, and if you do go, you're guilty. Just face the facts. You're big enough to face facts. Whatever people say, whatever they want to say, that's all right with me. I'm with you." So I went.

According to Farkas, the committee was not interested in her prior government service—including Johnson's Program for the Handicapped—or her knowledge of languages and European politics.

When that note came in, everything else stopped.[8] Then when they said they had to think about it, there were a bunch of reporters outside. "What happened?" "How about it?" "Did you buy the job?" "Blah-blah-blah." I kept on saying, "No comment. No comment, no comment." I wouldn't talk. I just refused to get in any argument with them, that's all.

Later, I guess it was March, [the State Department] called me back again and told me that I had passed [in] the Senate and they'd like to brief me. If I ever felt that I didn't want to do anything, it was that.

Well, I went to the different desks [for briefings]—European desks, you know, and economic also. I think the legal division, too. Then the cultural things and the state of Luxembourg and some of its interests. They also told me what they would like for me to do while I was there.

I wanted to know, first of all, about the economics of Luxembourg, what its situation was in the EEC [European Economic Community], and so forth and so on, and I wanted to know more about NATO because there were a few people in NATO who were responsible to me, so I didn't want to go over and not know what I was talking about. I had a good briefing.

Ruth Farkas taking the oath of office as ambassador to Luxembourg, 12 April 1973. Looking on are her husband George (holding Bible) and her four sons. Marion Snooks, protocol officer, administers the oath while Kenneth Rush, deputy secretary of state, officiates. *Courtesy of U.S. Department of State.*

Farkas was sworn in on the eighth floor of the State Department.

There were a lot of people there. I didn't invite very many people. My family was so damn angry, and I said, "To heck with the whole business." My sons, of course, were there with their wives, my grandchildren, and my brothers, but that's all. I didn't invite another soul.

Farkas decided that the DCM was one staff member who would have to go, since he was "so directed by Kingdon Gould" (her predecessor) and accustomed to running the embassy a certain way.

[For instance], a certain telegram came, and I don't know where I was. I wasn't out of the country, but I was someplace in another city. It wasn't important, but on the other hand, I didn't think that he had the right to do it—he answered it. And I told him, "Don't you ever dare do that again. I'm the responsible party here. Not that what you did is so wrong, but the fact of the matter was that it could have been wrong." And he'd better know that "I'm the ambassador now and you're no longer the chief here." So that's when I decided that maybe it was best to change.

You know, it's a difficult thing. He didn't know me, didn't know my abilities—or disabilities, for that matter—and so I guess he figured, "Well, maybe I'd just as well answer the thing." I was a little bit miffed.

Farkas reported that she had "wonderful rapport" with her FSOs. In fact, her relations with her staff were excellent, according to staff members, who said Farkas gave unstintingly of her time to help anyone with personal problems.

What I would do, and a lot of ambassadors never do, I invited them to dinner every once in a while. Let their hair down, talk to each other, talk to me. You know, I'm a person, they're persons. I think it was very helpful. And even with the marines, I went to their place a few times and had lunch or dinner with them. After all, they were youngsters, and their parents' sons. I have sons.

Increasing American business opportunities was one of Farkas's main objectives.

I was asked to see if there [was] a way that we could have Luxembourg importing from the United States, and inasmuch as my husband was in the department store business, and knowing a lot about import-export, and looking at some of the things they had and the prices—because Luxembourg had very high prices even then—I thought there was a way that they could go to the United States and learn about some of the things that we could send them.

They did import a lot of things. You know, they're known for their steel. They have one of the biggest steel mills—Arbed—and things like that, but they didn't make clothing or shoes. Those were all imported [from] France,

Spain, different countries, but I could see that they had nothing from the United States, and we could have done a lot with them.

I once asked my husband to help me, and he said, "I have nothing to do with your job." I did have a meeting, though, of the top merchants in Luxembourg. I told them that we would be very happy to help them go to the United States, and go to the Department of Commerce, and be directed to some of our best manufacturers and purchasing offices, and, sorry to say, Commerce didn't do anything.

Farkas chose her second DCM with care.

I spoke to some people I knew in France who were partially in government. And then I spoke to somebody I knew in Belgium through my sister-in-law's family, and I finally decided on [Peter Tarnoff]. He was terrific. At that time, he was principal officer in Lyon. I didn't ask anybody [in the department] about him. I had him come to see me, and I liked him. I liked his ideas, I liked his viewpoints, a clean-looking young guy. And I took him on. They offered me somebody else first. Forget it.

He was with me for two and a half years, I guess. He was everything you would want. Spoke French beautifully. He had gone to the Sorbonne for a while. His father originally was with Macy's, if I'm not mistaken—one of those department stores—so we could speak the same language in a certain way. I would write my own reports, you know. Sometimes if I'd want to write a report to the government that I felt was more than [narrow] political [reporting], I would say, "Peter, just go over this," and he always did very well. He was really good.

Of course, you can't make an overall, general rule, but I do think that [FSOs] sometimes hesitate making a decision because it's not within the format of the diplomatic peripheries. That's why I liked Peter Tarnoff so much. He just figured, "If I'm wrong, I'm wrong, and what the heck!"

I opened up the first cultural center in Luxembourg, because I felt that the Russians were doing such a job and we weren't doing anything. I said to my social secretary, "Miriam, we've got to have something." "Well," she said, "let's see if we can't get some building." We got the building from the government. I think it was an art gallery, first floor and basement. We got 3,000 books first, and then we had some pictures and things like that, so we'd have an art show. Then we started to have children's books, and it really became a heck of a wonderful center because, you see, Miami University from Ohio had their junior year there. They really enjoyed it. I couldn't imagine not having something cultural for the Americans who were there, or for Luxembourgers interested in Americans. And they're so interested, these Luxembourgers. They adore the Americans, I tell you.

Although the news stories pictured her as the prototypical political ambassador, she never considered herself "political."

I was diplomatic—I never did anything political. I never was out for this Republican or that one, no. What I did was mostly in the cultural area, or diplomatic service, like UNESCO's Science Commission. Being on the executive committee of the Science Commission is not political.

When I first came, I went to the prime minister [Pierre Werner]. The Communists were talking all this kind of nonsense, and I said to him, "If you feel that you're unhappy or dissatisfied—if I'm questionable—I can leave before we have any problem." He said, "Absolutely not. We're looking forward to having you. We're very proud of your background, and we know you're going to make a great ambassador." I must tell you, he was just wonderful.

George Farkas was rarely in Luxembourg, which meant Ruth was obliged to "serve as my own host and hostess."

I felt comfortable doing it. I was brought up in a family where my mother was head of a big business, and at home with my own husband we had to do a heck of a lot of entertaining to foreigners and businessmen. I brought my own help, so my cook knew exactly what she had to do.

My husband went there first, came back to me, and he said, "Honey, that place [the residence] hasn't been redone for God knows!" Of course, the ambassador before me had too many children and couldn't live in that house. When my husband saw it, he said, "It's sad. You might be able to do something with the furniture, but you'd have to have it recovered. The electrical wiring is dangerous." He was very aware of that, having department stores, you know. So he said, "Unless the government does something about rewiring and repainting that place, and putting some bricks in where they're out, and taking that ivy off (because there was ivy growing over the windows and in the windows), you can't go there. You just cannot." The government gave me $80,000, but I want you to know it cost me another ninety.

Farkas found that her State Department entertainment allowance was far from adequate for herself and her officers. To make up the difference, "I dug into my own pocket." When her officers entertained officially, "they'd always tell me how much they were using, and if they needed more, I'd give it to them, you know."

[When I arrived] things were running all right, except that the Russian ambassador didn't like [the first DCM] too much. When I first went there, it was very interesting. You know, you have to meet all the ambassadors. His deputy said, "The ambassador only speaks Russian and German." I said, "Really? Well, I'll speak French, if he could." He said, "No, no. You speak French, and I'll interpret." Well, I couldn't do too much about it. So I spoke to him in French, and whatever he said [in Russian] I still don't know. A lot of the other ambassadors were cordial, but they shunned him to a certain extent. He'd been there a long time. He was the doyen.

I don't know why, but he sort of took a liking to me, and one day the embassy called me up to ask me if I would accompany him and a couple of other ambassadors to the Unknown Soldier in Luxembourg. Well, I didn't know there was an Unknown Russian Soldier in Luxembourg. Nixon was someplace off in the skies. I never was able to talk to him. I said, "Well, I've got to figure it out myself." I was thinking about it: should we honor a Russian Unknown Soldier? And then I said to myself, "Well, at that time they were our allies. It was their unknown hero." Just then, the French ambassador called me up and said to me, "Are you going?" I said, "Well, it's not the biggest thing. There's no secrecy about it, and it will please him no end. After all, he is the doyen. Maybe we can get somebody from Ireland or the Netherlands." I think it was the ambassador from the Netherlands who came. Three of us accompanied him. He was very grateful because the French ambassador had said, "If the American ambassador will come, I'll come. If she doesn't come, I'm not coming."

After that, he called me up one day and wanted to talk to me about something, and I said, "Why don't you come alone? Don't you understand some French?" He said, "Not much." I said, "I understand some German, so we can get along." He said, "Well, perhaps." So that's when I said to Peter, "Look! Look out of the window. If he comes with his deputy, you're going to stay in the room. If he comes alone, you stay out." And he came alone, surprisingly enough.

After that, he was most cordial.

I got to know who was important and who wasn't, and I got to know the person who could do most for me when it came to doing a very needful, political thing for my own country. I got to know the people from Arbed, then people from Thyssen who have interests with the cigarette manufacturers. And Thyssen—I made sure I did something with that, not only the steel mills, but I got to know heads of these mills. The head of one of the biggest metal international works in the world was living in Luxembourg, by the name of Henry Leir. He's a great philanthropist, too. It was really one of my own men who told me when I first got there. He said, "There's a man who is terribly powerful with the prime minister and with the government, and also with the grand duke and grand duchess, and it would be a wise thing for you to cultivate him."

So I cultivated him and invited him to my home, and it was very worthwhile. In fact, on his seventy-fifth birthday—he had done me a big favor—I asked him what I could do for him, and he said, "Give me my seventy-fifth birthday party in your residence." His wife said, "Now don't ask that. You know she's got enough to do." To me she said, "Don't you do it for him." I said, "Yes, I shall. Just give me the names of your friends." Which he did, a lot of people in government and whatnot, so it didn't do us any harm either. I gave him a wonderful party and I think he was most grateful.

In Farkas's opinion, Luxembourg's tiny size does not reflect its importance to the United States.

First of all, I think Luxembourg, as far as we were concerned, is not only part of NATO but was very important to the EEC, and while we weren't part of the EEC, remember that we needed import-export, so it was terribly important for me to see what they were doing and to try to cultivate things so we could do something.

In fact, one of my biggest disappointments was that our government had asked me to see if we couldn't get something really big going, and I became very friendly with the head of the steel mills. One night he called me up and said, "I have something to tell you. We are thinking of building rolling mills." Now, rolling mills are things that make the steel flat, and they cost $215 million a mill. He said, "This is the first time we're going to let the United States bid for it." I said, "Oh, gosh. Isn't that something." He said, "We're very pleased with what you're doing here." I immediately called our Department of Commerce. Forget it! I said, "We need someone to give us some kind of financial basis for what we might be doing." Nothing happened. Sent another telegram saying, "I'm waiting." Of course, France was bidding, Germany was bidding, another company was bidding. Why couldn't we? Finally I sent a telegram to Kissinger, and I said, "The ball is in your court." [The American companies were] too busy in the [Middle] East. They couldn't bother with it. I was really mad. We didn't get it.

Commercial affairs were not Farkas's only priority. She saw much of her diplomatic work as building goodwill "in as many ways as possible."

When I did this [charity ball] for the [mentally handicapped], although I was personally interested, certainly they knew that we, as people of the United States, were not only interested in doing diplomatic work, we were interested in their people, their country. They appreciated it.

I went to visit the Institutes for Aging to see what we could do for them. Also, at the university, I gave two of the graduating groups graduation parties. I came and spoke to them. Once a year, in May, I would have a big [open house] and invite as many students as I could get, and we'd have a big roundup. I would have a buffet for them, and we'd sit and discuss what was going on in other countries in education.

Although her years in social work and in arranging charity benefits stood her in good stead, when it came to government budgeting, her experience in private business led her astray.

When I came to Luxembourg and asked to look over the budget of the previous year and saw things that never had been spent, I said to my administrative counselor, "Look, we don't need as much money as they give us." And I was advised, "Don't send any back, because once you send it back, you'll never get it again." I said, "Well, I'm sending it back." I sent back $10,000. Never got a thank-you for it. But then, a year later, when Mr. Kissinger wanted to come with some men and we needed more space, and I was going to partition some of the office off for them, I asked for some

Ruth Farkas with Attorney General Edwin Meese III, Washington, D.C., March 1986. Farkas was chairman of the board for the Center for the Study of the Presidency. *Courtesy of Center for the Study of the Presidency.*

money and they wouldn't give it to me. I did it to myself—it was like déjà vu: "I told you not to do it." He [the administrative counselor] was right.

When Gerald Ford took office on 9 August 1974, Ruth Farkas, following custom, submitted her resignation. It was not accepted until a year and a half later, on 23 February 1976, and not publicly announced until 4 May 1976. The delay was to allow adequate time to ready her successor's appointment so the two announcements could be made simultaneously. When the news was released, Ambassador Farkas was in New York on leave. She had had lunch with her grandson, Allister Farkas, and they had "stopped to buy a newspaper to find a movie, and there on page 3 or 4 was an item that she'd been replaced." Young Farkas was indignant at this impersonal way of terminating his grandmother's ambassadorship but noted that she "didn't so much as flinch."

A career officer who served with her at Luxembourg described Ruth Lewis Farkas as having the "highest integrity. Very intelligent, very thorough, very serious about what she was doing. There was never a question of lack of integrity or seriousness or sincerity or determination to do her best." [9]

7

CHAMPION OF WOMEN'S RIGHTS
Mary Seymour Olmsted (1919–   )
Papua New Guinea 1975–1979
Solomon Islands 1978–1979

The 1972 Herter Award, given to senior officers of class 1 or 2 in recognition of "extraordinary accomplishment involving creativity, and intellectual courage and integrity, including disciplined dissent," cited Mary Olmsted for "her intellectual courage . . . not only evident in the reforms she has been able to help win from a conservative system but in the fact that she is the first senior woman FSO who voluntarily put her name, her rank and her career on the line to help remove discrimination against women."

The character and integrity Mary Olmsted exhibited during her leadership on women's issues at State was nurtured during her childhood in rural Florida by her parents, who were of English and Scottish extraction. Both were college graduates, her father a mining engineer and her mother a high school teacher. Young Mary attended the Episcopal church and Sunday school, belonged to the Campfire Girls, and found schoolwork in the local public schools "a breeze."[1]

She was guided toward a private women's college in New England by her parents, who wanted her to experience life in a part of the country where, they felt, academic standards would be highest. She selected Mt. Holyoke, partly because her paternal grandmother and great-grandmother had attended courses there. She graduated in 1941 with an economics major, having partially worked her way through with waitressing and clerical jobs. The war had not yet begun when she went to New York to work in the security analysis division of a large bank. After a couple of years there, she moved over to the National Bureau of Economic Research and took courses in statistics at Columbia University.

Her entry into the Foreign Service was, she says, "happenstance." In 1945 a friend who had gone to work at one of the wartime agencies in Washington brought her application forms to enter government work. She completed them and took "the least presentable down to the Department of State, because I felt they would not hire me."

To her "great amazement," she was hired as a junior economic analyst in the Foreign Service Auxiliary and was sent to Montreal. There she took the first postwar Foreign Service examination, designed for veterans but open to a few others. She passed the two-day test, then passed the oral examination the following spring. As was expected of a proper young lady in 1946, she wore "a new dress and a new hat and a new hairdo for the occasion."

Her first assignment as a Foreign Service officer was to Amsterdam as a commercial officer. "There was a rotational program, established at the request of the four young officers who were in Amsterdam. Initially it was only the men who were rotated. I said I wanted to be rotated, too, and after a little delay, they agreed I could be."

She moved on to Reykjavik, Iceland, where she did political work for the first time. This she enjoyed very much and hoped to continue, but with her next assignment, to Vienna, she once again found herself in economics. By this time (1952) the service was moving toward the cone system of specialization and away from the cultivation of generalists, an orientation that had prevailed since 1924. Locked into economic work, in Vienna she was given "one backlog after another" of work left behind by staff officers who were forced out at the time of the great reduction in force. She found it very dull work and was not alone in her dissatisfaction. The early Eisenhower years were difficult for the Foreign Service; according to Olmsted, "Morale was terrible."

While in Reykjavik she had applied for Russian language and area training, but "it was decided in the department that I would not get [it] because at the time they were not assigning women FSOs to Moscow. Therefore, they weren't going to train them in Russian. So instead, they assigned me [in 1955] for political training at Fletcher [School of Law and Diplomacy, Tufts University]."

Back in the Department of State, she was assigned to the Bureau of Intelligence and Research (INR), doing work in East-West trade, then was seconded to the Department of Commerce. (She had requested the Department of Labor.) There she answered correspondence and wrote for the Foreign Commerce Weekly. During this "dull period" of being shunted around from one office to another, she certainly "never spent much time thinking about becoming an ambassador."

Her next assignments were to the Bureau of East Asian and Pacific Affairs (EA), as an international economist, and then to New Delhi, again in economics. At Fletcher she had developed a great interest in the Third World, and when offered Delhi, she "accepted with alacrity," although technically it meant her career took a step backward. She had just been promoted to class 3, and the job was a class 4. Olmsted retained her personal rank and salary. New Delhi proved to be a broadening and rewarding post for her, as it had for Carol Laise.

The embassy had quite a large economic section, and the new person usually gets the dregs, and I did. But I caught on to the fact that in a large and very complicated and very different economy like India's, you can't start out at the top. You've got to learn. So I took advantage of the situation and, again, I cleaned up some backlogs of work, but I managed to keep moving so that I worked in one area of the economy and another and another, and after a while I became the person others were turning to, because I had the broadest view of things.

I did a great deal of traveling and saw a lot of India [and] managed to get away from the New Delhi cocktail circuit fairly often. I enjoyed it very much, a very, very enriching experience. I probably did more in the way of original reporting—more of the analytic reporting—there. In addition to that, for the first time I moved into a semisupervisory job. I became the deputy to the economic counselor, and it was a fairly large economic section. I did a good deal of the liaison work with AID.

As a result of her efforts, she was selected to attend the prestigious Senior Seminar in 1965. After serving a tour as senior economic officer for India, Nepal, and Ceylon with responsibilities for food and grain shipments to head off famine in India, she was sent in 1969 to the planning and research section of the Office of Economic Opportunity (OEO). This was a real change of pace in that she now was concerned with economic development in her own country. While at OEO, she became interested in women's issues at State.

I had a telephone call one weekend from someone whom I had known slightly. She said that a group of women in the department were becoming concerned over the fact that there was great activity going on in the formulation of new policies, and women were being left out, that no consideration was being given to the role that women might play. She said that a group of them were getting together for brown-bag lunches to talk about it. She asked me if I'd like to join them. So I packed a brown-bag lunch and went over, and that was the beginning. There was only a small handful of us, but as we continued, we became larger and began formulating what we were going to do.

Over a period of time, I became the chairman of this group, which was then called the Ad Hoc Committee to Improve the Status of Women in the Foreign Affairs Agencies. We [called] on Mr. [William B.] Macomber [the deputy under secretary for management] on the twenty-sixth of August, which was Women's Suffrage Day, and presented him with a package of proposals, some of which he accepted on the spot; others he said would require further study. That encouraged us tremendously. One of the things we persuaded him to do was to hold an open meeting for women in the Department of State and the other agencies, and it was a meeting that took several hours. This proved very successful in drawing out women who had previously stayed on the sidelines. Some of the things that people stood up on the floor and said, things that were debated, made the department realize that they had got to get moving on the things that women were talking about.

The department had been required by executive order to take certain steps regarding women employees. One of the parts of that package was the establishment of a federal women's program with some woman at the head of it. The department had not bothered to do that until we became active, and then suddenly it did appoint someone for that job. There was some debate among us: did we need to continue now that there was a women's coordinator? We decided, yes, we did need to continue, because a little pressure from the outside always helps. So we formalized our status to become the Women's Action Organization [WAO] for State, AID, USIA. [Although] many women felt that they would hurt their careers by going into an organization such as the Women's Action Organization, I found that was not true.

I think it was around the beginning of '71 that I became the first president [of WAO]. Then I was taken into the Office of Personnel, on the Board of Examiners, and then I became deputy director of personnel for policy, position classification.

[Personnel] was a new field for me, but I found there were many aspects of it that I thought were indeed well worth the assignment. I went in with the group that was put into personnel shortly after the suicide of Charles Thomas.[2] It was a very tense period. There was a great deal of pressure brought to bear on us.

In 1973 the director general of the Foreign Service left, and Olmsted became acting deputy director general. In July 1973 a memorandum crossed her desk. "It was a request from EA for authorization to open a new post. Papua New Guinea was soon to become independent and our embassy in Australia in charge of the area was finding it difficult to be informed about developments and believed State should open a consulate in Port Moresby."[3] She routinely initialed the request and sent it on, but the more she thought about it, the more interested she became in having the job of consul general at the new post. She put in a bid for the slot and immediately ran into sexist opposition. How could a woman in her fifties open a new post when the task called for a man in his thirties? How could she be effective in a male-dominated society? How could she cope with the difficulties and uncertainties of a remote Pacific island? But with the help of friends in the right places, eleven months later, in June 1974, she was on her way.

The first task was setting up the new post, from scratch.

The department sent in an advance team consisting of the young man who was to become our administrative officer and another young man who was sent out from the department. They looked around to try to locate both housing and office space for us. Then my secretary went out a few days before I did.

We moved into some rather shabby quarters over a lunch counter and a bookstore. There was no furniture in our quarters, so we borrowed three battered desks and five chairs from the people we were renting the space from. These were straight chairs, not swivel chairs. As I say, these offices were a bit grubby. They were carpeted with large squares of blue and bluish-green cheap carpeting, and curtains were orange and white. They were broken down into little rabbit warrens, a whole passel of little rabbit warrens. The floors creaked when we walked across them. One day when we had three visitors and all of our staff of three were there, one person had to stand because we only had five chairs, so I told the administrative officer, "For goodness' sake, go out and buy a few chairs locally."

We also bought a large heavy table to put our telex on, got the telex installed, and that linked us up first with Australia and later with Washington. We felt a little bit more in touch with things. Then one day our shipment from Tokyo arrived. When a new post is opened, they always ask one of the large embassies in the area to make up a shipment of things that a new post will need. Well, obviously Tokyo cleaned out its attic when it made its shipment for us. This great big lift van full of boxes arrived. We opened them one by one, the stationery, envelopes, consular forms, seals and rubber stamps, and all kinds of things that we needed, like paper clips. We couldn't get any paper clips locally. They also sent our flags. One was 19 feet long, and we had to open it up through the doors of three offices to see what size it was. I'm sure it was the largest flag in all of Papua New Guinea. We found exactly one use for it all the time that I was there: we strung it up on the Bicentennial Fourth of July.

[The staff] tended to be quite young and rather gung ho, and I sometimes had to hold onto their coattails. I'd rather have that sort of a person in a post like Port Moresby than those who had become old and cynical and even embittered.

It was considered a very exotic place, and the word got back that the assignments there were good assignments. They had the chance to do real

Consul General Mary S. Olmsted proposing a toast at a reception to mark the opening of the new consulate general in Port Moresby, Papua New Guinea, July 1974. Sir Maori Kiki, foreign minister of Papua New Guinea, is at right. When the country proclaimed its independence from Great Britain, Olmsted became the first U.S. ambassador. *Courtesy of Mary S. Olmsted.*

things. I had an economic officer who had completed the work for his Ph.D. and was on his first assignment. He set up his own little shop and presented me with an outline of what he wanted to accomplish, and I told him to go to it. He had a very free hand, and he found it a very rewarding assignment.

We had a brand-new local staff with no experience whatsoever, and the junior officers, I thought, did an excellent job in training the local staff and encouraging them. My secretary taught them touch-typing, and the officers encouraged them to take correspondence courses, one in commercial work, another in consular work, from Washington, and helped them with it, and they helped them with their English.

There was a very high rate of turnover among the local employees in Port Moresby, not only of the diplomatic staffs but throughout. After a young person had been on the job for six months, he looked around for what else he could get that would be new and interesting and pay better. By giving them more responsibility, by teaching them, by giving them increases, we held onto ours. It turned out to be very effective.

I lived in Port Moresby, on the side of a hill overlooking the Coral Sea, an absolutely spectacular view of the curving coastline and the little islands dotting the harbor. From my patio I could look 180 degrees around the horizon. Below me, at the left, there was a fishing village on stilts built out over the water. To my right there was the curve of Paga Hill. I was in a very modernistic house which was built by a Greek Cypriot as a bachelor's pad. You could see that a bachelor had built it, from many of its shortcomings, but it was an interesting house.

I hired a houseboy named Kisini, who stayed with me all the time I was there. He had only a little training. This young man, I'm sure, was still in his teens when he first came to me, and spoke very little English. I had an Australian friend who had had a plantation in the area where my houseboy came from, and he spoke the language. When I ran into real problems, I'd telephone him and he would play interpreter over the telephone. (*Laughs.*)

A surprising number of things were available locally, and yet there were gaps in supplies that were also surprising. I can remember one of the young married men on the staff came back after he had gone out to do some Christmas shopping and reported that there were nine brands of French perfume available in town. *Time* [and] *Newsweek* were both available on the newsstands, the Australian edition of both of them. There were some of the other American periodicals and also a number of Australian periodicals.

The government of Papua New Guinea was "a modified Westminster-type government," with a prime minister chosen by a vote of Parliament, which numbered about 100 members.

It's a very primitive country, very, very undeveloped. When they conduct a national election, it takes three weeks because they don't have enough trained people to hold it simultaneously in all parts of the country. Therefore, election officials will go by small plane, even helicopter, by canoe, and on foot to reach these remote places. Everyone is given a chance to vote, and the ballots are kept sealed until the election is completed, then they're counted. There are 750 different languages spoken in Papua New Guinea. They have an enormous language problem. [Elections are by] the whispering vote, as they say. (*Laughs.*) They whisper to the person who is marking the ballot whoever it is they want to vote for.

Regard for Americans among Papua New Guineans was high for several reasons.

The largest missionary presence in Papua New Guinea is the American missionary presence, and there are many people who had Americans as their teachers. There are, I'm sure, many people who think they would not be alive except that there was an American mission hospital or clinic in their village, and they could go to it and get a cure for their ailment. Consequently, I think that Americans are well regarded. I also think that the older people who remember the Second World War regard Americans highly. The Japanese were quite cruel in their treatment of the local people, and there was quite a contrast between the way the Japanese treated them in most places and the way the Americans treated them.

When the American troops came in, they brought with them just vast quantities of matériel and things like refrigerators and candy bars and everything in between—much more than the Australians ever brought in. It was the first time that the Papua New Guineans realized that there was a country that was more powerful and richer than Australia, and that impressed them.

Another thing that impressed them was the fact that there were black American troops and there were black officers. John Guise [the governor general] will say—I've heard him say it—that he remembers when he saw American blacks giving orders to American whites in the military, *and they were obeyed*. He said he saw them doing what looked like, to him, highly skilled technical work. This was one of the factors in starting the stirrings of independence, because the people started looking at each other and said, "That man's black, and look what he's doing. Why can't I do it, too?"

Independence was the sixteenth of September 1975, and that's when the post became an embassy. We had a little ceremony elevating the consulate general to the status of embassy, and we unveiled our plaque, which read "Embassy of the United States," in place of the one that said "Consulate General of the United States." I automatically became the chargé d'affaires. I had hoped, of course, that I would become the ambassador, and I had decided I would not stay on as DCM if they appointed somebody else. I didn't know what was going on back in Washington. Our communications weren't all that good; nobody had visited recently to bring us up to date on things back there, so I just sat back and waited to see what would happen. I knew I would be very disappointed, because I liked Papua New Guinea and I wanted to stay on. I felt I could handle the job, but I also know that there's many a slip when it comes to ambassadorial appointments.

I think it was sometime in late October that I got the cable saying that President Ford wanted to appoint me as ambassador, and was this agreeable with me? (*Laughs.*) I sent back a very quick cable saying, "Yes, I'd be delighted." My name was eventually sent up to the Senate, and I was confirmed in absentia.

The Solomon Islands, then still ruled by the British, came under Olmsted's jurisdiction, and she visited from time to time, making the four-hour flight from Port Moresby. When the Solomon Islands became independent in 1978, Olmsted was named its U.S. ambassador.

She described a day in the life of the American ambassador to Papua New Guinea and the Solomon Islands.

I often began the day with a quick swim in my little pool, and then had breakfast. After breakfast, my driver came and took me to the office. The security people used to tell us we should use a different route going to the office every day, but that was quite impossible. There was one way to get there, unless one went perhaps 20 miles out of the way to take the ring road around Port Moresby, so we followed the same route, driving along the coastline of the Coral Sea, looking out at that magnificent view. I never got tired of looking at it.

Once in the office, I would look at the cables and read the newspaper when it was delivered to me. Then the day would begin. There would be things to discuss with various staff members, perhaps a staff meeting, or perhaps just individual discussions. There would be people outside the office to see, perhaps someone to call on in the government, or perhaps a discussion with a colleague from the diplomatic corps. Often I had lunch in town with someone, but I also stayed home, occasionally having luncheons, as was appropriate for the occasion. We had a surprising number of visitors from the United States in Port Moresby. So I might have a visitor to talk to or to take on a call. Then I would perhaps have a cable or two to write, and the work of my office staff to review and sign, and then the day would end. We did not often work overtime in Port Moresby. We opened at 8:00 and closed at 4:30 because athletics and sports were very important in the lives of my staff. Many played golf, some were boaters. One very enterprising young officer built his own sailboat, did a beautiful job on it. Squash was popular with some members of the staff.

There was a rather lively social life in Port Moresby. People did quite a bit of entertaining because there really weren't a great deal of other things to do. There were a couple of theatrical groups which put on plays from time to time, and I always went to those. The National Arts School regularly had showings of their students' work, along with a little reception. I regularly went to those.

I had a beautiful view of the Coral Sea from my patio, and I found that small cocktail parties at sunset were an effective way to entertain. It was a good way to entertain visitors—a small enough party so they'd have a chance

Ambassador Olmsted and guests on the patio of the embassy residence in Port Moresby, enjoying the spectacular view of the Coral Sea. *Courtesy of Mary S. Olmsted.*

to talk to people and could enjoy watching the setting sun over the Coral Sea, which is a lovely, lovely sight, and then watch the lights come on around the coastline as the sun went down. Sunset came very quickly and darkness followed promptly, as we were close to the equator. Very dramatic.

I found that I circulated in several different groups. First the official group, the government and diplomatic corps. It seems to me we had a diplomatic corps of six or seven [countries], which then expanded after I left. The Papua New Guineans were not terribly enthusiastic about having a lot of foreign [embassies]. They didn't see the need for them, and they weren't intending to open up a lot of posts themselves. We were really a close-knit little group and we did have our little get-togethers.

Another was the business community, which I, frankly, did not enjoy as much as some of the other groups. The business community tended to be people who were not terribly well educated, not very broad in their outlook; [they were] interested in making money and going home. Another group was the university, and I did make a real effort to cultivate contacts in the university. The faculty of the university was like the UN, there were so many different nationalities there. And another group that I circulated in was the arts and crafts group, the people who were interested in the arts and in the artifacts and in buying and learning about the New Guinean artwork, particularly from the Sepik.

Mary Olmsted's sensitivity to local mores was an enormous asset in a land where the people were unaccustomed to women in positions of authority.

Papua New Guineans are very conservative people. They don't jump to conclusions. They don't go off on rash tangents. So when I arrived, they were a little taken aback, but they thought it over very carefully and waited to see what kind of a person I was and how I fitted in. After I had been there for some time, Washington appointed Anne Armstrong as ambassador to London. When the Papua New Guineans learned that London had an American ambassador who was a woman, and they did, too, they rather felt that put them in the class with London; that was pretty nice.

I think it was an advantage that I was both a foreign woman and an older woman. Older women do have a status in the traditional community that a young woman does not have. I saw my role as developing a good working relationship with the foreign minister, Sir Maori Kiki, and with his immediate subordinate, who was the secretary in the Department of Foreign Affairs. I was fortunate in that both of these men were married to women who were educated and who were strong figures.

I thought that one of the most important things I could do to establish good relations would be to portray the United States as having a sympathetic and friendly interest in a small emerging country. Consequently, I spent a great deal of time on what was essentially public relations work.

The chancery is very close to the street, and behind us we had quite an area of land which was being used for nothing. Every time I looked at it, I began wishing we could somehow develop it. So eventually we came up with the idea of putting in a small amphitheater where films could be shown, and lectures and education and so on. It was slightly terraced, and benches were put in. There was a little stage with large logs behind it to form the background for it. There we had American films twice a week, free. Sometimes we had things by invitation only, but a lot of them were open to anyone who wanted to come.

Eventually we opened a library. We had a very active program of leadership grants, and we certainly managed to send to the United States a lot of people who became important in government. That was, I felt, a very important contribution that we made.

At the time of independence, lots and lots of small ceremonies were taking place: the introduction of the new currency, the turnover by the Australians of certain military equipment. The diplomatic corps was invited to these things, and I made a point to go to them, to demonstrate my interest. Not all of the diplomatic corps did, but I was always there. When they introduced the new currency, I had a $20 bill that I could take up to the teller and change into the new currency, and the finance minister said later it made him feel very good to see someone changing an important currency like American dollars into *kina*.

I tried to entertain more broadly than I think a diplomat ordinarily does. They had a women's conference in Port Moresby, drawing in women from all over the country, and I had a reception for the women and displayed some photographs and printed material from the American women's movement. When I gave large receptions, I tried to include university students and some of the more junior people from the government. I did a lot of traveling, and we visited schools. I visited places in the country that most diplomats don't go to. I took a seven-day trip in a dugout canoe on the Sepik River, and spent the nights in little *haus kiaps* [huts on stilts] along the way and looked at the artwork and the *haus tambarans* [spirit houses].

[Once] when I went to the Southern Highlands, it was announced on the radio that a big important visitor, a foreign visitor, was coming from Port Moresby to be present at this ceremony. They told me that the announcer had a very hard time saying that a woman was important. It was very difficult for him to bring himself to do that. Finally, he managed it. (*Laughs.*)

Although not a significant power, Papua New Guinea's vote in the UN was important to the United States.

I was in touch with the government of Papua New Guinea on various items that were coming up in the UN, and asking for their support in such matters. I found, generally speaking, that either they would abstain or would be willing to vote along with us. There were a lot of matters that they felt they did not want to get tangled up in, and they didn't want to devote their rather scarce resources of trained manpower struggling with certain international problems that they felt did not affect them. But on the other hand, where there was something that would affect them or that they had a broad interest in, they were certainly willing to listen to what I had to say and often did support our position.

Despite their favorable relations with the United States, the Papua New Guineans came to believe that Americans were meddling in internal affairs and promoting the Bougainville secessionist movement.

Bougainville is the most easterly of all the islands out from the main island. It's the furthest away from Port Moresby. The people there generally have a darker skin than most Papua New Guineans. The Bougainvillians generally call other Papua New Guineans "redskins." They felt that they were different, and they felt that they had been neglected because they were the furthest away.

Well, when Papua New Guinea reached the point of becoming independent, Bougainville started talking about becoming independent from Papua New Guinea. There were three leaders of this movement: one of them was a Catholic priest, one of them had been a Catholic priest but left the priesthood in order to marry an American woman who had been a nun, the third had at one point studied to become a priest but had not ever entered the priesthood. All Papua New Guineans. Bougainville was very strongly Catholic, and the Catholic bishop was an American citizen. Other Americans were also in the church hierarchy as missionaries. Consequently, there was a certain involvement of Americans in the secessionist movement right from the start. I don't think the church ever officially sanctioned the secessionist movement, but it was known that there were considerable sympathies [for it] among many of the people in the Catholic church.

The central government became increasingly perturbed over the "American" role. It was very important to the central government that Bougainville should not secede. The psychological impact of secession would lead other parts of the country to want to secede, and in addition to that, the royalties being paid to the central government from [a major] copper mine were a very important part of the government's income. They feared there was CIA intervention. I kept telling them that there was not, but the rumors went on and on.

I was at a government reception one evening, and one of the senior Australians came over and told me that there had been a cabinet meeting that day at which the CIA's role in the Bougainville secessionist movement had been discussed. It was extremely hard to prove a negative. I saw the prime minister, who was, I thought, very cool towards me, and I said [to myself], "I've got to do something about this," so I went over and talked to him. I pointed out to the prime minister that there was very little American interest, just a minuscule American financial interest in the Bougainville copper mine. I said, "We have just no reason to want to support the secessionist movement."

Of course, they were concerned over the fact that some of the secessionist leaders were going to the United States to get sympathy at the UN. The day after I saw the prime minister at the reception, I called on the foreign minister and discussed the matter considerably further with him. I explained to him that it would be extremely difficult for us to refuse to issue visas, particularly to the secessionist leader who was married to an American citizen. So I said, "We'll have to go ahead and do it, but we will keep you informed." Therefore, after that, I always let them know if we had issued a visa to any of the secessionists, and I think they appreciated that.

But there were all kinds of wild rumors about the Eighth Fleet being just over the horizon, with 30,000 men on it ready to take over Bougainville. Just incredible rumors going around. I was very particular that CIA people should not visit Papua New Guinea. Some of them wanted to, and I had rather strained relations with our embassy in Canberra because I just said, "We can't have it."

Another thing that happened about that same time: two warrant officers from the [U.S.] Army were going to the Solomon Islands in connection with a long-standing scientific project, but we received no notice of their arrival. One of my young officers happened to be having a drink at a bar and fell into conversation and discovered these two American military men were going to go to the Solomon Islands, stopping overnight in Bougainville on their way, and carrying all kinds of strange boxes and parcels in connection with their scientific mission.

I said, "Get those men down to my office now." He did so, and they came in, and they were very reasonable young fellows, just doing their job, not at all aware that there was any problem connected with this. I said that they would just have to stay in Port Moresby a few days longer and take a direct flight to the Solomon Islands, do their business there, and take a direct flight out and not stop in Bougainville.

As time passed, the Bougainville issue was settled, and Bougainville stayed as part of Papua New Guinea, and the secessionist movement died down, and everything blew over. But it was a very uncomfortable period.

The United States had no AID program in Papua New Guinea, having decided that Australia, the "big figure" in that part of the South Pacific, should also maintain the major aid role. Because of this policy, "it was my job to say again and again and again, 'No, we are not going to supply aid to Papua New Guinea.'"

It was rather an interesting situation, rather unusual in the American Foreign Service, to recognize consciously that another country is the big power in a given area, and that we are definitely playing the smaller role. It did pose some problems for me. On the one hand, I wanted to follow the policy, which I felt was the right one. On the other hand, I did not want to appear to be in the hip pocket of the Australian high commissioner. I made every effort to keep [him] informed of things that might come to my attention that he might not know about, but at the same time I never went from the foreign minister's office to the Australian high commissioner's office on the same trip. I always saw to it that there was some lapse in time [between the two visits].

In reflecting on her impact as a woman ambassador, Olmsted made two important points.

I think that I was able to demonstrate a friendly interest of our large and important power in a small country, and I think they appreciated that. I think the fact that I was a woman did make a difference. I think women are more willing to listen. In dealing with Third World countries, I think that sometimes men, particularly the younger men, go in with the idea that they are to be the big wheel, the big cheese in the country, and try to, well, even throw their weight around a little bit. I think a woman is much less likely to do that.

Not long before I left, one of the people that I dealt with in the government said to me that if I didn't know it, I would be interested in knowing that my appointment there had caused a good deal of discussion within the government of Papua New Guinea. The conclusion that the government people reached was that if a big and important country like the United States was sending women abroad as their representatives, giving them high positions, Papua New Guinea should also have women that it could name to high positions. He said that my appointment there had given a real impetus to the improvement of the position of Papua New Guinean women.

When I left, I felt considerable satisfaction in believing that the United States government had made its official presence known and recognized in a way that was entirely acceptable to the Papua New Guineans. I thought that the opening chapter of our relationship had been a good chapter.

The visitor to Port Moresby can still find tangible evidence of the high regard and deep respect felt for the first U.S. ambassador by seeking out the short thoroughfare that bears the name "Mary Olmsted Street."

8

CONSUMMATE POLITICIAN
Anne Legendre Armstrong (1927–   )
United Kingdom 1976–1977

Anne Armstrong, the first woman to represent the United States at the Court of St. James, a top diplomatic post, took the tools of a successful U.S. politician, elevated them to an art, and emerged as "a very popular ambassador, both within the embassy and within the country—maybe the most popular [in Great Britain] that we've had."[1] Her talent for representation was manifested by a manner that was open, frank, and friendly and enchanted the British man in the street.[2]

The British found her background, her looks, and her husband all "romantic."[3] They gave her nicknames—"Annie Oakley" and "Auntie Sam."[4] They loved the fact that her husband, Tobin Armstrong, was a Texas rancher with a 50,000-acre spread, and that the couple had five grown children, including twin sons. Flattering articles about the Armstrongs, singly and together, often appeared in the British press. She was greatly in demand as a speaker and a ribbon cutter throughout the country.

Armstrong had had a remarkable career as the "ultimate" politician, moving up from precinct worker in South Texas to top positions in the state Republican party. The 1960s and 1970s were good years to be in Republican politics in Texas.

I used to kid Sissy Farenthal, who was a Vassar friend of mine, a very liberal Democrat, because Sissy had to go through [the] big entrenched bureaucracy of the Democratic party of Texas with many males in place who weren't about to want her to rise. I didn't face that. I was in a highly fluid situation where there was opportunity for rapid rise. You could get leadership opportunities rapidly, and you had challenges just thrown at you as fast as you could handle them.

Armstrong had little trouble balancing politics with her family life on the ranch as long as she was in local and state politics and could commute from home. Her husband was firmly wedded to the ranch and had no desire to live elsewhere.

These were my time-consuming activities. I didn't do the things that I might have done as a wife in a big city; I didn't do symphony this day, USO another, disadvantaged children another. I had two big things I was doing—my family and politics.

Having lived on the ranch since he was a little boy, [Tobin] adores it. It's everything, from his family tradition and the way of life he loves. He was in charge. That is his family's ranch and had been for generations. It wasn't so much my home as with most wives; it was his family's place. And he's a wonderful father, that's the other thing. Besides feeling this is his home, he's just a terrific father in every aspect of his kids' lives.

She went on to become co-chairman of the Republican National Committee with Sen. Robert Dole, to which her husband agreed only reluctantly, as she would have to be away from home for long periods. She was a keynote speaker at the Republican National Convention of 1972 and became President Nixon's counselor with cabinet rank, making her the highest-ranking woman in the Nixon White House and the Republican party.[5] By 1976 her meteoric rise had made her a serious contender for vice president on the Ford ticket.

Through much of the Watergate fiasco, she staunchly defended the president. (A wit said she sounded like the social director on the Titanic.)[6] To her credit, when the tapes revealed Nixon's involvement, she then called for his resignation. The scandal of Watergate did not touch her, and her popularity in the party did not wane.

Watergate was a horrible experience. President Ford asked me to stay on, really to help get the White House and him through that period; plus, in a

Anne Armstrong, May 1973, before becoming ambassador to the United Kingdom, considered the United States' most prestigious post. *Official White House photograph. Courtesy of Anne L. Armstrong.*

way, I wanted to sort of cleanse myself, as it were, so I stayed a few months with him. It was just a wonderful experience in every way. He was marvelous to work for.

By the time Gerald Ford nominated her, in December 1975, to be ambassador to Great Britain, women chiefs of mission were no longer a novelty (she was the eighteenth), but the announcement drew attention because, except for Clare Boothe Luce, none had ever been given a class 1 post.[7]

I was totally thrilled and totally surprised. I knew I wanted very much to do it, but it took quite a while. I couldn't have done it, or wouldn't have done it, if my husband hadn't agreed that he would go, and that meant then we had to find somebody to run the ranch in his absence, and we had to find someone that the rest of the family would be happy with. That took about three weeks to get all those things settled.

We had our eldest son working on a ranch in Venezuela, and he had just started the job a few months before; he adored it but agreed to come back. My husband was so upset by the idea that he literally got sick and lost weight beforehand in the months before we went over. He said that he would try to be there for all the most important times that I needed him, [but] he would have to go back every month to help our son with the ranch and other business interests. The way it turned out, he went back once from England to Texas and never went back again except when we both went on vacation. He was very happy, very busy, [and] made the friends that truly are our best friends now. He agrees with me that was, if not the best time in his life, one of the best times.

I remember that [the members of the Senate confirmation committee] were very reasonable and that I was asked very fair questions. I thought it was a good experience. The State Department had prepared me very well. I think they have a good program for the administration nominees. I felt well prepared and at ease. It would have been even better had I known more about what was going to be expected of me later as an ambassador, but at that point, there wasn't any cram school for what an ambassador should know.

That would have been very good to have given me before all these meetings at the CIA, or with the New York business group, et cetera, took place, because you could have assimilated a great deal more. A lot of it hit you so fresh and strange that you really didn't take it in as well as you might have. It would have given me a framework.

Armstrong's swearing-in ceremony was unusual in that it took place at the White House.[8] "I was close to the President and Mrs. Ford, [and my nomination] did highlight a high role for a woman."

When Armstrong went to Great Britain, she was open-minded about her goals as ambassador and knowledgeable about her strengths.

It is our closest ally, or certainly one of the top two or three. I hoped to further cement those relationships. I realized there'd be some economic problems over there. At that point I really didn't know what my role was, but England was in the depths then, had to get an IMF [International Monetary Fund] loan, which just seems unbelievable today. As far as the issues, I didn't know that Croatian terrorists overhead in a plane, hijackers, would be an issue. I knew Northern Ireland would. It was not clear to me what, if anything, an American ambassador could do. I saw England, too, as a hub of many of our activities—military, economic, NATO, otherwise—so I hoped to be able to be useful in areas that weren't even strictly London, as it were.

And I guess, drawing on my own past, I thought I'd probably be pretty good [at]—and then this turned out to be maybe the thing I was strongest at—portraying the United States to your host country. I'd had a lot of experience doing that. I had not had a lot of experience in negotiations or running an embassy. I had been able to run volunteers—thousands of them—but that was my limited managerial experience.

When she arrived in London, she did not know what to expect, and many people thought she would fail. Not only was her view of the world parochial, but she mistrusted the career diplomats, beginning with her DCM, who had served her two predecessors and had himself already been an ambassador. The signs were not good.

But she could make decisions, and she listened, however unwillingly at first, to advice from the professionals. She was also bright and a quick study. Ronald Spiers, her deputy, was in the unenviable negative position of having to tell her what not to do and what things couldn't be done by the embassy. The clash of their two forceful personalities created shock waves throughout the embassy.

Armstrong followed some of Spiers' suggestions, specifically his advice to mingle with people from all British social levels and all political parties, but it was obvious that she was hostile and that he did not have her trust. Part of this appears to have been an "us versus them" attitude on both sides. She was asserting her authority and believed her Foreign Service staff was resisting. Her personal secretary attributes a "snickering" posture to them, and says, "They resented a woman coming." She adds that Armstrong let it be known before she left Washington that she was the boss.[9]

Relations between the ambassador and the deputy continued to deteriorate until finally, believing things could only get worse, Spiers went to Armstrong and recommended she tell Washington she wanted a new deputy. He explained this was often done and the department would understand, adding that she could be sure it would not affect his career. She replied, "No, but it sure as hell will hurt mine." He likens what followed to "breaking the sound barrier." The air was cleared, the resulting rapprochement was complete, and Armstrong went on to a highly successful tour of duty with Spiers. She was smart enough to realize her emerging popularity in Great Britain was partly because she had followed her careerists' advice. She came to trust her staff, and she relied on them to carry out the embassy's substantive functions while she concentrated on the representational side.

I had had some of my [initial] fears assuaged by people assuring me of the caliber of people who'd be working for me. No matter what job I'd had, you certainly can't do it all, even when you know a field as I knew U.S. politics. Ron Spiers couldn't have been a better complement to me—I mean, the consummate pro. Poor Ron, he'd already trained Walter Annenberg, Elliot Richardson. As you know Ron, there's nothing put-on about him. He wasn't too happy about this job, but he gave it his all; he would never hold back. And although it wasn't the challenge he was looking for at the moment—and he told me so—I couldn't have asked for a finer DCM. At first, I thought he was awfully prickly, and I didn't particularly take to it, but as the weeks went on I did appreciate him, and I wouldn't have changed him. At first I thought, "Oh-oh, I don't think that this flint and steel, or oil and water, is going to mix at all." But it did. And our counselors, with one exception, were very strong, and therefore that makes the ambassador strong. They were not only professionally most able, but also the chemistry was right in these instances. It was just a top-flight embassy. We really had fantastic people.

The problems we would have often happen in big posts, of course. Treasury and your economic ministers don't often get along. There was some of that problem. The Henry Kissinger syndrome of conducting diplomacy behind the ambassador's back. Henry kids me; he still hasn't got the story straight. We had a big blowup once. I picked him up at Claridge's, and I'd found out he was having some meetings with the foreign minister that I was not privy to, so I blew my top and told him, "That better not happen again." Henry tells the story and claims I cried. Well, the last thing I was going to do was cry then. I might have bitten him, but I wasn't going to cry. So after that, that went better. But these were things that happen to ambassadors in many, many posts. In London, they're often glamorous because they involve a Henry Kissinger.

Although London has long been accounted one of the most socially demanding assignments, Armstrong did not find her representational duties too burdensome.

London is so sophisticated that the demands on the ambassador, as far as the formal calls, et cetera, are less than they would be in a smaller post. The other ambassadors have plenty to do, and they really care very little if the U.S. ambassador calls on them, whereas in another post, it's a very important matter. So the entertaining was not a surprise, and I didn't feel it was out of line. I didn't get exhausted.

[I had an] excellent staff. Just as in the chancery, the residence was splendid. I didn't run the best residence in London. I didn't get a good enough chef. I had able help with the guest lists and the entertainment, and the entertainment was fun. It was not as elegant as I am sure Evangeline Bruce did, or Lenore Annenberg, and so I could have done better there.

"Yes, I know," Armstrong said when reminded that these hostesses' husbands were the ambassadors, not they themselves. She insisted that her own full-time job as ambassador included setting "one of the best tables in London . . . that's management, too."

[Tobin] was splendid at thinking up groups of people or who would be exciting in that group of people or who'd leaven the loaf in that one, but as far as menus and chefs, that's not his bag. He'd have a good idea for a theme for a party, or he'd hear somebody from the United States was coming, in politics or culture, and he helped a lot that way and was a marvelous host. He was one of the reasons people had a good time.

I loved [the representation part of the job]. True, the most boring would be the cocktail parties in town. That's boring for most people, but at least when you're an ambassador, you have a mission usually, to see a couple or three or a dozen people and ask this or that, so you're often there for a purpose.

Armstrong was wary of falling into the trap that ensnares some ambassadors to old world capitals of cultivating only the aristocracy. "I think having been in politics in the U.S. was a big help. I mean, you wouldn't think of representing the Republican party by going to see Madam La-de-da and her pals, and thinking that was Chicago or Peoria or whatever." She recognized, too, that the American Bicentennial provided unusual opportunities for her to represent her country in a positive light.

To me, the most moving and impressive thing I did was at Westminster Abbey. They had me read the Thanksgiving service, and they had the service in honor of America. That was an absolutely magnificent ceremony. I read Governor Bradford's famous description of the first winter of the Pilgrims. I read that, and I read a lesson, too. I read lessons all over England and Scotland and Wales. They liked ambassadors to do that. I'm an Episcopalian, so that fits, but the Presbyterians had me in Scotland, too.

Armstrong felt that "the good ol' drinks party" served her purposes better and made the best use of her entertainment allowance.

What people want to do is see that beautiful house [Winfield House]. [Cocktails] would not serve the purpose of making warm friends or conducting negotiations in a conducive social venue, [but] it served getting a lot of people to say, "I met the ambassador and her husband and their children, and we saw that gorgeous house," et cetera. So we did more of that than anything, and that served [the] purpose of [accommodating] the huge numbers of Americans in London [and] the congressmen that want their constituents entertained.

However many Americans Armstrong entertained, she almost always had British guests as well.

I could count on one hand, I think, the times we would have just Americans, and then it would not have been a big party. No, I think that's a key function of an ambassador's entertainment, unless there's a very good reason—you know, if you're having a caucus of congressmen who want to talk privately. But those occasions, obviously, are not where the ambassador learns a lot or where the ambassador teaches other people very much about what's on America's mind. Then the dinners are better. I did very few lunches, mainly because we did quite nicely at the chancery, and it was just easier for the counselors, rather than having to stop work and go—because it took a good 15 minutes—back to Winfield House. We had many lunches at the chancery.

Tobin Armstrong rarely participated in the chancery luncheons. Both he and his wife knew "that wouldn't have been right."

The only time he had anything to do with embassy business was with agriculture, which he's thoroughly competent in. And [Earl L.] Butz, who was then secretary of agriculture, had given him a commission to try to promote U.S. exports. He wasn't paid, but he did it well. He did it in England, and he went to Poland, some Iron Curtain countries, Greece. He would work occasionally, maybe a couple of days a month, with the agricultural attaché; he'd try to go to the agricultural shows. It was a part-time job that maybe took a day a week. But otherwise, he did not have anything to do with embassy business and would not have wanted to; he knew better than that. That was never a problem.

Armstrong and her husband were "well off" enough to pay for the occasional "something exceptional" ("you know, yellow roses or champagne") out of their own pockets. Otherwise, Armstrong found the ambassador's allowance was "enough to do it very nicely."

You'd never be criticized. We had California wines, but they were very good wines, and I was happy to do that anyway—things American. We had wonderful American art that year for the Bicentennial. A friend of ours lent us a marvelous Remington & Reynolds collection of bronzes and pictures, which for Texans was just [perfect]. I always had a little trepidation: how will these things look in that Georgian house? They were absolutely stupendous. And in that foyer, those bronzes—it was sensational! And we got help from Art in Embassies [the State Department service that provides American artworks for display]; they were very useful, too.

Walter H. Annenberg had redone Winfield House not long before.

It was in the most beautiful shape. Elliot and Anne [Richardson] had been there since, and there was scarcely a thing to do. I remember saying before I went, "Well, of course, I'll put my touch here and there." It would have been a mistake. Upstairs we painted the library, and that was a little worn. That was the only thing we did. Put some music in and changed the pictures, because the walls were bare. But Wildenstein's [an art gallery] pitched in. A friend who's a decorator with a very fine firm in New York went over with us. The only disappointing thing was, all the walls were not only bare but [there were] the alarms—because Annenberg had fantastic art, so the pictures were alarmed. Here were all these dreadful gadgets hanging out of the walls. But within a couple of days, Wildenstein's had lent us enough. We gave a dinner party within two nights, I think it was.

In 1976 Armstrong and her husband accompanied the queen of England on a tour of the East Coast.

It was so interesting to see the different ways the cities would manage it. Philadelphia amused her. It horrified me. [Frank] Rizzo was mayor, and Rizzo's idea of a proper greeting for the monarch was to have more policemen than I have ever seen in my life, arms akimbo like this, from the dock to downtown Philadelphia, with their backs to the queen, facing the crowd, as if there were imminent danger of a riot any minute. It was really something. And, of course, nothing happened. They were happy crowds.

Boston did it magnificently. I think [Michael] Dukakis was governor then. They had their police people—they weren't police people, but they were from the local towns, and probably sheriffs or other sorts of law enforcement people—done in colonial costume. So it was attractive rather than a downer. Everywhere, I was very proud of America.

Back in England, the Armstrongs' contact with the queen was mostly confined to ceremonial occasions. They did have one "personal visit" with her at Sandringham.

King Constantine of Greece, Princess Margaret was there, the Queen Mother, Prince Philip, and I guess that was it. We had a very informal, delightful time—luncheon. And then she puts on her bandanna and her low shoes and takes me out to the Landrover, and off we go to see the horses, and the corgies are piled all over. We had just a delightful family time.

A very different picture of the queen was on board the *Britannia*, when she had President Ford and Henry Kissinger in conversation after a party, and for the first time I realized how knowledgeable she is in foreign affairs; it really was an eye-opener. They were talking about the complexities of Cypriot politics, which, of course, is Byzantine, all sorts of subjects, and the queen was an expert on all those subjects.

Another important Englishwoman at the time was, of course, Margaret Thatcher.

She was the head of the shadow government. She commanded my respect then, and I think I knew her well enough not to be at all surprised at what she's accomplished. A most commanding woman [who] makes an instant impression of power and authority. The first time I met her, she'd invited me to her quarters. She was just back from a trip to Israel, and tremendously impressive with her grasp of the issues, her analysis of the personalities, and she was very pleased. She had accomplished what she went for. Then we got to know her after that.

Since then, I have a better insight into her as a wife. Ron and I tried and tried to get her to come for dinner to Winfield House, and she was slow to accept. Finally we got her, and it tickled me so afterwards. You know how the English are very polite about seeing you literally to your car when you're their guests? So Tobin and I, as hosts that night at Winfield House, took Mr. Thatcher and Mrs. Thatcher to their car. Mr. Thatcher gets in the driver's seat and drives, and Mrs. Thatcher gets in the backseat and he drives her. I thought Tobin would die, because he liked her so much, but this was quite a blow to him. [Laughs] She probably had some papers back there that she was going to attend to. Since then we have learned that Dennis is a very happy husband, that she is a wife very dependent on him, that they're a marvelous pair. But that was kind of a blow.

Armstrong was never aware of being in any personal danger.

In those days there was not the problem of terrorism. Yes, there were still sandbags around some buildings because there'd been a bad rash of bombings several months before we got there. And several months before I left they changed the curtains in our offices in the chancery to those mesh curtains that catch glass. So there were a few steps taken, antiterrorist steps, but there was not the fear for the ambassador that there has been in recent years. We had a guard dog that ran around Winfield House at night, but it was really quite relaxed and amateurish compared to what people have to do now.

Maybe it's partly because of the big, beautiful house and the upstairs rooms. I never felt put-upon as far as lack of privacy. And those gorgeous grounds. You could take a walk—you've got several acres there to walk around—Regents Park, so I never felt hemmed in. And, of course, the British people are such civil, wonderful people. They'll leave you alone usually. Or if they bother you, it's in a nice way. Their politeness is famous, and justly so. So if you were walking down Stratford-on-Avon and you were sightseeing, if they had anything to say, it would be something complimentary about your country, or, "We're so glad to have a lady ambassador," or something like that. It would never be hurtful or intrusive.

As with Mary Olmsted, being a woman was part of Armstrong's great success as an ambassador.

It certainly contributed to being well known and being a novelty, and so you certainly got your foot in the door as far as getting people's attention. You were noticed the minute you arrived. Ambassadors can do good jobs in so many different ways, I've learned. One of my strengths was knowing how to deal with the public and enjoying it, and this was the kind of a post where that could be useful. In many countries you wouldn't think of doing that. I think it helped to be a woman.

Her husband, however, did not go to the lengths that Henry Luce did—sitting with the women while his wife sat with the men after dinner.

We didn't do that, we didn't separate the sexes. Now, I had to make up my mind whether I was going to take a stand on that in other people's houses. I did not. The only women's issue I took a stand on was at a club. They had a separate entrance for the women, and I did take a stand there. I said, "If I'm coming to speak here, we're all going in the same entrance." But as far as separating after dinner, if we were in somebody's house and [they] did it, I did not squawk. Each woman has her own way of doing things, and I have not been as confrontational as some women I respect very much, who get things done by making more noise.

After Carter defeated Ford in 1976, the new secretary of state, Cyrus Vance, graciously told Armstrong to take her time leaving, but she, knowing her mandate had ended, departed right away.

Had Ford been reelected, you know it's reasonably certain he would have asked me to stay on. When he wasn't, obviously I was going to go, although they were very civil to me. So it couldn't have been more nicely handled.

For 90 percent of the ambassadors, [staying on] would have worked, but I had been highly politicized. But it was beautifully handled, with the utmost tact. Vance was completely fine about it, and all the State Department people were. It just couldn't have been easier for all concerned.

I tell you, the only truly unpleasant thing that happened the whole time I was over there was at the very end. After Carter was elected, we get a phone call that I am to leave the country because [Walter] Mondale is coming. I said, "What? I'm ambassador for the vice president-elect,[10] and I'm ambassador for all Americans." "No. You get out of the country."

Ken Rush was ambassador to France, and he called and said he was getting out of France, and could he come stay with me? I said, "Well, I've just gotten a phone call that I'm supposed to vacate." And so I said to Ron, "Ron, you tell them I want to see a cable to that effect. Put it in writing." And it never came, and so I stayed. Rush left. All the others left. There were some others involved.

The foreign minister came out to meet Mondale and said very nice things about me as I was standing there. On purpose, because I'm sure the British were privy to this.[11] And, you know, that isn't the way diplomacy works. I doubt, from the way [Mondale] talked he even knew about it. Somebody had done it. But then there was an unfortunate set of statements by one of Mondale's people after a party that the prime minister [James Callaghan] gave them, and he had served them some famous old brandy or famous old wine. Anyway, the next day the press person said, "Well, the vice president never would have been elected if he spent that kind of money on an obscene party."

Well, poor Mondale by that time was in Tokyo. And so Mondale called me and said could I explain to the prime minister that, of course, those weren't his sentiments and that he was terribly embarrassed about this statement. They had not invited me to that party and had said it was a stag party. I found out later there were women there. But anyway, I called the prime minister and said, "The vice president—this is certainly not the way he feels. It was a beautiful party. He's so upset that he's called from Tokyo to make sure that you understand this."[12]

Armstrong's opinion of the Foreign Service was transformed by her experience as ambassador.

I figured they'd be intelligent, that I knew. And that certainly proved true, [they were] the most intelligent group of government people I've ever worked with—very hard-working, very loyal, without ever being two-faced, the ability to put all their efforts behind whoever is deserving of it at that point. I am a great admirer of the Foreign Service.

9

THE AMBASSADRESS WHO BECAME AN AMBASSADOR
Mabel Murphy Smythe Haith (1918–   )
Cameroon and Equatorial Guinea
1977–1980

Mabel Murphy Smythe Haith's tour as an ambassador provides an excellent example of the pluses a career in academia can bring to a diplomatic assignment.[1] Her appointment to Cameroon was apt; she had had a longtime professional interest in Africa, and as a writer and lecturer in African studies, she was an acknowledged authority on African cultures and politics. Unlike most noncareer ambassadors, she did not come cold to her assignment: she had accompanied her husband on his tours of duty as ambassador to Syria (1965–67) and Malta (1967–69).[2]

Haith is an eighth-generation descendant of Catherine Cleveland, a free woman and member of a prominent family in Sierra Leone who emigrated to America in 1764 on a ship—possibly owned by her grandfather, a British slave trader— that was carrying a cargo of Africans to be sold as slaves in Charleston, South Carolina.[3] Haith has reestablished links to her African cousins. The family is still prominent in the leadership of the country, and in an interesting parallel, one member became Sierra Leone's first ambassador to the United States.

Both of Haith's parents were college graduates. Her father, orphaned and raised in Boston by relatives, taught English at black universities and later ran a printing business. Her mother's career as university hostess (equivalent to dean of women) at Atlanta University did not blossom until her three daughters and one son were raised, although she was active in civil rights and in 1930 was a delegate from Georgia to the national NAACP [National Association for the Advancement of Colored People] convention.

Home was a warm, supportive place where the children were encouraged to use their abilities to the full. Haith was the scholar among the children, but the

119

whole family was bookish. All four children studied musical instruments; Haith played the piano, violin, and cornet.

Summers were spent visiting her maternal grandparents in South Carolina, where "Granddaddy" owned prime property in the heart of Camden and ran a grocery store that specialized in fine comestibles to tempt the winter resort people. Family ties were constantly nurtured, fostering feelings of security and belonging and the firm conviction that those in better circumstances should assist the less fortunate.

Although raised in a community somewhat sheltered from racial conflict, Haith was "very, very aware" of the evils of segregation.

There were some horrendous things happening around us, and yet it was possible to protect us from the worst of it because we lived in a vast black community, so complete that we didn't see outside it much and we didn't come in contact with the element that would be most difficult. We just weren't where we'd come across working-class whites, who would most resent competition from blacks. We had both white and African-American teachers in school.

We had the black newspapers, which headlined all of the lynchings, and there were many more than one might imagine, even in those years. During the summer vacation, my best friend and her older brother went to the playground after church. They were the children of the minister and lived some distance away. Her brother, who was a senior at Morehouse College, took their little brother to the swings and began swinging him back and forth, and she was standing there. Some white men came in and said, "That's the nigger." They believed that he was the one who had said something to one of the whites, and they murdered him. They shot him in front of his little sister and brother, and he had been in church at the time that the incident happened. But it was so outrageous and they had been so careless of establishing his identity and he was clearly not guilty, for the first time in the history of Georgia [a white person was] sentenced to prison for murdering a black person. The *first time in history*. Now, they were given only two or three years for it, but it was such an astonishing change from what had been customary.

In discussing her early life, Haith stressed her mother's influence.

She's a natural leader, much more so than I am. She had a funny kind of understanding of a kid like me. She understood that I would sometimes not say what I really wanted, and she was a creative listener who found out what you meant underneath and encouraged. She never made a secret of her pleasure and her pride. No matter what small thing I had done, she always cared about it and celebrated it, and that gave me a great deal more confidence than I naturally had. I tended to be a shy little thing, but she made me feel that underneath I was very confident.

Haith was scholastically precocious, and at 18 she had completed her coursework at Spelman College in Atlanta. Having won a scholarship to Mt. Holyoke in Massachusetts, for the first time she left the Deep South. The atmosphere at the New England school affected her profoundly.

It was a funny thing—I felt I belonged there. I had a sense of belonging greater than I had had in many other situations, because most of the students seemed to have the same kind of goals and concerns that I did and the same kind of family background and so on. When I was growing up, very often I needed to be a little careful of what I said so as not to hurt anybody's feelings, or to stimulate comparisons, and I got very good at it and at not appearing to be too bright or too intellectual. In the South, there was the southern womanhood kind of symbol of not outdoing the men, and I could look as impressed by somebody's very modest intellect as anybody else's.

Haith graduated from Mt. Holyoke at age 19, and after two years teaching at Fort Valley High School in Georgia, she married Hugh Smythe. She accompanied her husband to Northwestern University, earned an M.A., and then, when he volunteered for wartime service, went to the University of Wisconsin, where she finished her Ph.D. in economics. She taught at Lincoln University in Missouri for three years, then the Smythes moved to Tennessee, where both taught at Tennessee State. This proved, in her words, to be "an eye-opening kind of experience," because they came to realize that the aim of the administration in enriching the faculty and the course work was nothing more than "an attempt at providing separate education that would keep people quiet," that is, keep the African-American students from asking to go to white universities. Fed up with such politics, Haith says, "we went to New York and decided we were simply going to stay out of the Deep South." In New York Hugh worked for the NAACP and Mabel taught at the New Lincoln School, where she became principal of the high school after two years.

In 1951 the Smythes and their young daughter Pamela moved to Japan. There each taught at a different university. Upon their return to New York after three years, Mabel undertook work for the NAACP on the school segregation cases and was deputy director of research on the team led by Thurgood Marshall. Their work led to the Supreme Court case Brown v. Board of Education of Topeka, in which the court struck down segregation in the public schools. She described this period as "a high-water mark in my life."

By that time, the movement for more attention to Africa came along. Jim Robinson [a New York City pastor] ultimately developed the Crossroads Africa program to take American students to Africa for the summer. In 1958 he wanted me to take the first group to Nigeria, so I was leader of that first group. As soon as we were identified as people with an interest in Africa, we were asked to participate in lots of things. For instance, AID was sending a group of teachers to East Africa, and we were asked to come to Columbia University and speak to them about some of the cross-cultural experiences they might expect.

One thing led to another. For instance, Julius Nyerere [Tanzanian nationalist] came over; I remember a meeting at which he, before the independence of Tanzania, talked about how he looked upon his country and his leadership in that country. When Tom Mboya [Kenyan nationalist] came over, we met him; when Kenneth Kaunda [Zambian nationalist] came over, we met him. So we got to be part of the "Africa crowd." It was a heady time, and there were a number of conferences, a number of attempts to educate people on the meaning of Africa and its importance to the United States, or its lack thereof, so we became known as Africanists and remained Africanists the rest of our professional careers.

After their joint book on Nigeria was published in 1960, Hugh Smythe joined the U.S. mission to the UN, and from there, in 1965, was appointed ambassador to Syria. Once at Damascus, her husband sensed some resentment from the career Arabists but found this was by no means the prevailing feeling.

We had a middle-level officer who said to my husband, "I have learned more from you than I have from anybody else up to this point." Once [Hugh] sent in an analysis that our policy toward the Middle East was less sensitive to certain aspects of Arab views then it might have been. A neighboring ambassador sent in a response saying, "We concur with Ambassador Smythe's comments." Some of them wrote to him and said, "We could not have said that, we who are permanent members of the staff."

Haith said she, too, was aware of that resentment toward political appointees.

I think the point is whether you are serious in working there. If you are there [only] for the public relations and it's understood, fine. But if you are there to work and you have a serious attitude, I think they are understanding and appreciative.

The Smythes had an exceptionally active social life in Syria, which put a heavy burden on the new ambassadress.

We counted one year the number of social events we had gone to—800. It was nothing for me to have a coffee to go to in the morning, Hugh would have a luncheon, we might or might not have a dinner, but we surely had a reception, and sometimes two receptions, sometimes a reception and a dinner, and sometimes still another thing.

My staff could get a reception for 300 ready in two days. We had 11 people who could be tapped for waiting on two days' notice without any question, but we used our gardeners as well as our household staff. It was good training for me, by the way, to have that behind me.

[Our daughter] was doing a year abroad [in Spain] when we were ridden out of town on a rail in Syria in '67. It was with Hugh that [Syria] broke off relations [on 6 June 1967] during the Six Day War. We were evacuated to Athens. One couple was attending the air show in Paris, and they came back with no real understanding of precisely where their children were. Our safe haven was Italy, but it was easier to fly people to Athens and dump them and go back and get some more and get them out fast, so those who were going on to Italy had to do a second trip. It must have been a little stressful to be 13 and not know where your mother was, or to be parents and not know where your 13-year-old and 15-year-old were.

But the odd experiences have never had me feeling as if I'm really in imminent danger. I always felt as if it couldn't be too bad most likely, and so I've had the privilege of having a front-row seat at some of these events and, at the same time, not feel too upset about what was happening to me and mine. When our daughter was safely in Spain, we simply cabled her from Rome to come on to Rome instead of going home to Damascus when school was out.

It was a couple of months before they decided where [Hugh] was to go next, and that was Malta. Pam and I were going to stay in New York while he went on to start with Malta, because this was going to be an election year. We weren't sure how long he would be there. I finished up the school year while he did his first five months in Malta, then I joined him.

I saw as much as I could, and Hugh included me in as much official traveling as possible. Hugh was a very active person who didn't like a sedentary life, so [in Malta], when he wasn't doing NATO things or traveling around the country, he was visiting parish priests or factories or something. Toward the end of his tenure there was a little back-and-forth in the newspapers. Somebody wrote in and said the newspaper didn't seem to have much to write on except the American ambassador. Why did they pay so much attention to the American ambassador? The truth of it was, it was the only game in town. He got to be well known, and when he'd visit a village, as our car would go through the streets, people would reach out to shake his hand. I said, "Are you running for public office here?" It was very funny.

We got involved, as embassies so often do, in social betterment things. [The Sixth Fleet] would come ashore, and instead of leaving sailors with nothing to do, we would ask them if they would paint and repair a camp for children or the home for the mentally handicapped. If they didn't have things to do, you'd have someone calling up complaining to the embassy that they left 18,000 beer cans on the beach last weekend, and we'd tell the navy to have them get out there and clean it up.

Every time a ship came in, [Hugh] had a list of jobs that they could do. And, do you know, there was an orphanage where they were so glad to see these big men—they were bigger than the Maltese—and they would let the kids climb up on them. Of course, many of them missed their little brothers and sisters and enjoyed playing with kids. I remember the discussion over whether they would be able to do something to a big, old-fashioned wood-stove that would make it work, or whether it would be better for them to try to make a new stove. I had no idea that our fleet had foundries that could make things. You have to take off your hat to them and know that they would be able to survive no matter what happened.

I'll tell you something else: the competence of our admirals impressed us. There have to be some bad and incompetent sailors and officers somewhere on the way up, but they certainly weed them out before they get too high.

Hugh was to be in Malta—this was '68—another year, but Nixon had already been elected, so there was no point in his going back on a long-term basis. So we just went over there for the summer again, in the summer of '69, and took part in his farewells to the diplomatic corps. That was the end of diplomacy for a while.

Haith agreed that the department should offer courses to help new diplomats understand the need for sensitivity to other cultures, but she pointed out the danger in the opposite tendency.

Some Americans are so anxious to make friends, so ready to listen to the other side, that they forget they're representing the United States, and I found some who went overboard in imitating other countries. I was visiting a country once and the cultural affairs officer had me over to dinner, and he was so proud at having trained his four-year-old son to kiss my hand. Well, I cringed. It's so un-American, so unrecognizable. I think we go overboard when we think we must take whole things that are really not normal and comfortable in the United States.

After her husband's return from Malta in 1969, Haith went to work for the Phelps-Stokes Fund in New York. She also began a four-year stint of consulting work for Encyclopedia Britannica, primarily on the problem of making its publications "acceptable from a black point of view."

I ran into Franklin Williams, who was then at Columbia University—and he was becoming the president of the Phelps-Stokes Fund—and wanted to have a new *Black American Reference Book* published. Frank wanted me to come on board to edit it, and I accepted. I spent the next six years dealing with the project. I spent part of my time running some African programs for Phelps-Stokes and organizing exchange programs with Africans.

In February 1977 Haith was at a Phelps-Stokes meeting in suburban Virginia.

When I returned to my hotel one evening, there was a telephone number to call and a Mr. Vance had telephoned. The only Mr. Vance I could think of was Cy Vance. [*Laughs.*] I knew his wife. She and I served on the board of the New York Urban League together. I knew who he was and had heard him speak.

Vance asked her to be ambassador to Cameroon.

Now, I had had a rough winter. . . .

A very rough winter indeed. Before the meeting in Virginia, Haith had been on a trip to several countries in Africa in connection with the Phelps-Stokes exchange program. While there, her daughter managed to get word to her about an event that would change her life.

One of my old acquaintances who was stationed in Ghana met me at the airport and said, "I'm going to take you to my house, because your plane doesn't leave for five hours." So we went home, and he said, "I have some news for you. Your husband is in the hospital." [He] gave me the news that it was cancer, that they had not been able to get it all. Hugh would undergo chemotherapy, and if we were reasonably lucky, he had a couple of years yet.

So I hung onto the "years," and I [came back to New York and] went in to see him. He was feeling cheerful enough. He didn't know how bad it was, and for a while he gradually improved. Long before my appointment was announced, he had gained enough weight and barely enough energy so he had gone back to work. By the time they announced my appointment, on April 25, he was doing better so far as the public was concerned, but he had started his downward spiral. He was getting sicker and sicker and losing weight all the time. He couldn't keep food down. A week after [the announcement], he went into the hospital for the last time and lived less than eight weeks.

But you know, he took so much interest in my briefings and whatnot. He wanted me to go to Washington and come back and report to him on who had said what, and so I would do this. I would go down on Monday morning and come back on Friday afternoon, and in between I kept in touch by telephone. I had been passed by the Foreign Relations Committee, but I was

Mabel M. Smythe (later Haith) being sworn in as ambassador to Cameroon by Stuart Rockwell, protocol officer. Karen Pamela Smythe holds the Bible for her mother. Smthye's face reflects the stress and sorrow she was suffering because of the condition of her terminally ill husband, former ambassador Hugh Smythe. She served both as ambassadress at her husband's posts (Syria and Malta) and as ambassador in her own right. *Courtesy of U.S. Department of State.*

postponing the swearing-in. He said, "That's foolish. You don't get on the payroll until you're sworn in. Go get on the payroll."

He went in [the hospital] on May 2. I passed the Senate Foreign Relations Committee on the fifth of May. I was sworn in on May 27, and he died on the twenty-second of June, so he lived merely a month afterward. And after surgery, except for the last three days, he was in intensive care, so I couldn't stay but ten minutes at a time, but I could get in to see him every two hours.

It was a real strain, and it wasn't possible to do anything useful like planning ahead. So I'd work for a couple of hours and dash down for ten minutes, and I also organized my work so I could carry work and sit there and do it and go back and hand my secretary stuff that had to be typed. It was an unreal time.

I wasn't getting any training in Washington to speak of, except French. I was an Africanist, so that some of the information that I would normally have been given was already in my possession. I had already done the diplomatic wives' briefing course when Hugh was an ambassador, and people were very understanding. I'll tell you, I don't quite know how I managed the whole thing. How ironic to have this pinnacle of your life come with the nadir!

Cameroon, once a German colony, was divided between France and Britain after World War I. The French portion was granted independence in 1960, and in the following year the smaller British portion opted to split, with the southern half joining Cameroon and the northern half going to Nigeria.

I saw the most important part of my job [in Cameroon as] building and maintaining good relations. The business of making friends was more important than pushing specific policies. The policies followed the friendship, rather than the other way around, and we happened to have some things going for us that were very useful.

For example, we were interested in helping developing countries through giving them advantages in selling to us when they were the chief suppliers of some product or other. Cameroon did not realize that it was our chief supplier of wrapper tobacco for cigars, and as the primary supplier of that, they were in a position to ask for a tariff reduction on their product. We were able to point out that they were eligible for a tariff reduction.

There were many times when they were not aware of some other international provision that we could help them understand. They simply didn't have the staff and the people who were trained to do certain kinds of jobs.

The AID program was one in which I had a great deal of interest. As an economist, I had been interested in economic development for a long time. The thing about the AID program that particularly appealed to me was that it was in the process of being Africanized, in a sense. We had enacted legislation, thanks to Sen. Hubert Humphrey [D-Minn.], that required joint action between the host country and the United States AID program in selecting projects, in carrying them out, and in staffing them, and it was the policy already in our AID program in Cameroon to have a Cameroonian co-director. It was, in some ways, trying to be a model program for our AID agencies around the world.

AID had established centers for training young farm families in improved cultivation methods. Originally, AID brought one family from each village within a ten-mile area. According to Haith, "If that person didn't have a great talent for leadership, people would say, 'We never did it that way,' and wouldn't listen too much to one speaker."

So they started taking five to ten families from a village to live in the community for a year. They'd see all of the phases of cultivation, flood control, or control of insects or whatever, and then they went back, carrying with them a pair of oxen, a set of tools, and seed[s]. In general, the average of the farms of people who had had the training turned out to be much more impressive than the average product on the other farms. People didn't have to preach. All they had to do was work and let people see what happened.

[There was also] the ambassador's self-help program. I had $90,000 a year to allocate to small local efforts to do something that would benefit a village. There was a former Peace Corps volunteer who had invented a simple machine that would shell the peanuts and the hulls would go out one way and the nuts would come out another. If they didn't have to spend two hours shelling them, they could spend one hour going to a meeting and becoming literate. So there were some literacy classes, there were some classes in sewing, [and] other things that they could attend at a meeting house *if* they had a machine.

So I made a proposition: if they would earn the money for half the machine, we would pay for the other half. That made our $90,000 go a little farther and, at the same time, it was not handing down something. They put forth some effort and could say, "We earned this."

[It was] tremendously rewarding, because Cameroon was a country where people were determined to move ahead, and where Westerners were particularly pleased to see a kind of caution in the way they moved. Unless you have a somewhat conservative approach, much of what you put out is likely to be dissipated before you organize a discipline to use it.

After a "dreadful" first month, Haith straightened out the domestic problems and chores she had no time for by hiring a house manager. Though her social life was not as frenetic as it had been in Syria, "it was lively."

I had an American community that was inclined to entertain informally, and we enjoyed being together. Everyone was friendly. We were there to relate to the people of the country, to make them know more about us, and help us know more about them. We were not there to become better acquainted with other people's ambassadors.

The first party to which I was invited after I arrived had four Cameroonians present, and two of those were our employees. So I sent around a notice that we were there to make links with the country. We had a very limited representational budget, and it would be reserved for those entertainments for largely Cameroonian guests, so don't expect compensation if one was not entertaining Cameroonians.

That first embassy party brought in a lot of people who were not used to being at the embassy, who didn't really understand how embassy entertainment went or what to do with it, and among our employees were the ones who were not usually included. I included all the drivers, everybody, at that first party. This was my getting-acquainted with them. It set one kind of tone. They felt at least I was not unapproachable, and that we were serious in our interest in knowing more about Cameroonians and how they felt.

I tended to have focused events, discussions, very often. Because of my academic background, I tended to get involved with lecturers who would come over from various universities, perhaps more than might otherwise have been the case.

Then the shooting war began heating up in Chad, and there was a very real possibility that we'd have to evacuate the U.S. embassy in Chad. We had chartered a Cameroon Airlines plane, and it was waiting in northern Cameroon with orders to fly to N'Djamena and pick up our people and evacuate them to Yaoundé. The only trouble was, word had come that there was too much shooting; it wasn't possible to have them come.

So I went down to Douala, stayed for a reception, and took the first plane back in the morning, something like 7:00 in the morning. I went straight from the airport to the embassy and sat down and was looking over my mail when someone came in and said, "We'll have to go back to the airport. They have just landed a plane from N'Djamena." So I went down to the airport, and here was a plane. No one had been allowed to disembark yet because nobody had any clearance or anything; these were refugees. I got on board the plane, and here were all these people. It was a cargo plane, and they were sitting knee to knee, four rows longitudinally down this plane, all the American workers in the embassy and some third-country nationals who worked for the embassy. I just opened the door and said, "Welcome to Cameroon," and one lady burst into tears. She was feeling safe for the first time. You see, those cargo planes don't have windows and you couldn't look out. She didn't know where she was.

Part of Haith's job was trying to persuade the Cameroonians to vote with the United States in the UN.

I would sometimes make representations directly on specific issues, and explain what our point of view was and why we held it and what the payoffs were for them, and before the General Assembly we would have someone come out to go down the whole list of major issues that were to be discussed.

I had been watching African policy for a long time and had been concerned that we seemed so ill informed about African points of view. [Conversely,] I found with my African graduate students at Northwestern that I was *appalled* at some of the things that they took for granted, but then I realized if I had been taught from the time I was a child that the United States is *the* chief capitalist country in the world and that capitalism can be defined as exploitation of people, not caring about human rights or anything other than profits, we would understand the difficulty they have with giving us the benefit of the doubt.

One way Haith responded to the African belief that Americans are racists was to show the televised version of Alex Haley's Roots *to motivate a discussion about the problem.* Roots *presented the history of Haley's family from its African origins through generations of slavery in the United States.*

We started off by having the Cameroonian employees of the embassy see it first, and we asked them, "Do you think we ought to show it?" Some of them said, "I'm not so sure. It's pretty strong stuff." Others said, "Yes, show it, but know to whom you're showing it, and explain to them some questions about this." I was asked to chair a panel of people who would talk about it.

So we had this invited crowd. They watched the first two hours or an hour and a half of the program, then we turned the lights on and sat around for discussion. Well, it was absolutely fascinating. I had asked the black Americans and Africans in the embassy to come over and feel free to comment. One question from an African that was extremely interesting was, "We can't understand why you glorify that primitive life that we're trying to get away from." [*Laughs.*]

So I explained the romanticism in dealing with Africa, that it sprouted from a sense of being able to be proud of one's heritage now, after so long a time of being deprived. If there's one thing I pride myself on being able to do, it's [to] handle controversial material through a dispassionate exposition of the factors involved, and it works every time. One other person who came to the embassy was a very provocative kind of speaker, considered leftist by Americans, but such a lover of the United States that he was a little too defensive if Africans would attack. It was very interesting to see how he would explain things, while thinking of himself as very critical of American ways of doing things.

I think the more varied Americans they can send out who can criticize and not have me upset by it or anybody else upset by it, the more [the Africans] begin to understand what we mean by our free press and freedom of discussion and inclination. And they are impressed by it, they are very much impressed by it. The more we show, the more easily they accept the fact that "Americans are crazy": they'll let you say anything, they'll accept it, but they hate to hear you object to something that they really love and feel strongly about. Somehow it works, and they keep on being able to accept some things that are good about. Somehow it works, and they keep on being able to accept some things that are good about Americans.

Building rapport with Cameroon's president, Ahmadou Ahidjo, was a gradual process.

He is a Moslem, a devout Moslem, but African Moslems are not Arab Moslems. He said, "You will be a role model for our women." And do you know, within six months, 10 percent of the National Assembly was made up of women. I'm not suggesting cause and effect, but he was aware of the emphasis on human rights from Carter.

I learned later on that he had been a little concerned about this ambassador who was coming. In the first place, a woman, and it must mean a wild-eyed radical of a woman. [Laughs] But human rights, as it was then being enunciated from Washington, sounded strident to many ears in one-party countries. The idea of having a civil rights advocate come in and criticize what was or wasn't happening in Cameroon was a little unsettling, but apparently there was not a feeling that this would be enough to refuse agrément, and they ended up responding with reasonable dispatch, I think.

[The president] got so that there were times when we would talk essentially alone. He would have an interpreter around, but most of the time he could manage with my French and I could manage with his. He didn't attempt to speak English, but he declared that he could understand it and was quoted as saying to his cabinet that he understood it and they should learn to understand it, because it was a bilingual country.

Cameroon has more to offer American businesspeople than most developing countries, because they do have an infrastructure in place. You don't feel as if you're starting from scratch. There are a number of people there who are interested in cooperative ventures, and I think this is the time to pursue them.

When I first went there, there were four or five oil exploration projects and other [companies] who had contracts to assess the oil properties, but we didn't have many resident businesspeople. As time went on, there was a little accretion. There were people who were investing in things like the new sugar factory and the new leather factory. The more success they had with small investments, the more other people were interested in hearing about Cameroon, and by the time I had been there two years, I was seeing three times as many businesspeople as I had earlier. Do you know why? Because Chase Bank Cameroon had opened up. Once you have a bank, so that you can do banking more easily, once you have a critical mass of people who are devoted to American business, everything is easier.

Haith rated her experience as an ambassador "pretty close to the top" in her overall life story.

If I had to characterize myself, though, I'd have to say that I'm more jack-of-all-trades than a specialist at something. I've come to terms with the fact that if you are highly gifted in one stream, you're more likely to have a great impact in what you're doing. But on the other hand, I just enjoy so many things about this world that I'd be very hard put to specialize and stick with my last and try to become great at one thing.

10

FROM SOCIETY TO DIPLOMACY
Anne Cox Chambers (1919–)
Belgium 1977–1981

Her name consistently appears on the list of the top ten richest people in the United States. She sits on the boards of the Cox Broadcasting Corporation, Coca-Cola, and several other major organizations and is a leading art patron and philanthropist. She uses the Concorde to fly family and friends to her vacation home in the French Dordogne and conducts her business in both New York, where she has a luxurious Sutton Place apartment, and Atlanta. When time permits, she takes friends to Belize to show them the Mayan artifacts she knows so much about. Yet Anne Cox Chambers was a "painfully shy and awkward" child who enjoyed solitude and a world of imagination.[1]

The daughter of James M. Cox, three-time governor of Ohio, Chambers was the first of two daughters by Cox's second marriage, to Margaretta Blair, 20 years his junior. Her other sibling, a half-brother, was 18 years old when she was born in 1919. Home life centered around her father, "an imposing figure." The family, of English ancestry, was Episcopalian, but the little girls were raised by a German Catholic nanny who passed on her beliefs about sin, which made little Anne even more fearful and timid. She held her parents somewhat in awe. They were not demonstrative people, but philanthropy was woven into the fabric of family life.

In the 1920s the family shuttled between Dayton, Ohio, and Miami, where Governor Cox had built a winter home. The children went to a Dayton school during the spring and fall, and to one in Miami in the winter months. It was assumed from the moment the daughters were born that they would attend Miss Porter's School in Farmington, Connecticut, where their mother and grandmother had gone. Chambers's parents did not encourage any particular aspirations in their daughters.

One of my roommates in boarding school and I were discussing that. Amanda said, "Nobody ever told us to be somebody, so we weren't." Miss Porter's School was then a finishing school. It was not even college preparatory. I wish I had gone to college. We weren't even thinking of that. I certainly had nothing in mind, and I was married when I was 20.

The winter after I finished at Miss Porter's, I went with two other girls to spend some months living with a family in Paris. That was very much a thing to do, particularly [for] girls who had gone to schools which were not college preparatory. That was the beginning of my love for France. We lived with a very aristocratic family who had fallen on hard times, and we grew to love them. We'd have French lessons and then we'd go around to the Louvre, the museums, to Chartres. All of this in French. It was a wonderful experience.

Chambers made plans to return to Europe, but by 1937–38, "Mussolini was rattling sabers" and her father cancelled the trip. She briefly attended Finch, a junior college, but was not a serious student and did not return. The following year, she enrolled at "something called the Residence School, run by an Irish lady named Mollie Hourigan, and we lived in a brownstone. The only class that we actually did there was learning about operas and maybe piano. I went to a cooking school, and then I guess we had French."

Later that year she accompanied her parents to the festivities surrounding the world premiere of Gone with the Wind *in Atlanta.*

When I got there, our hostess said, "A friend of mine is having a luncheon for your parents." I met my first husband [Louis Johnson] there at the luncheon. He was studying in New Haven at the [Yale] graduate school. I went back to school after New Year's, but we were engaged by February, so I just gave up school and came home and that was the end of my education.

I did the provisional course of the Junior League, and my mother-in-law got me in her garden club. That was supposed to be something very big. The next December was Pearl Harbor. Even before that, I guess, I volunteered at the British War Relief. We went in the navy soon after that. Just after the war started, I had my first child.

After the war, James Cox put his daughter Anne on his board of directors, an act that "didn't mean that I had anything to say, but it was some sort of acknowledgment. Daddy felt strongly that women should not be involved in the business.''

The only thing I've ever done that made my father really proud was when I was elected president of the Peach Tree Garden Club. I told Daddy [just when] he was going to have lunch with Mr. Woodruff, who was "Mr. Coca-Cola" in Atlanta, and he said, "I told Bob Woodruff you're the only Yankee, ever, to become president of the club." That really pleased him very much.

My marriage was not very happy. Their father really never paid any attention to the children, so we didn't do things as a family, [but] I thought a woman's happiest years were being with her young children. I never thought of going beyond.

During the years that I was being the typical young matron, I did start playing golf, and I really loved that. I was never a good athlete. I had to really work very hard, but I really, really did, and that was one of my great pleasures. I played a lot. By this time, I was married for the second time and my husband [Robert Chambers] loved to shoot, and there was wonderful quail shooting, so I started shooting. I was 50 years old. Well, I got really into the shooting, and I really got good. I had the most wonderful teacher, and it was such fun. It was less trivial than it sounds. It became a great part of my life. I really did become a good shot, and I was terribly proud of myself. [My teacher] died, and afterward I said to someone who had known him, "You know, he gave me almost the first self-confidence I ever had."

Anyway, my father and he were great influences, and the third person was Jimmy Carter, because by appointing me to that job, my life became really changed.

At the time, Chambers was very active on the board of the Fulton National Bank (now the Bank of the South), as well as on the boards of Central Atlanta Progress, the Atlanta Chamber of Commerce, and the Atlanta Music Festival Association.

Since I first could vote, every presidential election I would go down and volunteer and do whatever. I was keenly interested in every Democratic election, and in 1966 many of us were very concerned about the possibility of Lester Maddox becoming governor of Georgia. So I said to my friend Philip Alston [subsequently ambassador to Australia], "Is there anyone on the scene rising in this state to combat this terrible tragedy?" And he said, "There is a young man in the state legislature, a state senator. I'd like you to meet him. His name is Jimmy Carter. I think you'll be impressed with him." I think I met him at [Judge] Griffin Bell's house. And I was impressed. So right then I started working. That year he was defeated by Lester Maddox. I remember after the election Charlie Kirbo [a Georgia lawyer] said, "If we had had $20,000, we would have won." I didn't have the kind of income then that I do now, but still I said, "Charlie, why didn't you call me? Don't ever let that happen again."

Philip Alston and I were the only people any of our friends knew who had supported Jimmy Carter through the years. [A friend] said, when I told him I was going to become an ambassador, "Do you realize that all of your friends thought you and Philip were crazy?" I said, "Sure, but this has been my political history all through my life."

After his father's [presidential] defeat in 1980, I was at a luncheon with Chip Carter. It was kind of the first old group. Chip said to the group, "I'll never forget the time that Daddy came home with a check from Anne Chambers. It was the biggest check anybody had ever seen."

In 1970 Carter was elected governor of Georgia.

My house is right across from the [governor's] mansion. When they moved in, he said, "There are funds either for a tennis court or a swimming pool." They couldn't decide, because the family liked both things, and I said, "Why don't you build a tennis court, because I have a pool." And that's what happened. So my family, who played tennis, went over there, and, oh, it was quite an unusual scene: the policemen were stopping traffic and the governor would come across with Amy on his shoulders in their bathing suits. When they came, I rarely went down; I just left them by themselves. They're [Jimmy and Rosalynn] both very reserved, very hard-working.

I was very involved in the [presidential] campaign and worked very hard. My husband and I were in New York, and Bert Lance [an Atlanta banker and subsequent director of the Office of Management and Budget] called me and said there was going to be a rally in Wall Street. It was the building where George Washington had spoken, and he said they were having Democratic celebrities, [Cong.] Bella Abzug and Lauren Bacall and Robin Duke [wife of Ambassador Angier Biddle Duke], who speaks beautifully. He said, "They want someone who is from Georgia who knows the Carters as a friend and neighbor, and will you do it?"

I was paralyzed. Absolutely. "Oh," I thought, "If this means so much. . . ." I had some months before started doing transcendental meditation [TM]. The morning of this rally, the phone rang, and it was the young couple who had been my teachers in TM, and I said, "Oh, I can't talk to you now. I'm in such a twit. I've got to make a speech in Wall Street, I've never done anything like this in my life. I'm just too nervous to talk." She said very calmly, "How long is the drive down to Wall Street?" I said, "I don't know, I guess 20 minutes." She said, "When you get in the car, just close your eyes and meditate, and that will calm you down." And it really did. So I did do that speech. I was rather excited about it. That was the first speaking like that that I've ever done.

In the early spring after Jimmy Carter's election, Anne Cox Chambers was nominated to the ambassadorship of Belgium. She took the State Department's ambassador's course, "commuting to Washington and learning for about a month."

I even went out to Virginia to the office responsible for decorating embassy residences. I went to the Pentagon. I met with Stansfield Turner [at the CIA]. There were seven newly appointed ambassadors. We had a two-day seminar on terrorism. The first thing we were told was that our government never pays ransom. I think it was like saying, "Anybody who wants to leave can leave now." I remember Sen. [Mike] Mansfield [nominated as ambassador to Japan] saying, "If someone is really out to get you, they're going to."

The hostages were taken in Iran while I was in Belgium. What it did for the morale was just awful. [The staff] knew some of the marines. Then the younger ones and my secretary would start getting letters: "Get out of the Foreign Service; we're worried about you. Think of the children."

The American Foreign Service Association (AFSA) raised objections to Chambers's nomination.

If it hadn't been for Ed Djerejian, deputy assistant secretary [for European Affairs], I don't think I would have gone through with it. He was in the northern European area. He's the one who took me around. He was just wonderful and very simpatico. He told me this association was going to object to Phil Alston and me and say we were not qualified. This was just after Ted Sorensen had been turned down, and this upset me very much.

I went home for the weekend, and I returned Monday, and I said, "Ed, I'm not going to be another Ted Sorensen. I'm going to withdraw my name if I'm not qualified." He said, "It has nothing to do with you personally. It is against any political appointees—career people feel threatened. Don't be bothered by it." Well, I was, and several times I know I became discouraged. Someone said to me, "Why in the world would you want to take on a job like that, just to do pure drudgery?" This was after the Foreign Service Association controversy, and I had felt some sort of hostility from some of the regular Foreign Service people. [Then] this person breezed in and said, "I just want to tell you something that I don't think you hear much. I think it's wonderful to have, sometimes, political appointees who are close to the president. You could get information across that we cannot."

And I must say that I, again, felt antagonism during the first few months at the embassy. Once there was something that was crucial to us. No one could get through to the State Department, so I called Jody Powell [the White House press secretary], and no matter where he was, he called me back. This time he called me back from Air Force One. The whole staff was impressed with that.

Chambers was to be ambassador to the king of Belgium. The other two U.S. ambassadors in Belgium were Representative of the United States to the European Communities (USEC) Deane Hinton, and Tapley Bennett, the U.S. permanent representative on NATO. Both of these men had the rank and status of AE/P and were stationed in Brussels. There was also the supreme commander of the Allied forces at Supreme Headquarters Allied Powers Europe (SHAPE), Gen. Alexander Haig.

Before taking up her post, Chambers received invaluable advice from former Secretary of State Dean Rusk, whom she knew through the Southern Center for International Studies. "You're one of three American ambassadors there, but since you're the ambassador to the king, you're the ranking ambassador. Just remember I told you."

The other advice he gave was such a wise bit. I had known Tap Bennett pleasantly, but not well. Rusk said, "You can lean on Tap for advice and help whenever you need it." And I leaned heavily on him.

When I was leaving for Brussels, I said, "I couldn't stay away from home for four years. I'll maybe stay two years." I couldn't imagine being away for four years. Those four years went so quickly!

Liz Carpenter, press secretary to Lady Bird Johnson, visited Belgium when Chambers was there. "I think it was genius that she went, because in Belgium they do business on hunting parties. She was an accomplished marksman, and so they included her, those male ambassadors, and that's where a lot of business was done between ambassadors.[2]

There was an article in a Brussels paper, maybe the chamber of commerce magazine, about me before I came. One of the things the article said was how much I liked shooting, and that was a great plus, because immediately I had invitations for that coming fall, and every weekend I went on these wonderful shoots. They were very pleased about that.

I had met the Saudi ambassador and he called me one day and said that he and the Lebanese and the Iranian ambassadors had leased a shoot together and invited me to come on a Tuesday. I was very self-righteous and said, "Oh, Ambassador, thank you so much, but I only shoot on weekends." He said, "Madam, when three ambassadors invite you to shoot, you do not refuse." I said, "Good, I'll tell my staff that I was invited."

Tim Towell, who was my first secretary [political section] and who was such a help to me, was the one person who was really honest, and he said, "You could often do more good, get more information, walking down a country road with your gun over your shoulder, and the Saudi's gun over his shoulder, than at the most formal national day celebration."

Chambers renovated the residence before her arrival in Brussels.

My friend Robin Duke, who had been an ambassadress three times, said, "Take some of your own possessions. That really makes you feel good. Take some of your favorite plates. You get awfully tired of looking at the eagle on the official plates." One of my daughters was going to be in London, so I asked her to go and take a look. She wired me and said, "All the walls are gray, and [if] it's raining when you get there, you're going to take one look, burst into tears, and come home." The decorator who was helping me at that point really did it all over. I paid for all of that myself.

Relations with her DCM were strained from the beginning. He made little effort to smooth her path, and even his arrangements for her arrival displayed a minimum of courtesy and were a far cry from the usual treatment accorded a new ambassador.

We arrived at the station in Brussels, and the DCM and his wife met me, and we went in and had a glass of champagne with the station master, and that was all. [At] the residence, [I] was introduced to the domestic staff, and then the DCM said, "Your first appointment is at a certain time tomorrow." My secretary said that she went to him that morning and said, "Aren't you going to go to the residence and escort the ambassador?" "Oh," he said, "she can find her way." And so that is the way it started off.

Ambassador Firestone had left nine or ten months before I was appointed, so you see the DCM had been in charge. I think he thought, first, [with] a political appointee (I had no experience, obviously), and a woman, that he was going to continue to be in charge.

I felt—I don't know if "hostility" is the word, but certainly I didn't feel any respect. I felt no cooperation, and I didn't feel that I was informed. As I say, he'd just say, "You're doing this and this."

One of my first appointments was [with] General Haig. I had my schedule, and it said I was going with the military attaché, who I liked very much. Well, that morning, Sharon [Stilke], my secretary, said that the DCM was going along. I said I didn't understand that, I thought it was just Colonel Lawrence. She said he just decided he wanted to go. So when we got near Mons, the driver said, "Would you like the flags on the car?" and the DCM said, "No, that won't be necessary." I said that I would like the flags. I realized that was just really the last straw. It was a morning appointment, and then I was to stay for lunch. So I got there, and very quickly the secretary came and said General Haig would like to see me, and the DCM got up at the same time. The aide said, "The general will see the ambassador alone." We talked for an hour and a half, and he cooled his heels. Then Al Haig said, "We'll go and have lunch," and he added, "I must say that I was quite surprised to be notified that your deputy was coming along." That was when I realized there was just *no way*.[3]

You know, when I was having trouble with the DCM, I had asked Tap Bennett to come for lunch, and I was trying to think of how I could bring it up to him, and he, in his forthright way, asked, how was I finding the staff? I said, "Mostly very good, but not all—some real problem." He said, "You mean at the top?" And I said, "Exactly," and he said, "I've heard that." I said, "You know, I just really don't think I can keep this man." And when I told him what was going on, he said, "Of course you can't." George Vest [assistant secretary for European and Canadian affairs] was my immediate boss [in the department], and Tap said, "You just tell George Vest what's going on." So that's what happened. But Tap gave me the strength [to ask for the DCM's transfer]. To have that support, being such a new ambassador, was just about the most important thing that happened in the first months.

I arrived in June, and then in October, the then-prime minister, Leo Tindemans, who is now the foreign minister, was going on an official visit to Washington, and so, of course, I went with him. When I arrived back in Brussels, I, again, arrived by train. All the officers were there, at least ten people with their wives, and I said, "But this is wonderful. What's going on?" They said, "This is the way your arrival should have been, and we all knew that." They were just appalled by that DCM's reception at my arrival.

It took a while for Chambers to establish her authority. One of the things she was up against was the pervasive male chauvinism of Belgium's traditionalist society. It was so deep-rooted men were completely unaware how offensive their actions could be. For example, when Chambers called on the Belgian foreign minister, Henri Simonet, to make a démarche (statement of policy), she took along her political officer to listen and take notes. Simonet, ignoring Chambers, addressed his remarks—at length—to the male officer, who was extemely embarrassed: "My answer was to avert my eyes and look at my notes and try to become a nonperson. That might remind him that he should be talking to the ambassador of the United States of America."[4]

But there were bright spots as well as difficulties in those early days, including official visits to Washington.

When the king and queen came, I, of course, went with them. First there was going to be a luncheon at the White House. Somehow I got word that the Carters had planned to just have the king and queen, just the four of them. Fortunately, I got wind of this, and [since] that would be considered inappropriate, I [got] on the phone, and I said, "This just simply will not do." So they put on an elegant luncheon. It was in April, and it was all the White House vermeil, and the flowers were dogwood. George Vest afterwards said, "I've been coming to lunches and dinners at the White House for 25 years, and this was the loveliest."

Chambers had been given no particular instructions by the department's Belgian desk before she left.

Ambassador Firestone had had the F-16 to do and successfully completed that. No, not until, as they say, the "miss-eyle" [missile] crisis came along.[5] Then we, along with the NATO ambassador, were busy with it the last year, year and a half. But that was most discouraging because, first of all, the Belgian government takes so long to make up their mind. They were very influenced by the Dutch on it. When the Dutch Parliament turned down the missiles, then there would be a backslide, and I'd go over to a minister and say, "The State Department would like an answer." "Oh, everybody's on holiday. No one's here." That's probably the most frustrating thing. You know how those European countries just close down in the summer.

President Carter's initiative promoting human rights struck a responsive chord in King Baudouin, as Chambers discovered when she presented her credentials.

The king took me in the room by myself. He had really done his homework. He's very impressive, his knowledge, and such dedication. President Carter had, just before I came, made his speech at [the University of] Notre Dame on human rights, and he mentioned that, and he said that he hoped to meet the president, because his whole philosophy on human rights was so impressive and so the way he himself felt. I always felt that Carter's stand on human rights, on the Panama Canal treaty, and [the] Camp David [agreement on the Middle East], all were far more appreciated in Europe than in this country.

Chambers found that a significant part of her job was staying abreast of the American business community.

At that time there were more than 1,500 American companies [in Belgium]. I visited all of the big plants. The chamber of commerce is very anxious for the ambassador to be involved in that. That's very important. And the Fulbright Commission, too. I was on that board. I think it's the custom for the ambassador.

There were many things going on in Antwerp and Ghent. There were American firms, so I visited places like that. I went to a newspaper plant. I loved those things, and I'd see other parts of the country.

Because of all of the American involvement in Brussels as well as the whole country, I was asked to attend openings, in the World Trade Center, and the book fair, and the automobile show—everything, because there was always an American emphasis in all of these.

Chambers described the Belgians as "very formal people."

I would say that I had a warmer relationship with [Prime Minister] Leo Tindemans than with Mr. [Wilfried] Martens [the subsequent prime minister]. Mr. Tindemans had been away in the summer, so I hadn't had him to dinner. I asked if he would like an official dinner or would he like to come just with his wife and my husband and me? He said he preferred that, so I asked him to come to my little house that I rented in the country outside of Brussels. He was very pleased, because it was the last Flemish area near Brussels. It was surrounded by the French-speaking part of the country, and he was very pleased that I chose it. I remember I served brussels sprouts and he refused to eat them because of the word *brussels*.

I had a closer relationship with Henri Simonet, who was the foreign minister. His was the opposition party, and I was amazed when the prime minister went to Washington on that official visit [that] Henri Simonet, as the leader of the opposition, insisted on coming along. He said that their views had to be presented to the president, to the department. To me, with our form of government, this was just amazing. You know, would the leader of the Democratic party have gone to Reykjavik? I found that very interesting.

I don't know if I told you my terrible faux pas when President Carter came. *That* was very much reported, and on television. He had been, I think, to seven countries, and Belgium was his last stop. The three U.S. ambassadors, naturally, were at the plane, and I was first in line since I was with the king. When he got off, he kissed me. The next day at my staff meeting, one of my officers said, "We were very proud to see you were the only ambassador on this trip to be kissed by the president." Well, obviously, I was the only woman.

The next day was Saturday, and I was at a shoot near Antwerp, and there was a man who was always kind of teasing me and sort of flirting, and he said, "Oh, I know what you were up to last week." We were at lunch in the middle of the shoot, and we were speaking French. He said, "Ah, I saw you being kissed by your president as he stepped off of the plane." Then I said, in French, "Oh, yes, my country team was very proud that I was the only ambassador to be kissed by the president." Well, I said the word in French, and you know the difference. [In French slang, *baiser*, to kiss, is a euphemism for having sex.] I didn't know what I had said, and everyone was laughing. I mean, there were these hoots of laughter, and my husband, who was at the other table, said, "What in the world did you say?" "Well, I said something awful." On Monday my French teacher came. I said, "Brigitte, your reputation is ruined. You're never going to have another pupil. This is just terrible." And when I told her, of course she turned beet red.

One thing I started doing, which apparently hadn't been done, was to say to each section chief, each department head, "Ask who you want." And then we had sort of working lunches in the residence. The labor man, for instance, said he'd never been asked to do that. My whole staff was very pleased about that. [They invited] people who wouldn't have been invited to the embassy otherwise. I know it was interesting for me.

As she grew into her role as head of mission, she came to feel part of the Foreign Service and developed a great respect for its personnel.

I talked to Philip Alston about this. We were both, from the beginning, so impressed with the dedication and how hard people in the Foreign Service work. I don't think it's recognized enough, and certainly it's not done for money. I have never met in any profession a more dedicated group—really dedicated, hard-working people. As I say, at first I felt some antagonism, but I truly think [after] maybe a year, in almost every case, I felt that I had established a rapport.

Several of Chambers's staffers took pains to stress her graciousness and thoughtfulness, and they invariably mentioned the parties she gave at her own expense for all members of the embassy, including host country nationals. Chambers also developed excellent rapport with the official and diplomatic community. One of her social successes came from an unexpected quarter.

When I arrived, we didn't have formal relations with China, and the ambassador at that time, oh, he was so stiff. Then he went home, and he was replaced. Of course, we all wondered who was coming next. The new one really was pretty much the opposite. He was a big man and very friendly. He wanted to make an appointment to call on me, and my political officer suggested that I ask him for tea instead of coming to the embassy, because of this strange relationship. When I asked him to come for tea, he asked if he could bring his wife.

Well, he was pleased to see that I had some Oriental things. Then he said he understood that I liked Chinese food, and I said I absolutely loved it, so they had us to a dinner. We would sit at a round table and have a lazy Susan with all of these marvelous things on it. He would ladle out the soup, and I remember one time he ladled out something, and I asked, "Oh, what is this?" And he said, "It's sea slugs. It's very beneficial for elderly gentlemen. It makes them young again; very spirited." I said, "Does it do the same for elderly ladies?" Well, he had a sense of humor. He said, "Oh, you may just run back to your embassy instead of riding."

I got a call about three one morning saying that we were establishing formal relations with China, so, of course, I called him first thing, and he was very, very pleased about this. I said, "Now I can have an official dinner for you," which I did. And he never missed a National Day celebration, and I never did either. That's really one reason we became so friendly. He'd say how appreciative really small countries were, and he said, "You know, other ambassadors need not go, but if the American and the Chinese ambassadors come, that is a great compliment."

The Belgian government looked to her for support in obtaining landing rights in Atlanta for SABENA, the Belgian national airline.

SABENA wanted to establish a direct route [from] Brussels [and] the FAA [Federal Aviation Administration] had to [give approval], so I would try to explain that. [The Belgians] would reply, "Oh, your president is aware of this, and you're a friend of his." I really sweated out that summer because if this hadn't gone through, I would have been the culprit, and I didn't want to go home. I got a lot of credit for [the eventual approval], and I didn't deserve it. [SABENA] is owned by the government, so they cared very deeply. [The approval] was not because of me, but it was a plus [for me], a mark of success.

After the king and queen had gone to Washington, I went to call on the king. President Carter had sent him a book, so I gave it to him and he opened it. It was a book about the South. He looked at it and said, "I have something for you." I couldn't imagine what it was. He walked over to a table, and there was a long box containing a decoration. It was the second highest order of the Ordre de la Couronne. It's one of those big beautiful things you wear with sashes, and I was just overcome. I was only the second American ambassador to ever receive it. That was just staggering.

Her greatest success may have been voiced by Amedou Ould Abdallah, the Mauretanian ambassador to Belgium at the time: "She brought the king's ambassador up to the level of [USEC] and NATO [ambassadors]. At the same time she brought with her all the other king's ambassadors from around the world." Expressing the view of the diplomatic community, he explained: "She came against the odds. [At first] the Belgians were not impressed. They were very happy to see that in the end the ambassador to the king was very powerful, very important, where he used to be marginal compared to [USEC] in negotiating on agricultural end products or to NATO [on] peace disarmament. The ambassador to the king used to just [be a] ceremonial role. With Anne, it was made very significant. They knew her power in Washington. In my opinion, the center of the American presence in Belgium was Anne."

Asked if he had perceived rivalry among the three U.S. ambassadors and General Haig, the envoy replied: "There was no rivalry. They were very close to each other." He described how she included the others in her functions, went to them with problems, and behaved very discreetly. "She went low-profile. The way she did with her staff, she did with her colleagues, two professional diplomats, [and] with General Haig. I don't remember her having any function without Haig." About her staff, he said, "She felt comfortable. She had no conflict, and so they felt comfortable. This impressed outsiders. It was clever of her, because she had the support of her base. This was one of her best achievements, administratively." [6]

I had no idea how my life would change when I came back here. All the wonderful things that have happened, and are still happening to me, are because of those years. I think just being interested in varied experiences brings great rewards. Everything just leads to other wonderful and exciting things. As I say, I'm just constantly surprised. I'm always feeling a bit like Cinderella.

Former ambassador to Belgium Anne Cox Chambers, at a ceremony held by French officials in New York City on 15 June 1993, to honor her as a Chevalier de la Legion d'Honneur for outstanding work in international affairs. *Courtesy of Anne Cox Chambers*.

11

CINDERELLA FROM THE BARRIO
Mari-Luci Jaramillo (1928–   )
Honduras 1977–1980

Mari-Luci Jaramillo began at the bottom of the economic ladder and, by extraordinary feats of persistence, endurance, and application, rose to become "The Honorable." Hers, more than any of the others, is the ultimate American success story, for she had the longest way to climb and had to strive every inch of the way.[1]

Although not the first woman to be named chief of mission to a Latin American country, she was the first actually to serve there.[2] *She was, in addition, the first woman Hispanic ever to represent the United States abroad. As women proved themselves in one geographic area after another, there seemed always to be yet another culture for which the tired cliché could be aired: it would insult the host country; she wouldn't have the respect of the male leadership; America would lose face in the host country; and so on. The idea of machismo, firmly embedded in Latin American culture, was the main argument the diplomatic establishment had used against sending women as chiefs of mission south of the border. Only the Middle East was considered less congenial toward women in positions of authority.*

For these and other reasons, there were grave doubts about Jaramillo's ability to represent the United States in Honduras. She was unschooled in the intricacies of diplomacy and had been named, perhaps cynically, to provide "diversity" to President Carter's appointments. (As both a minority and a woman, she was a "two-for-one" nominee.) The Foreign Service, represented by its professional organization, the American Foreign Service Association, initially opposed her. Nobody really expected very much from her. Her future deputy thought the choice was "terrible" because at that time, 1977, Honduras was governed by a group of military men who had a reputation as hard drinkers and Jaramillo was a known teetotaler. (In fact, she is allergic to liquor.) He thought the appointment made no sense at all. Today he says, "I was dead wrong."[3]

Jaramillo surprised everybody. Another officer at the post with her has said, "She won the hearts and minds of all Hondurans from the president on down."[4] *For that post at that time, she was custom-made. Culturally, she was one of them; she understood the Hondurans through and through. Her fundamental integrity and strong sense of decency and loyalty won the total trust of the Honduran leaders. Through her actions, her empathy, her ability to listen, her ease with their language, she convinced the Hondurans that the United States cared about the people and country of Honduras.*

Why did it matter if the people of a tiny impoverished country came to trust its huge neighbor to the north? Two reasons: (1) Still engaged in the cold war against communism, the United States was trying to encourage democratic forms of government throughout the region as an anticommunist bulwark, and badly wanted a peaceful transfer from military to civilian rule in Honduras, with honest orderly elections. Honduras's two political parties, the Liberals and the Nationals, were trying to outjockey each other, and the military was dragging its feet. (2) President Anastasio Somoza had been overthrown in Nicaragua by the Sandinistas, who were supported by the Communists, and overnight Honduras, which borders Nicaragua, was on the front line.

Mari-Luci Jaramillo helped the progression to democracy immeasurably. She was a key player behind the scenes in ensuring progress toward an election and was rewarded by having it take place on schedule. She reassured the civilians and military that the United States cared about the security of the Hondurans and saw to the beginning of U.S. military support for them.

To her embassy Jaramillo brought "leadership with a light touch," according to one officer. He added, "I felt I was with an IBM research lab or maybe a well-run university. I was never in an embassy where responsibility was delegated as clearly. It was my most positive experience in 25 years [in the Foreign Service]."[5]

Family values imparted at an early age were the key to her determination and drive.

In the Hispanic culture, people that are good to you and live in the area become a part of your family, too, so then you have the whole barrio. It becomes kind of an extended family, and you can go in and out of homes just as if you're going in and out of your own. It's just a beautiful feeling. That meant you had roots, and you knew everybody. But wherever you were, people knew you, so you didn't misbehave. [*Laughs.*]

When her mother would say, "We are going to go for a walk," Mari-Luci knew that meant going in the evening to pick up sticks that they'd seen in the daytime, for their stove. "I look back at that now, and I think why didn't we just pick [them] up in the daytime?"

You know, there was a sense of pride, that you didn't let people know that you really needed to pick up sticks from the street in order to keep warm. There was that sense that you didn't ask for help. The help came from your friends, from your family, but in ways that never made you feel ashamed. For example, I know that I always wore dresses that my mother would take apart from women's dresses, wash them, iron them, and then make [into] my clothes. And she was told, "We're giving you these clothes because you're so handy and so good with that needle, and you are so clever in making things." She wasn't told, ". . . because your kids don't have any clothes," see?

My parents thought that if we got an education we'd get out of poverty. They lived it, both through my father's example of always reading and studying and learning more, and my mother providing the environment. We came home and had to study. We couldn't do anything until the homework was done. To this day I hate to cook. I am one of the few Hispanics from a poverty base that doesn't know how to cook, because my mother insisted that we study and she do the work. We couldn't come home if we didn't have straight As, so you worked very, very hard at school.

A lot of people have asked how come I became such a strong woman in pursuing what I wanted to pursue and doing what I wanted to do, having had the model of a mother who took all this? I think that maybe that made me strong, because I decided then that I wouldn't put up with that. But I learned all the skills of how you continue doing something without upsetting someone else, which comes to play beautifully in office politics. You still get away with what you want to do and you've offended no one.

[My] early ambitions were, I want to do well in school, and I want to get a job, and I want to make money, and I want to be able to eat whatever I want. When I grew up, I was going to have money to buy bananas.

I loved school. Still do. When I graduated from high school, there were three awards given, and I got the three awards. I was valedictorian of my class—the whole bit. The night that I graduated my father showed up [for the first time at any school function]. And that night, I was in the middle of the stage; kept going back for my awards. And it was kind of my night, and my father was there! When we got home, my father said that he was going to help me go to college. He said, "I will give you a hundred dollars."

[I earned the rest], every single penny. I'd work at night, I'd write other people's term papers, I'd clean houses, I'd waitress, I did everything, and I went to school. So that $100 that my dad gave me was the only free money that I got, ever, in my education. There weren't scholarships or grants or loans—none of that. I already had my master's when the financial aid picture came into place, and I was one of the first ones invited to go on a pilot study to learn to teach English as a second language at the University of California in Los Angeles. So one summer I had a fellowship, and that's it.

I started cleaning people's homes when I was 11 years old. I'd scrub the side porch and the back porch and the coal-bin in the basement for 50 cents a week. Can you imagine? Then I worked in my father's shoe shop after school and Saturdays. Those were my first jobs. I did a little bit of waitressing one summer. I worked in a parachute factory.

I became an observer. I picked up skills because I lived in a bicultural world and people refused to say that it was a bicultural world. I watched how teacher behaved, and I watched how the kids that she liked behaved, and then I acted like those kids, and then I was one of them. I learned behaviors that were different; they were rewarded in one culture and maybe weren't rewarded in another. I became completely, completely conversant in Spanish, which is not true of my generation. Those in power did not want us to speak Spanish.

At the university level, I have a lot of mentors, and all my mentors are men. Women say, "Why is this?" And I'll say, "Please don't forget, I'm the first Hispanic woman wherever, and what other woman is going to help me when there aren't any there?" The few Hispanic males that have moved in were the ones that helped me, Hispanic men that gave of their time to say, "Mari-Luci, look, this is what you have to do in order to get past that barrier. These are the kinds of questions that they're going to ask you."

Promotions have been very interesting. They always automatically came. The first job I asked for was when I graduated from the university. All the rest have just come automatically. I was brought from the first-grade classroom into the university. I became an assistant professor, an associate professor, a full professor, chairperson of the department, associate dean, special assistant to the president, and I've never asked for a job.

Jaramillo would eventually become a professor of education at the University of New Mexico. Before her academic career began, however, she had married young (when she was a college freshman) and had had three children. The marriage ended when her youngest child was a freshman in high school.

We lived with my mother and my grandmother in an extended family type of situation, and my children never had a babysitter. My children were always well taken care of, even when this mom was always studying or working.

After my divorce, I enrolled in a Ph.D. program at the University of New Mexico. It was a very difficult time for me because, as a practicing Catholic, I had the guilt that I probably had not worked at my marriage as hard as I should have. But I had a large group of friends who advised me that I should go to school, and so, while I continued working full-time, I went to school full-time also, and earned a Ph.D.

In 1972 I married Dr. Heriberto Jaramillo, a Colombian-American. He was born in Colombia. He, too, has a Ph.D. in curriculum and instruction. We have been extremely happy. He has been very supportive of my work. Not only did he give up his way of life, but he gave up his job, he gave up his profession. He went to a land [Honduras] where he could have been told, "Your wife supports you." He worked with the Peace Corps, he worked in the ministry of education, he worked with both the private and public universities. He was working the field for me, and he made lots of friends for the United States during those three years. He also helped me a great deal with the embassy staff because we were able to cover twice as much ground, make twice as many friends. A lot of my success is owed to him.

When we arrived in Honduras, we had thought that he could work in something—with a Ph.D. from a United States university, he could surely find a job. We quickly found out that everywhere he was offered a job somebody would say, "There might be conflict of interest there," because I was technically the boss of every American in the country. So we decided that we wouldn't even look, that we'd go ahead and do the best that we could without his working. The only thing that we promised ourselves [was] that we would not dip into our savings, that we would use every penny that we were paid so that we would have a successful tenure. But he worked constantly, right alongside me, day and night, and never earned a penny. I always felt that he learned what American women had learned a long time ago, that they just worked hard and yet were never able to earn any money.

I never aspired to be an ambassador. I don't think I really understood what an ambassador did, other than in very general terms. I've never been active in politics and I'm not rich, and I had always thought those were the two qualifications for a presidential appointment.

I had a call from Mr. [Warren] Christopher [deputy secretary of state] in my office where I was a professor. As usual, I had a number of students in my office that I had to shoo out when the phone rang. On the phone they said that it was a call from the State Department. I thought there was a mistake, because in those days I had a lot of calls from Health, Education, and Welfare. But, nevertheless, it turned out to be the State Department, and this voice was telling me that President Carter had reviewed my credentials and was very impressed and wanted me to be his ambassador in Honduras. I couldn't believe it. I didn't have any political connections. My reaction was, "Who, me? No."

Mr. Christopher was a genuine diplomat and said that maybe I'd like to think about it over the weekend, and to please call him collect if any questions came to mind. He told me that they wanted me in a hurry, but that it would be quite a long process because the FBI would have to check me out and then I would have to go through the [Senate] hearings.

So I hung up and thought about it for a little while. Was I hearing things? What was going on? I was terribly excited. Oh, he told me that, other than my doctor and my husband, I was to talk to no one.

So I immediately got on the phone to call my husband, and I tried to talk for the first time in code. Well, needless to say, my husband didn't understand what I was talking about, and so he said, "Meet you in the car in a few minutes." I got in the car, and he tried to calm me down because I was all excited. He was saying, "Slow down. Slow down." He made me go to the beginning. Where was I sitting? Who was there when the phone rang? To try to calm me down. We lived about seven minutes away from campus, and I was telling him all this, and he was driving. When we got parked in front of the house, he said, "And what did you say?" "I said no." He took the key out of the ignition, turned around, and said, "You said what?!" And I said, "What's going to happen to us, Heri, if I were the breadwinner? I know that you would just feel awful." And he said, "I know who I am. I'm a very secure person. I think it's common courtesy for you to tell your president that you'd be delighted to be considered." So I think that the diplomat in my family was him. I knew that he would support me regardless. Although in the back of my mind I kept thinking, "In three or four months, after he has to sit around all day, he's not going to like it." But I decided to take my chances. And he was just wonderful. He lived up to it.

So they got back to me from the State Department, and at that time I said I'd be delighted to be considered. It was very difficult because I am a member of an extended family where we have always shared everything, and it was very difficult for me not to tell anyone, even my mother, of this wonderful thing that might happen to me. It bothered me greatly, especially when one friend called me and said, "What have you been up to? I told you not to get so involved with this Hispanic movement. The FBI is checking you."

Well, finally the day came, and I had the Senate hearing and the confirmation. I was very excited about it. It was at the time when most of us, and me for sure, wore slacks suits all the time, and I didn't own many dresses. I only had one really nice navy blue dress that was a little too short for me because now the dresses were a little longer. And I remember tugging and tugging on that dress. And after, when you have the party that you have at the State Department for the actual swearing-in ceremony, I had my one navy blue dress, and everybody wanted pictures of me sitting here and me sitting there, and I'd yank on that dress constantly. I'd think, "Oh, my goodness, in order to be an ambassador I'm going to have to get a lot of new clothes."

Mari-Luci Jaramillo at her swearing-in as ambassador to Honduras, 26 September 1977. She is wearing the too-short blue dress at which she had to keep "tugging and tugging." *Courtesy of U.S. Department of State.*

Jaramillo was unable to take the ambassador's course or receive all of the usual preparation because the administration wanted her to leave immediately for Honduras. "It appears that because they had been without an ambassador for quite some time, there was an uneasiness amongst the staff."

I had heard in a lot of indirect ways that, number one, the media was going to eat me alive because I had no experience with the media; number two, the military weren't going to pay any attention to me because I was a woman. That boiled down to: I was going to be failure.

But I knew a lot of things: I knew that I had studied like crazy and I knew Honduras well, I knew I was bicultural completely, I knew that Hondurans were going to understand me, and I knew that I was going to show them that I would be the best that I could possibly be. I was so nervous. There I was with my navy blue dress, tugging on it, tugging on it.

When their plane landed in Tegucigalpa, she could see a row of people and someone with a bouquet of flowers. She said to Heri, "You know, they told me that the media's going to eat me alive. Look at the media."

Here are all these people, and the television cameras, and the other cameras. They asked us to come out first. Everybody just stayed in their seats and applauded. The word had gotten around that the American ambassador was on the plane. I came down the steps, and everybody kind of rushed, taking pictures and stuff. I had met the DCM in Washington, so he came up to me and hugged me, and then his wife gave me a big bouquet of gladiolas, or roses—big-stemmed. So I was carrying this, and that was a very nice gesture because, what do you do with your hands? You don't think of all these things.

So I'm playing with this huge bouquet of flowers, and I start going down the row of people. It's the high officers from the embassy, and they're all the Americans that I'm talking to. I'm looking at them straight in the face, and everybody smiled. When I got to the end there, then the protocol officer said that I had to go to the VIP room. I thought, "I wonder what a VIP room is?" Well, the media had all gone through another door, and there were all these people from the media. So I walked into the room—and I knew I was home. They all looked like me! [*Laughs.*]

I made eye contact—the kind of contact that you make with your cultural group. I had thought of two or three things to say informally, and I said my two or three things in Spanish, just very informally, my style. I decided that moment I was going to be me, I wasn't going to put on any airs. So I sat down, and then the questions started. And the questions would come, and we were doing fine. I've always been very self-conscious that I don't photograph well. At that moment that fear was gone forever because there's no way that you can pose. People are going to be taking pictures everywhere.

Jaramillo knew she needed to start off on the right foot with her new staff and prepared her initial remarks ahead of time.

I wanted to say it in both languages because I knew that there were some Hondurans in the group that spoke little English. I addressed the group in Spanish, and then I told them in English what I thought we needed to do together. They had had a hard time at the embassy. There was a lot of friction and a lot of unrest. Tension seemed to be high. I said I was a team player, and in order for me to look good they had to look good.

Another skill that I have as a teacher is, I remember people's names. I was introduced to people, and then the next morning I'd walk in and address them by their names. I personalize everything. I thank people for good work. I frown a lot if you don't do good work. I was very complimentary of good work, and people knew it. I went to work at 7:00 and 7:30 in the morning. People were shocked. Pretty soon everybody else was showing up at 7:30—never said a word. That's just my work style. I took many brown bags at lunch, and I worked right through the noon hour, just like I do on campus.

She decided that she needed to get to know the people and country as quickly as possible. With tireless enthusiasm, she traveled "constantly, just constantly."

I was a novelty. I was the first American Hispanic woman that had gone any place, so they felt that they were honored. I just have a lot of good luck. I quickly made friends across the board—the military, the church people, the businesspeople, the *campesinos* [peasants], the media.

By the way, the media became my real friends. I know that many times I didn't say things as eloquently as it came out in the newspaper. Oh, they were wonderful. And on television, they learned that I take horrible side pictures, and [so] if I look into the camera, they would capture it. They went out of their way to be nice.

In her belief that "you don't yank people out right and left," Jaramillo retained all of the existing staff, including her DCM and personal secretary. When her DCM's normal tour of duty was over, she chose Fernando (Fred) Rondon to replace him.

I went to Washington, and a lot of people tried to politick and tell me how great this one was and how great the other one was. But I was after a certain type [who] believed in hard work like I do, and [who] was completely bilingual and completely bicultural, because I felt that that way, whatever I couldn't do that person would do.

I did look around and see if somebody would suggest a woman. I had thought it would be marvelous if the ambassador and the DCM would be women. But, lo and behold! not one surfaced in the process who was free and all that, not one.

When Jaramillo first arrived, Melgar Castro was president of Honduras. She became close to him, but "he had aspirations of being something like a populist president" and was quickly replaced by a military junta. Jaramillo had a "marvelous working relationship" with the three junta members before it, too, was dissolved and one of its members, Gen. Policarpo Paz Garcia, became president. Her close ties with the junta, and particularly with Paz, enabled her to help convince them that a turn to a democratic form of government was desirable. With Paz, she "had a wonderful relationship."

We just became good friends. President Paz was not highly educated, very obviously from a rural background. He had been a war hero in the Salvadorian-Honduran [dispute]. And because we became good friends, he trusted me. He saw me as the cultural kind of bonding. You're not seeing citizenship, you're seeing identical cultures. You are seeing that you have the same belief patterns, core values. Because I come from a poor background, that quickly came through. President Paz and I met probably many more times than an ambassador and a president of a country will meet, simply because we were friends. I would call him at any time that I needed to speak to him, and he'd come visit me, and he would call me any time. Sometimes it would be on a daily basis.

[I was] very discreet. I had advance notice of everything that ever happened at high levels. And sometimes I had to fake naiveness in public places so that I wouldn't give myself away—that I had had privileged information for days on end before something had happened.

Encouraging Hondurans to hold democratic, free elections was one of Jaramillo's major goals. She pursued it by discussion— "mediation, consequences, talking out loud what it would mean to the country, talking the virtues of a democracy"—and by never missing an opportunity to persuade and educate.

At cocktail parties, you would drop a hint to one, and you drop something else to another, and then you pray like hell that those two talk to each other. So that it's not obvious.

I know that I could have chosen to be very obvious so I'd get a lot of public credit for it. I chose not to. I think that that's one of the ways that this country gets that reputation of having so many damn ugly Americans out there; [they] want to take credit. I think we go to serve our government, and we should hide in the woodwork. You do your thing without people knowing.

Jaramillo had never met President Carter before she went to Honduras.

[But] when I came up [from Honduras], I always got to see him because [my friends] Esteban Torres worked in the White House, and Abelardo Valdez.[6] I would get invited to go have lunch with them in the White House, and then I would get to visit with President Carter, maybe in a corridor or in a portico.

When I came up with General Paz, I got to go to all the formal things with President Carter. Then when I came back, I was in a big, big Hispanic gathering where President Carter was the guest of honor, and he was just wonderful with me. I always had the feeling that if I needed to talk to the president that I could.

The Carter administration's emphasis on human rights helped her reach out to Hondurans.

Can you imagine going into the hinterland in some place where you're with campesinos, these rural people that don't have anything, and you're out there in the middle with these people that have nothing in the world, have no home, have *nothing*—maybe a little shack to keep out of the weather— and they're standing there with the American ambassador in the middle of the field, talking about human rights, *their* human rights? And where would they have gotten it? They got it from Carter, that's where they got it from. I know when I came back I heard things like, "President Carter wasn't a very good president," and I said, "Listen, I've been out of the country. I don't know what's happened here, but let me tell you, he was wonderful where I was, as a world leader."

The consular field was her greatest frustration, and visa problems bothered her most, "not because you don't have highly qualified people and hard workers" but because the system is set up to compel consular officers "to discriminate against the poor."

You never say, "You're too poor to go," but that's what it really boils down to, and those people aren't stupid. Our officers are told over and over they've got to do everything they can to make sure that they screen everybody. This might be fine other places, but I know that in Latin America it comes out very, very rude. That was the area where I had to spend the most time settling people down that were very upset. Somebody's cousin had just been told no, and this, and this, and this, so [I] had to spend a lot of time healing wounds that had been caused there, and I do not believe that it was the personnel.

One method Jaramillo used to weld her people into an embassy family was to invite all of them—staff as well as officers—on a rotating basis to functions at the residence. She also held embassy personnel-only get-togethers, such as her "come to my shack" party, when she opened up the house and grounds for guests to use as they pleased, with no set agenda.

Mari-Luci Jaramillo, first Hispanic woman ambassador, in her "favorite setting--a classroom with children." Jaramillo was an outstanding--and unexpected--success as ambassador to Honduras. *Courtesy of Mari-Luci Jaramillo.*

Evidently, because there's no entertainment money in [Americans-only parties], ambassadors don't do as much of that—they always have to include the Hondurans in order for them to justify how they're going to spend the money—so [the staff] were very pleased, knowing that I didn't come from a rich background, that I was willing to have parties just for them.

The residence pool was open for everyone at all times.

It was open for the Peace Corps volunteers that came into town, too. Oh, they loved that. That was heaven. They would have been out for months in some little dusty place where they barely had enough water to take a bath, and then to come in and sit around the pool and the gardens, they loved that.

I thought that if the government people understood what tremendous work our Peace Corps were doing, they'd get more support. Whenever I went into a small community, ahead had been sent the message: the Peace Corps person is to be there to meet me with whoever was going to meet me, and that gave that Peace Corps person stature like it wouldn't quit, because he had to be there with the mayor [and] the [ambassador]. At the lunches or the dinners I'd insist that they sit with me, and so that gave them visibility in the community that their work was valued.

I tried at the beginning to hire a young Honduran lady to supervise the [residence] staff, because I realized it was going to be terribly hard for my husband, who hadn't done any of that stuff before, to try to do it. He was going to be in charge of supervising the buying of the liquors and what was needed. I hired a Honduran woman who was up high in the Honduran society and so knew what Hondurans would like and what they'd expect. Maybe she worked six months or so. It was the perfect thing for her to work because she allowed me to spend all my time on embassy matters and not have to pay any attention to the residence. Although I paid attention to it because I'm the kind that has to straighten out rugs and put out flowers, but I didn't have to worry that the food wasn't served attractively.

She had thought that I was hiring her so she could be my representative, and I started noticing that she would be fabulously dressed. All of a sudden I realized how it was developing. When she said she thought she'd done her service, I just took her up on it, and then I didn't have anyone. But I think it was perfect because it took us through that initial period.

5

Dealing with the husband of a woman ambassador proved to be no problem for the Hondurans.

It was so neat—they must have given him ambassadorial rank because everywhere we went he was always made the center of attention. I think that that was the way of the Latins showing him that he wasn't a lesser person, especially that he was the male. This is the way we got our invitations: from the American community we got "Ambassador and Dr. Jaramillo," from the diplomatic corps and from the Hondurans we got two separate invitations— Dr. Jaramillo one, and Ambassador Jaramillo the other. That way my name didn't have to be in front of his. That way he was not an appendage, he had his own invitation. Now, as you know, there's so many stag affairs, and I went to many, many stag affairs where I was the only woman with all the men, but for a lot of the stag affairs, they invited my husband with a special invitation. That was an accommodation for the male that they were doing.

The power of her position led Jaramillo to do "a lot of reflection."

I had to tell myself, "Okay, Mari-Luci, keep your feet firmly on the ground. You're a university professor. Somewhere from the high heavens this has fallen into your lap." And I worked under the assumption that maybe tomorrow I'd be called back, so I had to do my best work today.

But power didn't go to my head. I saw the access to power that that position has. It is a *miniature presidency.* You can do what you want to, you can order people around, you can do whatever you please. Within 24 hours, you can get rid of people without even having to justify it. The power is awesome.

That power in wrong hands is uncontrolled power. It made me very aware that that power was to be used for the benefit of my country. That it wasn't a God-given power or a personal power that I had because I was superior. That power went with the office and was to be used only if needed. I did a lot of thinking about it, and lots of thinking in the abuses of it, and understanding why people abuse power when it's handed to them without any kind of criteria of how it's to be used.

Besides handling power responsibly, another job requirement was living grace-fully in a "goldfish bowl."

When you're in the classroom at the university, you're a ham up there for that particular audience, and I guess what I had to learn was [to] become that person that I was in the classroom *all the time.*

I always [used to] put my own rollers on my head, but I was very conscious that I couldn't step out of my house because there might be a camera some-place through the fence, so I would always go to the beauty shop and get my hair done. It really was a fishbowl. I think it improved my self-image.

Jaramillo left Honduras in September 1980, after three years, to become deputy assistant secretary for Latin American affairs. She hoped to stay on under the new Republican administration.

Some appointments had survived change of political parties, and so some people said, "Oh, you'll surely stay." There was also the feeling that I would stay because there were so few Hispanics and because I had been very success-ful and lots of the State Department people liked me. But it turned out that those Republicans that tried to help me find a way to stay were not successful because [it] seemed that if you hadn't supported Reagan you were not a good American. All of a sudden, I saw that there was an about-face of some people that had been encouraging me to not disappear now not saying anything. I caught on immediately: somewhere, somebody [had] said, "We're not going to keep her."

I had decided that I would stay and honor my commitment, that I would stay until they told me to leave, but I was very scared of some of the things that I had seen and heard, of somebody arriving to work and their desk [had] been cleared. I was just petrified of this happening, and yet I felt this sense of honor, that [sometime] I would be told, "Thank you for your service. You have finished." I wanted to end my stay perfect. On the other hand, I was hearing so much that mine was a "political appointment," and I kept saying, "It was not. It was a presidential appointment. There's a great deal of difference. It has nothing to with political parties." But, of course, it did.

166

Finally, the word came, not officially, nor with thanks, but as a hint from a well-placed friend that it was over for her.

We were ready to move immediately. We had our car ready, we had everything in boxes from our apartment, we were ready to load and come. So we left and we drove straight through. We just stopped one night to rest a few hours, and then we took turns driving and came straight home. My university was ready to greet me with open arms. It was just wonderful. Had lots of community parties for me. It was just really, really nice—lots of welcoming. It was a beautiful coming home.

I think I never internalized the work that I was doing, or the position, until after I left it. That's when it really hit me. I represented the president of this country, and I did everything I was asked to do, and I didn't make a single enemy. Gosh! I really felt good after it was all over. I guess what I'm most proud of, that I represented my country at all levels, across socioeconomic lines. I tried to live the example of what American people are like.

12

SURVIVING A COUP
Nancy Ostrander (1925–   )
Suriname 1978–1980

When Nancy Ostrander walked into the American consulate in Santiago de
Cuba in September 1947, she was only seeking temporary work so she could
extend her vacation there. Hired immediately as a general clerk, she rose from
that lowly beginning, through a series of fortuitous circumstances and a lot of
hard work, to the eminence of American ambassador. Her upward progression
from locally hired staff clerk to chief of mission would never have been possible
in Constance Harvey's early days, but postwar personnel expansion programs,
one of which brought staff personnel into the officer corps, had radically altered
the Service.[1]

Ostrander enjoyed what would appear to have been a typical midwestern
childhood, enriched by a large extended family of aunts and uncles and cousins.
But her father died when she was an infant, and soon after her uncle, a coffee
grower in Cuba, lost his wife and sent his baby daughter to Nancy's mother
to raise. Along with cousin Eva came Esperanza, her nanny. These "Cuba
connections" awoke in Nancy Ostrander a "great interest in things international," although she did not travel to Cuba until she had graduated from Butler
University and saved enough money to pay her way. Three months into her
visit, that money ran out.

Santiago de Cuba was a very small post with too much work; Ostrander was
a godsend to the consul. She began at the very bottom of the personnel schedule,
FSS-14, salary $2,160 a year. In Santiago she received a grounding in the
nuts and bolts of the Foreign Service—passports, citizenship, estate law, and
accounting—and perfected her Spanish. She also did the liaison work with the
U.S. naval base at Guantanamo. Her initial consular experience was broad and
thorough, and when the embassy in Havana desperately needed an American to
straighten out its consular file room, Ostrander was tapped for the job and
received a sudden direct transfer on Christmas Eve 1950. That was the first of
many calls to "let Nancy do it."

In Havana she shared an apartment with a young woman who worked for the U.S. Navy, and in most ways she had a delightful time, with lots of dancing and a busy social life. She was not concerned with a career but enjoyed her work day by day. There was, however, a dark side to the assignment.

I was in Havana when the McCarthy investigations were going on, and it was absolutely devastating. It was unbelievable. As I recall, Havana was given a quota of the number of people they would have to lose, the number of Communists that would have to be found, the number of disloyal people. The embassy did this in stages, and the people who were to be fired were told on Fridays, Friday afternoon usually. I can remember work came to a halt every Friday afternoon for months, and we all sat there and stared at our telephones to see who it would be. Everybody was under investigation. The things that were called "questionable" were unbelievable.

You heard a lot of rumors about what was going on in Washington—that the State Department offices were called every week to say, "You haven't fired your quota of Communists." It certainly wasn't taken across the board. The accusation was, one in four in every office was a Communist. I don't remember that anybody was fired in my area because of being a Communist, but certainly they were accused of being disloyal for something in their background. A lot of people lost jobs. A lot of them lost jobs because of allegations of homosexuality, and I have no doubt that there must have been some in that embassy. Some of them I certainly would have questioned myself. I never would have questioned their loyalty.

These dismissals included a large number of persons dropped under the Eisenhower economy drive. Ostrander survived both McCarthy and the reduction in force (RIF), and when orders came in 1954 for a direct transfer to The Hague, she had risen to staff grade FSS-10. Her job supervising the records and communications section proved to be a "humdinger." No one had done it for six months, cable traffic was heavy and around-the-clock, and code clerks kept quitting from burnout. Her job again was to bring order from chaos, and she did, thereby furthering her reputation for untangling messes.

Most people hated the records and communications work. I found that I was the only person in the Netherlands that had an opportunity to read every single piece of paper that came into that American embassy. I had all those

[old] records and had to sort them out and decide what to destroy, so I had the whole inside picture on Indonesia. I had everything from the Netherlands-Antilles and from Suriname. Like it or not, I followed that whole period and had to understand it. I found that at the end of that tour in the Netherlands, I probably knew more [than anyone], because I'd seen it *all*, and everybody else was compartmentalized.

The snobbish attitude FSOs had toward staff officers is revealed in an incident from the mid-1950s.

I do remember in The Hague, the day the telegram came through that said that I was now commissioned, I could almost tell you the names of the officers who came around and for the first time treated me as if I were one of them, and who suddenly were treating me with a lot of respect and not standing at the door and yelling at me. And I have never quite forgiven those people. You know, they can yell at me if they want to. If I'm not doing my job right, why perhaps they have the right to yell at me, although I'd prefer for them not to. But suddenly to see this turnaround, it was an absolute eye-opener for me, because it never had occurred to me that the reason they were yelling at me before was lack of respect because of my [staff status].

Her next experience was as administrative officer in nearby Antwerp, then the busiest port in Western Europe. After two years in a thankless job, she managed a transfer into the consular section. She enjoyed her work there for a variety of reasons, including her participation in the international Vice Consuls' Association, whose members worked in the almost 50 consulates in Antwerp at that time.

It was really a marvelous, supportive group. The purpose of the organization was to have fun. That was its only purpose. Nobody above the rank of vice consul could attend unless they were invited by a vice consul. That included consuls general, ambassadors, anything. We gave out those invitations rarely, and they were very much coveted. Each month, one of the vice consuls sponsored a traditional dinner from his country. But the beauty of this was that whatever consular problem a vice consul from any of these countries was faced with, you had a support group. I don't know how many American kids who went broke in Antwerp got "workaways" with Swedish, Norwegian, and Danish vessels, because all I had to do was pick up the phone and say, "Have you got a workaway?" These kids got home without any expense to the U.S. government.

Ostrander's toughest consular job was in connection with the crash on 16 February 1961 of a SABENA flight approaching Brussels; all 18 members of the U.S. figure-skating team, en route to a world competition in Prague, were killed.

The site of the crash was in Antwerp's consular district. It was grim and gruesome, and the sort of thing that made me realize [no] consular officer should ever have to handle more than *one* plane crash.

I suppose [it's always difficult] to try to get the families to understand that it's an ugly picture and not to come and expect to find the remains of their dear ones looking as if they had died peacefully in bed. It's not going to happen. They are not realistic about it and cannot understand what you're trying to tell them.

[One man] brought his children. There was no way to stop him from wanting the coffin opened. Then he was so upset. How had I allowed him to do this? And you wish you'd had a tape recording of all [your] begging and pleading, "Do not do this."

I did learn that what a consular officer must try to provide for American citizens who get in trouble overseas [is to] try to think of that person as the person nearest and dearest to you, and ask yourself, "What would I want the consul to do for my husband, for my wife, for my mother?" This sort of thing. That sounds very Pollyanna-ish, but that is exactly what they're expecting, and you shouldn't lose sight of that. I have spent a lot of time in my career as a consular officer writing back what the funeral services were like, describing everything from the church service to the burial. I don't think I've ever gotten many thanks for that. People seem to think that's what is owing to them. Mighty few have said, "Thank you." You get so you don't expect it, and it's always a good surprise [when they do]. They hate what has happened and have to take it out on the American government. You happen to be the American government, so you're going to take it.

Ostrander had to deal almost daily with stranded Americans coming in and expecting the embassy to give them money.

This is what they say: "I always heard that if I got in trouble, the American government would take care of me." There are, of course, loans, but [only] loans in desperation. The government does provide, I think, a pittance that you have to repay if you're ever going to get another passport. If you're in a city where there's a large American colony, they often have a fund that the American consul can draw on for particularly worthy cases, but they're not going to support some bum, that's for sure.

Also there was a seamen's association, so if these people had missed their ships they could be helped out. Church groups. The Salvation Army would usually take somebody for a few days for next to nothing.

What I learned was how to make the contacts outside of the office, because you're going to need them in order to get the fairest deal for American citizens when they're in trouble. You've got to learn to think *outside*. Consular work also teaches you how to manage a large group of people to accomplish a specific purpose.

Such a responsibility was the immigrant visa section in Mexico City that Ostrander was in charge of in the 1960s.

After about six months on that job running the immigrant section, they set up a new job, which was to be the assistant to the head of the whole visa section [and] to take care of what I learned to call the "no win" cases—the cases that were going to make headlines whether you issued the visa or refused the visa. You were going to insult half the population and upset half the population no matter what you did. That was the job I got. It was awful. There were some 50 or 60 cases a day of those, and it was constant pressure. I learned to hate everything that the Mexico City consular section had to offer, while adoring living in Mexico City.

I can remember deciding it was time to go through the visa files and take out all of these refused visa cases as I came across them and try to get reversed some of the previous rulings of ineligibility at the time of [the] McCarthy era. I just poured them in as fast as I could, because we were insulting so many of the Europeans who had immigrated to Mexico and were living there. An awful lot of people in Europe joined the Communist party as a protest to Nazism. I did get a lot of them reversed. I doubt if any of those people ever realized that anything special was done for them, but it was a real job. It was all of the VIPs, you know—the poets, the writers.

It was a hard job, and I never want another one like it again, and I never, ever want to go back to Mexico City in the consular section. I was offered—

several times—to go back as consul general. No way. Just no way. Consular work in Mexico is unique. Even in the visa section we had to stand duty. We were averaging something like three deaths a day. It was just awful. When you were on duty, which was a week at a time, you were up all night, you were working all day. And they were horrible cases, really grizzly stuff. I remember an officer came to me and I showed her the roster. We had a lot of officers then, too; she wouldn't be on duty again for another six months. She looked at me, and she said, "Six months. With any luck, I'll be dead by then." I knew just how she felt, because it was that bad. [*Laughs.*] Yet we had a wonderful group there and I loved them all.

The next mess Ostrander was asked to clean up was in Kingston, Jamaica, which had become independent in 1962. The new immigration law that took effect in 1967 had moved the immigration quota for Jamaica from 200 a year (as a British dependency) to 20,000 a year, and the consul general had had a nervous breakdown trying to keep ahead of the flood of would-be immigrants. The new consul general, busy with administration, needed somebody to take charge of the consular work.

Nobody in his right mind would go into that mess, and I mean *mess*. So they found me, and I said I'd be happy to go.

The section had been two small rooms when there were only 200 a year. The bank next door had moved out, so the consul general had arranged to get part of their space. They had torn up the floors and it was a dirt floor, and raining a lot. They were trying to put tile down, but the tile layers had gone on strike. We had planks over the mud. I have never seen anything quite like that. It was a physical mess. If you opened drawers of desks, you would find applications for visas that nobody had ever even acknowledged, let alone tell people what the next step was. It was so far behind it was incredible.

I went home and I think cried every night for the first six months I was there. But I did bring order out of that chaos and found that there were an awful lot of really good local clerks and brand-new "retread" officers who were willing to sit down and do the job if somebody would just tell them where to tackle it. I had something like ten officers. They were ambassadors' secretaries who wanted to be commissioned, pouch clerks, former marine guards who had joined the Foreign Service, political officers who were about to get selected out but were given one more chance. Those folks were given a half-day's training and sent to me, into this mess. Well, you can imagine what their morale was. There were also two or three brand-new FSO-8s. I can assure you that this wasn't their idea of what should be the lot of somebody who wanted to be a political or economic officer. But they were good, you know. It brought to mind that a good FSO does whatever he's given to do and does it well.

Ostrander had a staff of about 25 helping her manage the concerns of over a million tourists a year.

Some of them needed help. They died, too, up at Montego Bay, and got into trouble and got into jail. When I look back on it, I think the first thing I did was call in all the local employees and say, "I'm sure that each and every one of you has good ways that we can streamline this." Then I got big charts on the wall to show where the bulk of it was going. Once they could see progress and once they realized a pattern, they were ready to just knock themselves out for it, and did so.

Far from buckling under the stress of the job, Ostrander "thrived," for a number of reasons.

You could see the progress, and I was getting credit for it, and I had an ambassador and a DCM and an administrative officer who were [supportive], and this just makes all the difference. I learned to love Jamaica. Not too many people liked Jamaica.

She enjoyed her own company and did not find it difficult to be a single woman living abroad; indeed, her impression was that life was harder for the wives of officers.

It seemed to me that they were always at home and unable to work and unable to get out of the house, and they were always, it seemed to me, trying to make do. They always talked about how bored they were. All of the difficulties of living overseas were sort of heightened because they had so much time to sit around and think about them, whereas I had my interest in my work and traveling around.

Being single—well, you have to be a good organizer, that is for sure. I must say that I used to laugh when new officers were moving into their residences, and their wives would call up and demand that they take two or three days off, and [one] would say she couldn't possibly do it by herself. But, of course, I always *did* do it by myself. I must say, I longed to have somebody that I could pick up the phone and say, "Come and help move the furniture." But if you don't have that, you learn to cope.

It used to irritate me to death when I was expected to call on the wives of the officers who were above me in rank, because I thought something was radically wrong there. Some protocol officers used to demand it of you. I got in some trouble in Jamaica for complaining that I just simply could not— in the mob scene I walked into in Jamaica—there was no way. Of course, I went to call on the ambassador's wife, and I went to call on the DCM's wife, but anybody else, I'm sorry, I will just have to meet them [socially].

After three years in Kingston, Ostrander decided it was time to return to home base and requested assignment in the visa office in Washington. To understand what she accomplished in Kingston, it is instructive to note that the slot she filled there as a class 4 now calls for a consular expert three full ranks higher in grade. She earned a superior honor award for her work there and was promoted to class 3. Without the award and the resulting promotion she believes she would have been a victim of the up-or-out provisions of the Foreign Service and "selected out" for not attaining the next rank within the required number of years.

I was assigned to be the deputy to the chief of the field operations division in the visa office. This was *really* dullsville. I didn't have much authority, and there really wasn't all that much to do. [The chief] was about to move on, though, and it seemed to me that what they had in mind was for me to understudy him and move into that position. So I did this, and that's just exactly what did happen.

We were then beginning to handle visa fraud, trying to come up with any sort of thing that would outguess those who were trying to counterfeit visas. Any rule that you come up with, they can come up with some sort of counterfeit. So you begin to wonder, maybe we just shouldn't have any rules, but we came up with counterfoil stamps and did a lot of work with the Bureau of Engraving to come up with things that couldn't be counterfeited.

By this time the women's liberation movement was coming into its own, and the rules and regulations were changing, and the State Department was really trying to do something for women. I can remember coming back and being absolutely astounded to see women wearing pants to work. No objection to it, but I had grown up in this dress code in the Department of State. Right on! If that's what they wanted to do, fine.

The powers-that-were decided at this time that women should be selected, even if only a token, to go to the war colleges. They also were trying to get consular people to the [National War College]. Anyway, I was selected to go, and I'm sure that's the reason I was selected.

This was not the first time women had gone to the war college, but their inclusion had been infrequent. In 1973–74, the government decided to send five women at once: one State Department civil servant, one State Department Foreign Service officer, one from CIA, one from the air force, and one from the navy.

The hierarchy kept calling us in every six weeks or so to ask us if everything was all right, and were the rest rooms all right? and how about the shower equipment for the places where we were supposed to be doing all our military fitness programs? But I loved the war college. I really did. I was terribly shy, though, and reticent. You know they want you to ask all these questions— I don't think that I ever put up my hand and asked a question.

But I analyzed, when I first went there, why is it I'm here? What is it they have in mind for me? And I decided the State Department wanted somebody who was preparing herself to be consul general. I figured the day I graduated I'd go right back to being a consular officer, which wasn't and isn't yet so highly regarded by the Department of State as it should be, and that they probably were training me to be a consul general in Latin America.

Economics was *terrifying* to me. The men who signed up for this course all were economists, and, of course, it was a snap for them. That whole course was done in calculus, which I did not have a clue about. I learned from that what a deprived child must learn when he suddenly goes to school and is absolutely out of it. It was absolute panic when I had to go back into that class. If the [professor] ever came near to looking at me, I would just go to pieces. Anyway, I got through it, and as a matter of fact, I came out learning quite a bit about economics, because of, I think, just sheer fear.

When I look back on that wonderful year at the war college, I learned that I *do* have something to offer. I couldn't imagine, when I went over there, that a woman consular officer would have anything to add, and I did learn that I certainly did. There were times when *I* was right and everybody else was wrong. Also, I think what it taught me was that a woman in this man's world has plenty to offer, because together you make a whole. Men will overlook a lot of the things that are first nature for you to think about, and they will also think of things that never would occur to you. You need both sides. And that certainly broadened my perspective 100 percent.

Any limitations that I might have felt suddenly fell away, and I realized that if the correct political situation presented itself, there was absolutely no reason in this world that I couldn't go to the top. I don't think I realized that before. Not only that I could do it, but that they would be quite right in asking me to do the job.

Assignments following a National War College year are usually choice, but in the mid-1970s there was such turmoil at the State Department because of the equal rights and women's movements that the assignment process was out of kilter. In 1974 Ostrander found herself a short-term assignment to personnel and was selected to run an unusual program to rectify former discriminatory practices against women.

At that time we had decided that any woman who had given up her commission only because she wanted to get married, could, up to a certain deadline, reapply, and we would take her back in. We'd see if we couldn't give her a commission at a higher level if she could show that whatever she was doing in the meantime was [professionally enhancing]. I ran that program, and I feel that I am personally responsible for bringing back some pretty good women into the Foreign Service. Jane Abell [Coon] was one of them.

When this assignment was coming to an end, personnel had nothing to offer Ostrander.

I finally said, "Look, I see that you're about to have a vacancy in career development for midlevel consular officers. I was pretty good at placement back in the old days, so I'm happy to step into that job, because I don't see

178

that you've got anything else to offer." Well, he was delighted, because not too many people wanted those jobs. I loved placement work.

I was sitting on panel one day when the first ambassador to the new country of Suriname was selected, and [I] realized while I was sitting there, by gosh, this is one that *I* would qualify for. There aren't many around, but this is one that I could very well hold my head up and proudly say, "There is no way you can tell me I don't qualify for this one, because I'm probably better qualified than anybody else, and if the job ever comes open while I'm around, I am just going to throw my own hat into this ring."

Her chance came in two years.

It was very apparent to me that what they were looking for at the time was somebody with a career both in the Caribbean and in the Netherlands, and if you had punched that in a computer, I think only one name would have come up, and mine was it. They were also needing to do something for consular officers, and they were getting pressure for women appointees. I drew up the list and added my own name and justified it. I don't know what happened. I'm sure [my boss] had to talk long and hard. But if the truth were known, I think probably what happened was that everybody else on that list had somebody [who] really did not want to see [him] on the list. So when it came right down to it, here's this unknown who is obviously qualified and would just solve a lot of problems. And besides, what harm can you do in a place called Suriname that nobody's ever heard of? Now I don't mean to downgrade this, but I wasn't asking for Moscow or Paris or London. Anyway, it worked.

Of course, my newspapers at home had gone pretty crazy with this, and my senator, Sen. [Richard] Lugar, telephoned me and said he wanted to appear with me [at the confirmation hearings]. He wasn't on the committee at the time. I wasn't particularly pleased with that idea because it looked like I was a political appointee. It's only the political appointees who show up with [their senators]. But his staff made it very clear.

I rode up to [Capitol] Hill that morning with Dick Murphy, who was going to the Philippines, and Terry Todman, who was becoming assistant secretary in ARA [Bureau of Inter-American Affairs]. So we got up there, [and] they said they hoped I wouldn't mind, they would take all these other people ahead of me. As a matter of fact, it was wonderful, because they wore themselves out on poor Terry Todman. They asked him a million questions. Dick Murphy, the shrewdy, had been up on the Hill and gone around to all the key people and said, "I want to brief you personally on any questions you might have on the Philippines." He went through very smoothly.

Then Dick Lugar arrived and introduced me, and I remember that sitting in the chair was Sen. [George] McGovern [D-S.Dak.]. I don't care what anybody says about Senator McGovern, that man was so nice to me. He said he had looked over my record, and he wanted to compliment me on how far I had come, and he gave a long discourse on how wonderful consular officers are, and how unsung, and how unappreciated, and here was one. Anyway, it was just a very, very nice introduction, and I was just relaxing like nobody's business, and it must have been very visible how relaxed he had made me feel, and I will always remember him for that. It was so kind of him.

In the middle of my hearing, the door opened, and a tour group came in, the loudest tour group I've ever heard. It was senior citizens, and all women. They were so absolutely delighted that a woman was being considered for something that they kept shouting at each other, "What's she doing?" "Where's she going?" On the way out, they yelled at me, "Honey, what is it you got?" [*Laughs.*]

I really felt a sisterhood that I had never felt before. They were absolutely *rejoicing* in my appointment, and it was doing something for each and every one of them. I had never realized that before. Also the folks back home—they were rejoicing. They were getting something out of it for themselves, too. And it was really kind of exciting that it made so much joy for so many people.

I took the Eastern flight to Trinidad and Tobago. The next afternoon I took the Air France flight, which island-hops Martinique and on down to French Guiana, but makes a stop in Paramaribo. It isn't exactly what you imagine of how you're going to arrive. It was packed full. People even in the rest rooms. There just weren't enough seats and not enough flights. I was met by somebody from protocol and by my entire staff at the airport. We had refreshments while they got my things through customs, and it was then night, and we [drove] through the jungle to get back. To me it was very interesting, because all the directional signs, the way the roads were set out, everything looks just exactly like the Netherlands, but you're going through the middle of the jungle.

Then I got to the house. Nobody in it but me. Just nobody. In Suriname you don't have servants at night. They go home. I was given the keys and just sort of turned loose, and that was the *greatest* disappointment of my life, that house. Every wall, and I'm talking about even those in the same room, was painted a different color. Let me give you a sample of one bedroom: there was an avocado rug, one lavender wall, one navy blue wall, one yellow wall, and one orange wall. There were two overstuffed chairs in it that had [pink] slipcovers. The bedspread was something [else]. I have never seen anything like that. Surinamers love this—the more color the better.

As I looked at it, I thought, "I can't live in it! And there isn't anybody here, and I don't even know where the john is. I don't even know where the kitchen is." I certainly didn't get any sleep that night. I wish they'd warned me. I wish they had said something like, "Don't worry, we'll do anything you want, we'll paint it. We're just not doing anything until you get here and have a look at it."

The next day, when I went to the office for the first time, the poor administrative officer said, "Can we do anything for you?" And I said, "*Paint* the house white!" They did that, and boy, what a difference it made.

Her fresh white walls gave Ostrander the idea of obtaining paintings from the Arts in Embassies program. But after six months of trying, she was still being stalled. She understood that Suriname's humidity was a factor but thought it made no sense to send art to the European capitals, "where they've got all the art you could possibly want," and neglect a country where "this is going to be the only opportunity for an awful lot of people to see anything in the way of good painting." She visited the arts program office on a trip to the department in Washington.

I was sitting there, being turned down by [the woman director], and the phone rang, and she answered it, and I heard her say, "The ambassador isn't here, but his wife is." And then the blood sort of drained out of her face, and she looked at me, and she said, "I do beg your pardon," and handed me the phone. And when I hung up from that telephone conversation, she says, "You can have anything you want." [*Laughs.*] And she sent me 13 very large paintings. I don't know how they ever got them into a plane.

All my artistic friends down there came over to help me hang them, and they all had such good ideas, and it really looked great. That night I held a grand opening. I gave something which in Suriname would be called an *opodoro*, which is an open door, or an open house, and invited everybody in the city. Even at that, people gate-crashed, because they wanted to see the paintings—very modern, a lot of color—anyway, that night even the president of Suriname came, and the TV station showed up to do a live on-the-scene thing.

Custom as well as her budget affected Ostrander's style of entertaining.

I started giving dinner parties at first, because it seemed the thing to do, but I soon learned that that wasn't going to do for me. You have the wives to dinner parties, and the money doesn't go very far when you're doing that. I didn't get much representation money. But also, after dinner they followed the custom of withdrawing, and the women were always in one end of the room and the men—who were the ones I was supposed to be with—were over somewhere else. And as much as I like to talk to the women—because I'm doing both roles—what I really was sent there for was to find out about the political side of things. Now, I could get some good things from the women on that score, but I needed to be talking to the men, and it just wasn't working.

So I decided, what I'm going to do is reserve the dinner parties for just social times, and I will go the luncheon route otherwise. And that's what I did, and that worked magnificently. Three or four times a week I had luncheons that usually started about 1:00, and then since nobody was going back to the office, they would leave about 3:00. I would have only one table of 12 or 14 people, in a circular table, and I invited only the men. There were times when I invited women, too, but it depended on what their job was. There were an awful lot of women doing an awful lot of very good work in Suriname.

Soeki, the cook, was superb. I could call him at 11:00 in the morning and say, "I've got to have a luncheon. Can you get something together for 14 people by 1:00?" And it was always marvelous.

[Soeki was] Indonesian. Well, he was great. He always wanted to check the menus with me, and he would come in a couple of days before. I tried to plan the luncheons at least a week in advance, and I would write them down on the calendar. He didn't fix my breakfast or my dinner, so he came for lunch. He would come in with his pencil and paper, looking very, very serious.

He would say, "Now, for the luncheon, the head of the Supreme Court's going to be here, and the last time he was here we had beef, so what do you think we'll give him this time? What do you want to start with?" I would say, "Oh, let's start with your delicious pumpkin soup." "Well," he would say, "I was thinking that maybe the clear consommé would be better on this occasion." And I would say, "Of course." Then he would say, "What, ma'am, do you want for the first course?" And I would say, "Are there any of those shrimp left over?" "Well, I was thinking of some of the *tukunari* fish." And I would say, "All right." And then, "What do you think for the third course?" "Well, let's go with your delicious cordon bleu." "Well, I was thinking maybe chicken kiev."[*Laughs.*]

Ostrander stretched her entertainment allowance of $5,000 a year by "fishing for the first course" herself.

Nancy Ostrander, ambassador to Suriname, with unidentified Air Force officer, 1979. The presence of Air Force planes in Suriname when a coup d'état erupted in that country was a serious problem for the ambassador. *Courtesy of Nancy Ostrander.*

[I] was very proud when I looked down at that and realized that I'd put that on the table. I had a good thing going with fresh vegetables, because at that time we had the air force refueling in Suriname, oh, maybe once every three months. So long as it was for representational purposes, they would provide from Wright Patterson [Air Force Base, Ohio], so I got lettuce and apples and all these fresh things that were absolutely impossible to get otherwise—and it was such a treat. Soeki could make that stuff last a long time. I always also made up a small basket of cauliflower and one sample of everything and sent it over to the president [Johann Ferrier]. Oh, they loved it. His wife told me that he always insisted, whenever that basket came, that he would make the salad himself. So you can make it do a lot.

[President Ferrier] sent me a parrot, which I loved dearly. He thought I was lonely, and I sure was in that big house. There's nobody to talk to. If you have problems with your staff, or worries about your staff, there's nobody to share that with, absolutely nobody, and you just live with it.

Ostrander had an experienced DCM with whom she worked well, but he fell ill after he'd been there six months and had to leave. The department did not replace him for another six months.

The [Suriname] government was on the brink of falling. Alcoa was on strike, so the economics of the country was falling apart. I ended up doing just about everything there was. The USIS officer left ahead of schedule with no replacement. The consular officer was transferred, and they were very sorry, but they couldn't get anybody down for another few months. That's when I got the flavor of what it's like in a post that most Foreign Service officers don't particularly relish serving in, [at] a time when you can't really send anybody to a post unless they select it. And I think that's probably too bad; the needs of the service ought to come first. I think everybody's preference ought to be in there somewhere, but it ought to be part of the equation, not all of it.

I talked to John Burke, who was [ambassador] in Guyana next door, going through hell over the Jonestown thing.[2] He was such a stabilizing force for me. He sent over his number-two man from USIS to help me out and in general offered me all kinds of support. I can remember he called me up one day, and he said, "Nancy, I just want to tell you that the fewer people there are in Suriname, the better the reporting gets." [*Laughs.*]

I had the code clerk, before he left, doing consular work, and he enjoyed it. I mean he was delighted with the opportunity to do that sort of thing. It was a time when we were so shorthanded that I was asking everybody to do everything. The consular officer, before he left, was doing some economic reporting and some political reporting.

It worked, but, oh, you know, you shouldn't be left that short. If they're going to open an embassy, they should staff it and support it. If they're not going to do that, they should have left Suriname without an embassy and covered it from Georgetown, Guyana, as many other countries did and do. The political situation was such that it was building up to the coup that finally happened. I couldn't report everything that occurred, but I tried to [do] a sort of wrap-up cable every week as to what had happened. I was doing what reporting I could, and it sure could have been improved on, but it was a pretty adverse situation.

Replacements for her DCM and staff arrived before Ostrander was faced with the event that taxes a chief of mission to the utmost—the overthrow of the local government in a coup d'état. The coup occurred on 25 February 1980, but the political and economic situation had been unstable for the previous six months.

Elections had been called, so we were in the middle of an election campaign, trying to report that. In January of that year, the sergeants in the military had gone on strike because they wanted to have their own labor union as they had back in the Netherlands when they were in the Dutch military, but that had been settled.

In February, however, a bunch of these sergeants actually went into the barracks and found the arms stores wide open and the clips in the machine guns, so they just took over the barracks and then went down and took over the rest of the government, shot up everything.

I don't think they killed more than six or eight [people], but still, I can remember that morning, 3:00 in the morning, hearing all the gunfire and waking and saying to myself, "It's Chinese New Year, and I wish they wouldn't shoot off so many firecrackers." "It couldn't happen in Suriname," in peaceful Suriname, where nothing like this had ever happened before. The guard out front was asleep, as usual, and so I thought, "Well, everything is calm and serene." He told me later, "I knew if there was anything wrong you would have awakened me." Can you imagine? [Laughs.]

It was really a bad time. The firing on the city and the bombs lasted for about three days.

A local radio station reported that the CIA had started the coup, an announcement based on nothing more than the appearance on the night of the coup of three U.S. Air Force planes, which were, in fact, stopping only to refuel.

It took all the ingenuity any of us in that place could pull together to get those extraordinarily expensive military aircraft out of Suriname that night. There were three of them, worth millions, and the airport was, of course, immediately closed. I still don't know how we did it. I remember a lot of work on our radios (which we weren't supposed to have). I sent the DCM and the administrative officer, with my USIS clerk, who knew how to get things done, to try to negotiate how to get the planes out of there and the air force officers, who were in hotels, back to the planes. I finally got them into my car and flew all the flags and managed to get them down to the airport. We're talking about 60 miles, and the road's closed and blocked and the shells [are] going all over everywhere. They got through.

By that time I had gone back to my house, and I got the word there. One plane got off, and then another plane got off, and then the last plane finally left, and that plane flew over my house and dipped its wings. I have never been so glad to see anything go in my life.

Nancy Ostrander presenting the seal of Suriname to the country's president, Johan Ferrier, and his wife. Ostrander worked the seal in needlepoint as a token of friendship and esteem; it carried much significance to Surinamese women, who were conditioned to believe that working women were unfeminine. That the American ambassador did needlepoint was evidence of the femininity of professional women. *Courtesy of Nancy Ostrander.*

Of course, nobody knew [the coup] was coming. Not even the [Surinamese] sergeants knew it was coming. They had decided that they were going to go over to the base and see if they couldn't get something going. I've heard they were hopped up on marijuana—I've heard all kinds of stories. But they certainly weren't expecting this. After about three days [the sergeants] had the entire government. They took the ministers prisoner and did not harm them. Once they got [control of] the government, there's no way they could give it back. They didn't know what to do with it when they had it.

I was extraordinarily worried about that because at the same time Sergeant Doe was doing his thing in Monrovia, and at night on TV we had pictures of the murder of the cabinet members in Monrovia.[3] I didn't think these sergeants were going to resist temptation, but they did.

As the coup unfolded, Ostrander was never actually in personal danger, "although I didn't know it at the time."

The two safe-haven areas I had staked out were gone. I had British friends who lived in the bush. I felt that, if worst came to worst, I could talk one of the Javanese boatmen into taking me upriver, and they could have gotten me up to the very forlorn coast, and somebody could have picked me up from there. All of that would have been pretty easy.

There were some 400 citizens, however, that I was responsible for. There was something that ran through my mind: "If you're not going to get out of this, you at least don't want it written up in the history books that you ran off and left 400 people and took the flag down." [*Laughs.*] It would be like only one person could leave the *Titanic*, and you elected yourself.

The world press also got to Suriname on that first day after the coup. They descended on the embassy. I found them a really lazy lot. They seemed to want it all handed to them—to have their copy totally prepared for them. We did our best, but we were sinking fast into a sea of work, and no help seemed to be en route. The U.S. cavalry was not galloping to the rescue!

Just when I felt we really couldn't handle this without help, the news broke that Diego Ascencio, our ambassador to Columbia, had been taken hostage.[4] The newspeople vanished into thin air—well, into the only plane still running. They went to Colombia and left me to deal with Suriname. What a relief! I was very worried about Diego, but if it had to happen, his timing was right for me and my small staff.

Ostrander never closed the embassy during these eventful three days. She also received no meaningful support from Washington.

I sometimes wondered if the powers-that-were even knew where Suriname was. When I first reported the coup by telephone, the regional director told me to "take refuge in the embassy compound and to call in the marine guards." My heart sank—he was not even aware there was neither compound nor marine guards. [This] was far from reassuring.

During that first morning, when the shells were bursting around us, my staff asked for permission to take down the flag as a safety measure. I did not give it. The insurgents were anti-Suriname government and anti-Dutch, but not anti-United States, so I felt the flag could be what saved us from a shelling.

Being a female ambassador elicited a mixed, though mainly positive, reaction in Suriname. Most of the male ambassadors were condescending at first. The Surinamers were more accepting.

The Dutch are so used to women as rulers, because of the long dynasty of their women queens, that [Surinamers] certainly accepted me in a position of leadership without any difficulties at all, even though they're no longer Dutch. Being ambassador of the United States of America would have put you in a position of authority there, no matter what.

Another thing, [as a woman] I could say, "Gee whiz, I don't understand this at all. Would you please explain it to me?" And no man could ever say that. His pride would never let him, although it would be true, and it was true in my case.

Ostrander stressed that each assignment is crucial to getting ahead.

Give it your all. And don't turn your nose up at it just because it's a little filing job. The background I got in The Hague, running their mailroom, was really what gave me the background that I needed to be ambassador to Suriname.

Especially in the Foreign Service, there's absolutely no dead-end job. It just doesn't exist. I never knew a good Foreign Service officer who didn't do a bang-up job, whether it [was] stamping visas or whatever. The really good ones seem to *milk* every job for what it's worth and never consider that it's beneath them.

If you want a life that is forever fascinating, stick with the Foreign Service. If you're the kind of person that's absolutely going to be destroyed because you don't get to be the president of the company, stay out, because very few are going to make it to the top. But if you're going to love those years for the marvelous opportunities they afford that you're not going to get in any other kind of job, why go for it.

13

SUMMIT NEGOTIATOR
Rozanne Lejeanne Ridgway (1935–)
Finland 1977–1980
German Democratic Republic 1983–1985

Rozanne Ridgway was the first woman to sit at a presidential summit bargaining table. At Geneva in November 1985, when President Ronald Reagan met Soviet Premier Mikhail Gorbachev face to face in a historic "first," the presence of a woman behind the scenes was also a historic first, one that went largely unreported by the press. Moreover, Ridgway, the assistant secretary of the Bureau of European and Canadian Affairs, proved as tough a negotiator as her Soviet counterparts. She continued to be the chief U.S. negotiator throughout the Reagan-Gorbachev summits.[1]

At long last, the institutional opinion of Ridgway concurred with the collegial: here was an extraordinary Foreign Service officer. Twenty years before, her career counselor had predicted she would end her career as a middle-grade consular officer. Her colleagues, however, recognized her special qualities early on. Her male superiors in Norway, aware of the institutional bias against women, discussed how to draft her annual efficiency reports so as to highlight her abilities.[2] Without exception, their comments about her today are positive and admiring. Moreover, when the faculty at FSI asked senior officers (including an all-male DCM class) to list their choices for the most effective leaders among FSOs, the name that appeared most often was Rozanne Ridgway.[3]

She entered the Foreign Service by examination in the summer of 1957, directly after graduating from Hamline University in Minnesota. She was only 21, and she did not impress the bureaucracy, which ranked her in the lower half of her entering class. Her first assignments, in Manila and Palermo, taught her valuable lessons about personnel and visas but did little to enhance her reputation at

Rozanne Ridgway, shortly before retiring as assistant secretary of state for European and Canadian affairs in 1989. Ridgway, the first woman to head a geographic bureau, was also ambassador to Finland and to the German Democratic Republic. As assistant secretary, she was the chief U.S. negotiator at the Reagan-Gorbachev summit meetings. *Courtesy of U.S. Department of State.*

State. Promotions were slow in coming, and she appeared to be heading for an undistinguished career.

Distraught by the crushing personnel prediction, she turned to George Vest, her immediate superior, for advice. He told her, "Whatever in the world made you go to a career counselor? Just do your work. Don't let up on your standards. Relax." She not only followed this advice but began to assert more control over her assignments. Her career began to accelerate.

Vest knew what he was talking about, and knew also how unreliable was the establishment's view of women. The year before, as a subordinate officer in the politico-military section of the European bureau, he had been looking for a junior officer to work for him. Personnel had sent him files of possible candidates, none of which he found satisfactory. He reports: "I called personnel and said, 'Don't you have any other files?' and the answer to me was, 'Yes, we have one more, but it's a woman officer, so we assumed you wouldn't be interested.' I said, 'Send me the file.' " The file was Ridgway's. Vest continues: "She was superlative. There was never any question from the first weeks that this was an extraordinary officer."[4] Ronald Spiers, who was in the same office, agreed. He thought so well of Ridgway that a few years later he asked her to be his DCM in the Bahamas, an extraordinary request from a male ambassador.

In 1967 she went as class 4 political officer to Oslo, Norway, where she worked for Ambassador Margaret Tibbetts.

She was terrific, but at a great personal cost for herself. She wrote most elegantly. She could perform all of this analysis just in an instant. Brilliant woman. She had a delightful sense of humor, which many people didn't see. Essentially, it was irrepressible, and it would pop out, some funny remark at a staff meeting. You never had the sense that Tibby was rewriting, was criticizing, was bringing her superintellect to something. She would let the process finish. She had to sit back and, I think, have many unchallenging hours in order to allow for the development of the people there. I've thought about it since, and I've tried to model myself as a manager in the same way.

She didn't need any of us, she could have done every bit of political analysis at this post, hands tied behind her back, and I'm sure all of the economic analysis. She didn't do it, she let us do it. She let us take the risks, and she didn't intervene in all of those funny little squabbles, even though the post was so small she knew about every one of them. But she let people grow, make their own mistakes, and have their own accomplishments. And the price was, she had a lot of hours in her office, and she must have been asking, "Am I going to die of rust on the brain?" But she paid that price. She would go walking in these wonderful yellow rubber boots that had white daisies on the side, because she had nothing to do with her time. It was not a challenging post for someone with that set of skills.

When Ridgway turned to Ambassador Tibbetts for advice on her next assignment, the ambassador recommended she accept a position as desk officer for Ecuador. Accordingly, Ridgway returned to the United States and set out to learn new work in a new area. She had no idea she would thereby make her reputation.

The year that I took over was the year that Ecuador seized 51 American fishing vessels. So I'm answering the telephone from congressmen saying, "What about my constituents who are in jail?" I'm on the phone to the ambassador down there, who's saying, "What is Washington thinking?" and I'm saying, "Washington is thinking that we are going to cancel the aid program," which we did. "Washington is thinking we are going to cut off foreign military assistance," which we did. He's calling me to say, "Well, Ecuador is throwing out the military group." And this issue which had been around as a funny little annoyance for 25 years suddenly got completely out of hand.

By the end of that time I moved up to the Latin American policy office as deputy director, continued to do fisheries. I learned how to do press conferences, went to the Hill with people. I developed Hill contacts I still have today and traveled throughout South America. Went to the OAS [Organization of American States] with the deputy secretary when there was a big case brewing there—[alleged] economic aggression by the United States against Ecuador because of this fishery war. Met a very wide variety of American domestic interests, the scientists, the ecologists, the packers, the fishers, the processors, the unions, all involved in these fishing questions. It was a wonderful three years of growing, you could feel yourself growing. I finally made class 3 in those years. I [learned] how to write, how to think, how to make decisions, how to analyze problems, all of which was building on what I'd learned from the superb group of people I'd worked with along the way.

Operating a one-person desk, Ridgway also encountered greater public visibility. She was "no longer five layers back where the paper started, but perhaps the person who had given the most recent bit of advice to the person who was testifying."

She earned the nickname "Tuna Roz" while on the delegation charged with negotiating tuna agreements with Chile, Ecuador, and Peru. She was becoming surer of her goals and beginning to understand what her special abilities could contribute to the service, and began to guide her own career. When she was offered a position as director of the basic course for entering officers, "the best we've got for you," Ridgway turned it down.

The phone rang, oh, a week later, and it was Ron Spiers saying, "How about being DCM in the Bahamas?" Now, the central system must have known [of Spiers's interest]. Why call me up and ask me to do the A-100 course, which would have been a dead-end? So whatever the system view of me has been, it's never been the corridor view. Back in those years, I don't think I would have done very well if the system had done all the placing.

To prepare for the Bahama assignment, Ridgway took the DCM course at FSI.

I was so grateful for that one week of being told about values in the Foreign Service and in other professions. I've never forgotten them saying, "There is no set of correct values, but you should understand your own institutional values." A week of that, a week of looking at case studies, and a week of being told how to keep the channels open with your ambassador. And the other little [suggestion] was, if your in-box is overflowing, you must be doing somebody else's job. I would remember that occasionally in the Bahamas, and sure enough, I would be rewriting stuff and it wasn't mine to rewrite. It was for other people to learn how to write.

After a year, Spiers, "a terrific ambassador," left, and Ridgway found herself in the position of being a career woman deputy to a male noncareer ambassador.

Looking back on it, I may not in fact have been as cautious as I should have been about making sure that it was *his* embassy and not *mine*. And I'm aware now of what can happen and how uncertain new ambassadors can feel. Whatever it was, I survived it, and nothing bad came of it. It could have. That is not a male-female thing, that's a proprietary kind of thing.

[As DCM], I was in a constant role of having to explain both the Foreign

Service and the Bahamas to someone who is very strong, very talented, [with] a national reputation in arms control matters [and] politico-military affairs. And here I am telling him what time a car can go and what time a car can't go, who the people are he should meet. Normally [it] would not have gone well. It didn't turn out that way.

Ridgway seems to have had an unusual ability to refuse assignments without offending authority. During years that were crucial to her advancement, she did it repeatedly.

I was called by the department and told I was going to the National War College, and I was also asked to sit on my first promotion board. So I came up here for the promotion board, and I stopped in at personnel and told them I wasn't going to the National War College, that I had had three years of politico-military affairs. They didn't have to tell me what a uniform looked like or what the issues were. They said, "Well, you've been selected for training, so how about the Senior Seminar?"

I came back to Washington to start the Senior Seminar, and I arrived a day late, so I was not present when the class picture was taken. An omen, I think. The second day of class, I had, at the first coffee break, a telephone message to call the under secretary for something. I met him for lunch, and he said to me that the deputy assistant secretary for oceans and fisheries affairs had resigned, and would I accept reassignment as a special assistant in that operation until they could find someone? I said no. I didn't want to go back to oceans work, I didn't want to be a special assistant, and it just didn't sound right somehow. He was quite startled and said he'd never had a Foreign Service officer turn him down before, and I said, "I'm sorry you can't understand, but that's just simply the way I feel about it."

I went back to class, and the pressure started about taking this position as "special assistant to the vacancy." I was the only one with the background in oceans and fisheries, and it was very important, and so on. Finally, Larry Eagleburger [then deputy under secretary for management] called one evening and said, "Roz, I'm sorry, but I'm going to have to order you to take this job and to leave the seminar." I said, "Larry, why don't you name *me* for the vacancy? I don't know who your candidate is, but I really believe that if you put my name out there, you would find among the industry as much support [for me] as anybody else you could be looking at." He said, "We hadn't thought of that. Let me look into it." It was on Thursday, and on

Monday he called me back and said, "We ran your name and the other name that we had, and the industry wants you."

So I left the seminar and became the acting deputy assistant secretary, and then the deputy and [also] the ambassador for oceans and fisheries affairs, because it has always been a position that carries both titles. The department resisted making me both the deputy assistant secretary and the ambassador because I was only an old style class 3. I pointed out that wasn't my fault, that was their fault. [*Laughs.*] So that got taken care of, and I moved into that job and spent the next two years really testing myself.

It was a field I knew, was comfortable with. [I had] a brilliant staff. One of the things I wanted to do was to get a staff of Foreign Service officers who knew a lot about fisheries and some fisheries people who knew about fish and [were beginning] to learn something about diplomacy, and put together a team. And we did. Within less than a year, we rewrote postwar international fisheries law, at least as it affects the United States.

It was during these negotiations that Ridgway met her future husband, Capt. Theodore (Ted) Deming. He was a member of some of the delegations to Japan and Mexico as the representative of the Coast Guard Commandant.

In the space of a year and a half, her team negotiated bilateral fishing treaties with 14 countries, including Japan and the Soviet Union, a remarkable feat that won her the additional sobriquet "Lobster Lady of the Bahamas." Then the administration changed, and she learned the hard lesson that politics can threaten a senior Foreign Service career, however apolitically that career has been conducted.

I thought I would stay on when Carter was elected. We continued to operate as before, but we very quickly learned that new people insist—frankly, even in the face of facts—[on doing] things their own way, and we had a very bad spring. I finished off a number of things, [then] I went in and said, "I'd like to leave."

I was eventually offered the embassy to Trinidad-Tobago, and I accepted. That evening I went out to visit friends, and we got to talking about it, and I got mad, and I said, "Wait a minute. I've done nothing but islands. I don't want to do *hyphenated islands*. I'm better than hyphenated islands!" I went through the atlas and came to Finland. I marched in the next day and said I didn't want to go to Trinidad-Tobago, I wanted to go to Finland. And I was named for Finland.

Ridgway never met President Carter during her tenure in Finland and as a consequence felt she had been left "without a rather important piece of diplomatic material."

I would have his picture out, which came to me just sort of printed with, "Best wishes to Rozanne Ridgway, Jimmy Carter," and someone would come in and say, "Well, I see you have a picture of the president. You no doubt have a great deal of contact with him." And I would say, tongue in cheek, "The last time I saw the president, he was quite reflective on such and such." Well, it was on television, but you know. . . . [*Laughs.*] But I never said, ". . . the last time he shook my hand," ". . . the last time I saw him personally." I did the best I could.

He didn't understand the office of the president, and none of his people did. It was a strange atmosphere. [Presidential transitions] always have a strange atmosphere, and I suppose it was no stranger than most. Certainly not as malicious as this [Reagan] administration when it came in. It was just kind of different.

In making the transition from "Roz" Ridgway to "Ambassador" Ridgway, she made some adjustments in her style. "I traveled in blue jeans but took an outfit with me, and in the changing of planes [in London], went into the public rest room and changed from blue jeans to a suit." Once in Helsinki, she was struck by the change in her own outlook.

I had dinner and wandered around this lovely upstairs bedroom in a state of disbelief. That wonderful, wonderful change, but a dramatic change. There is no way that I could have prepared for the difference between being a DCM, or a senior officer here in the department, and being an ambassador. You have got to go through it, and you can almost feel the tearing of the cloth that separates you then from the rest of the people as you have moved on. I sensed immediately that something was different, that my view was no longer *up to* a leadership but was the leadership view. And it wasn't uncomfortable. I almost became in my ambassadorial role, at least on ceremonial occasions, a third person.

The day I presented my credentials is one of my most vivid career memories. The day arrived, and I was in my best black bib and tucker, and we gathered at the residence, and the [Finnish] chief of protocol came in and said the

196

Rozanne Ridgway, 26 November 1976, after signing U.S.-Soviet agreement as deputy assistant secretary and ambassador for oceans and fisheries affairs. Although Ridgway was an acknowledged expert in the field, State was reluctant to grant her the titles that went with the position. *Courtesy of U.S. Department of State.*

equivalent of, "Your chariot is ready, madame." So we went out, and it was a gray day, but a gray day has wind also in Helsinki. And as I went out the front door of the residence, there in front of me was this array of limousines, the president's limousine, and the embassy's own limousine, which was going to be taking other officers. Each had a military driver. The lead car had this lovely official [presidential] flag of Finland, which is bright red with the gold lion rampant. The doors were swung open so that on the far side of the car each chauffeur was standing, and the car I was to get in had this gorgeous military decked-out attaché.

There are apartment houses nearby, and they always fly the Finnish [national] flag, so you had these blue and white flags snapping in the wind, and the neighbors all leaning [out] to see what the ceremony was, and I walked out, and I nearly fell apart. As we went through the door, the heels clicking, and the salutes and the white gloves, I said to myself, "This is not for Roz Ridgway, this is for the ambassador of the United States. And honey, the only way you are going to get through this is to remember that you are representing something, and so, hang on, because here we go." And I could feel my spine stiffen, I could tell I was barely holding tears back. There was a combination of elements of color and sound and ceremony that really was wonderful. We got into the limousine and proceeded slowly down the road, with the military attaché announcing to the palace where we were. Then we arrived in front of the palace. It's right across from the marketplace, again, all that color. But when the people saw the flag that was being raised and recognized it as the American flag, then they all started to yell and carry on, very positively.

We got out in front of the palace, into the palace gates, stood at the palace gates while they played the national anthem, and I reminded myself again, "This is for the office, not for you." And then to review the troops. Well, you try it in high heels on cobblestone. You have everything else going very nicely and you are hanging on and suddenly you realize that you are teetering as you review the troops. On in, and up carpeted palace staircases, through a room with military types all lined up, remembering to step over the transom. Finally into a very long ceremonial room.

As you cross the threshold and start down the room, you see the figure at the far end, and then you hear, "The honor to present the ambassador extraordinary and plenipotentiary of the United States of America, Rozanne Lejeanne Ridgway." And things are beginning to ring in your ear that you never imagined would be possible, and your name is associated with them. [There is] the pride we all have in our country, and the very real sense you have that you're representing the world's major power. I presented the letters of recall and my own letters of credence, and then we sat down and had coffee. And then I was all right. I never again, even in East Germany, never, ever felt the enormity of it all as I did on that occasion.

Ridgway soon realized that her old "oceans and fisheries" management style would not serve her well as an ambassador.

[At] my first staff meeting, I went in and everybody else had arrived. [They] stood up, and I said, "Oh no, please don't, please don't." It's very dangerous. Not long after that, I noticed that one of the marines [at the embassy entrance] was pretty slow getting to his feet when I came in through the front door, and then a little later he barely managed to get to his feet at all, and a few days later he didn't get to his feet. And I called in the NCOIC [noncommissioned officer in charge of the marine detachment], and I said, "I don't care whether he likes me as a woman or as an officer, but I am the ambasssador, and he will get to his feet or he can leave." And I found that if you become too chummy you lose that extra little bit of authority that sometimes you need to keep control.

I'd suggested everybody call me "Roz," and so they were at the stage where, out in public, in front of other people, they were calling me "Roz," and [then a management consultant from State] arrived. He just took one look at the embassy and said, "Roz, you've got to back off, you can't mother this place."

With the help of her DCM, Ridgway took this advice and put back up the "picket fences" that make the position of ambassador different.

The next time somebody shook hands and looked as if they were going to lean over and kiss me on the cheek, [I'd] just keep the elbow stiff, that's all it took. I didn't have to talk to anybody directly about it, and it hadn't gone so far that I had to explain to people that I was backing off.

There is [a mystique about the office], but there's also a remoteness which is not healthy, and you have to find your way to a balance so that you know what's happening in your mission, so people are aware of your humanity but don't encroach in such a way that it becomes destructive of relationships within the embassy.

In part because "Americans have trouble understanding neutrals," Ridgway saw her mission as one of facilitating "the Finnish-American dialogue, which has always been difficult." She arranged to give a speech in February 1980 to the Paasikivi Society (the Finnish Council on Foreign Relations). "I didn't want to give any more speeches on how nice the Finns are. I wanted to give speeches to the Finns on what the responsibilities of a neutral are and what the responsibilities of a global power are."

Finland [had] had to abstain on the vote in the United Nations criticizing Soviet entry into Afghanistan, and the Finns were tormented that they could not participate. They didn't know how to feel about that. That was a tough one for them, and they saw themselves as Afghanistan. The world had abstained on Finland [when the Soviets invaded in 1939], and suddenly all these [years] later [Finland] had to abstain on Afghanistan.

Come the evening, the Paasikivi Society was jammed, and there was the one seat up front, and the president turned up to hear this speech, obviously to give it his blessing. It talked about trade, it talked about the role of the United States, the history of the relationship, all kinds of things. But the line that mattered was the line that said, "The United States wants for Finland what Finland wants for itself, a *credible neutrality*. That remains the definition of American policy interests in Finland." And to this day, if you ask around, people will tell you that that speech, that occasion, is and continues to be the expression of U.S.-Finnish relations. It was a capstone to be able to have the stature to get up, to give a speech, to command the audience, to get the president there to bless this line, and to set, for what appears to be a lasting period, the framework within which we deal with each other.

Early in 1980 Ridgway was called home to be the counselor of the department. At first she was excited about the assignment, but within a week of her return she realized she was there because they needed a woman's face on the organization chart—and "it was the pits for a year."

I met with Cyrus Vance, who gave me a piece of paper and told me what my responsibilities were. However, he erased several of them and gave them to [my predecessor] who was leaving the job and [taking] these topics with him.

I asked when the staff meetings were, because the counselor is one of the principals of the department. I was told I would not be included in staff meetings. The counselor had been, but with the change it was decided the counselor would *not* be. I asked about the use of my car. I was told that the decision had been made that the counselor would not have a car. Dedicated cars would no longer be available. I never again saw Cyrus Vance, except the day he left. So I went back to my lovely office and tried to create a job, and I think I did fairly well. I took on Eastern Europe, which has certainly served me well, and I just sort of putzed around. I stayed busy, but it was never a real job. It was sort of an embarrassing period of time.

That first day in the office, and all the first bloom is there, with the staff and the paper and the like, and I was leaving the department, and I got off the elevator on the first floor and went past the guards and said, "Good night," and kept on walking and nearly broke my nose. I simply wasn't thinking. Nobody opened the door for me! [*Laughs.*]

The counselor position lasted until 5 November 1980, the day after the election of Ronald Reagan. Ridgway continued to work with her colleagues through the end of the year on keeping the Soviet Union from invading Poland.

It was clear that there would be all of these changes, and I didn't know quite how things were done. I guess I still don't. I had been the counselor, and I had hoped that maybe in the next administration I would have one of the senior jobs in the building, or an embassy. And none of that happened. Starting on the fifth of November, you get a combination of Carter people leaving, but leaving behind obligations that the next administration is supposed to pick up because that's the way it's always been done. You have a transition team that is moving in and meeting with department career officers to plan for the next administration, and they begin identifying talented people that they are going to place. I frankly expected that I would be taken care of. I was not, and I just sort of woke up one day and realized that I was plumb out of a job. Nobody had planned anything for me. Little Roz was going to get left behind. I hadn't been serious for them ever, and it was sort of kiss-my-fanny.

[But] I remained naive. On the twentieth of January, I was here along with [Assistant Secretary] David Newsom and [Secretary of State] Ed Muskie and Ed Muskie's team because the hostage thing was breaking in Tehran, and everybody was doing split screen: the inauguration and the plane at the end of the runway and all of that. And when the inauguration started and the plane still hadn't started down the runway and it was quite clear what the Iranians were going to do, Ed Muskie got up, tears in his eyes, and the staff the same. We all said goodbye. That was the end of his stewardship.

The next day the new team arrives, and there's a staff meeting, and I go into the staff meeting as the counselor of the department and introduce myself to [Secretary of State] Al Haig, and I blush about it now: I simply wasn't wanted. It was a rude new team. I thought I should be helpful. I had all of these things on Poland all done up with respect to personnel, with respect to the policy choices, handing them over, trying to provide for continuity. It was a joke. I realize now I just should have made myself disappear, but I also had nowhere to go, and the one thing that did turn out was the new team asked me to sit in the office of the Middle East negotiator because it was a large posh office and there was so much competition for that office among the new politicos coming in that they wanted to be able to show it on the space chart as occupied. So my secretary and I picked up and went down and plunked ourselves in that office. And that was the end of it—from a woman's face on an organization chart to a filled office on a space chart.

I just went home. I didn't have anything to do. I was saved by old skills. I got a telephone call one Saturday, and it was the under secretary for political affairs. The Canadian foreign minister had come to town to meet with Al Haig to prepare for the president's March 1981 first summit in Ottawa. Haig was briefed on the Canadian defense budget, NORAD [North American Air Defense System], you name it, and the foreign minister walked in and said, "If you don't settle the problem of scallops off of Georges Bank, the visit will be a disaster." Haig couldn't believe it. I'm told, in his own inimitable fashion, [he] said something like, "Who the hell knows anything about this?" There was silence in the room 'cause nobody on the new team knew, and [the career under secretary] said, "You sent her home."

So I was called in and was told to go fix it, and so I did. I started traveling among the Senate, the New England Regional Fisheries Council, Ottawa, back to New England, back to the Senate, to New England, to Ottawa, to the Senate, all around, and found a formula to save the situation. But I was dealing with an administration that didn't know the issues [and] wasn't interested. I couldn't get to people. They didn't want to see me, they just wanted this issue fixed. How could serious people have fisheries problems? They had no appreciation for it. They were all out there on this big global binge.

Finally [two senior FSOs] gave me advice: "Roz, you're just going to have to make your own decisions." Well, I've never minded taking risks. I just kept committing the U.S. government, with some support from Bill Clark [then deputy secretary of state]. And then the day came to make all of the package work, where we had everything prepositioned. The Canadians then [would have] a day in which to deplore, be angry, and say this is unfair and bad diplomacy. The president was to arrive, at which point the issue [would be] gone, everybody had had their little blowup, and the matter was settled. God, at the last minute, you know, Haig decides he doesn't know that he wants to start the trigger. Well finally, I just went to Judge Clark, and I said,

"You're going to have to trust me. This is all wired. This is wired in the Senate, in Ottawa, in the White House at the working level, everything is prepositioned, but you have to start it. You simply have to trust me." And it's very hard for [new political appointees to do], but Clark did, and it worked, and eventually what went through the Senate was passed 96 to 0. It was a bad chapter in American diplomacy that I had to repair with garden shears, not a scalpel unfortunately, and garden shears are not quite as genteel, leave a different size scar. I had needed a title to get that done, and so we created this special negotiator title, special assistant.

Eventually, famous people wanted that Middle East negotiator's office, and so I got a little corner that had been the staff assistant's office, and [my secretary] stayed with me at a desk there for two years. But [the job] wasn't full-time. I had Ted, had good friends, had family, and somehow or another I got through two rotten years.

You suddenly realize you married the Foreign Service and it didn't marry you. That you [have been] finding all of your identity off of the service and where you are in it, and suddenly it's not there. I suppose what I went through was my equivalent of a divorce after 25 or 26 years, with all the same effect, and it's not easy. I had nowhere to go, I wasn't 50, I couldn't claim a pension. Your pride is gone, your friends are suddenly not your friends, and you *really* know who your friends are. People who don't look at you, [who] decide, "I really ought not to have a cup of coffee with this person because I don't want to be sitting with losers." And believe me, it happens.

You disappear. You know, it's like Ralph Ellison's *The Invisible Man*. It doesn't happen only to the blacks in this society. In any institution or society, you're an embarrassment, so people don't see you, better off not to see you, and I think I probably came as close to just shattering under it as anybody can. I would not do it again, but there simply was not any choice—I was just a long way from being able to retire. They aren't the best years for a woman. You're 46 to 48, you've got all the trappings of success, and you are *nothing*. And it's humiliating.

Both Judge Clark and Larry Eagleburger had put her name forward for several positions, but nothing had panned out. Then the two got together.

Larry asked to see me one day and asked if I would accept the embassy in East Germany [GDR] and I said, "East what?" He said, "East Germany. That's all you are going to get." And I said, "Sure." I was pleased to get the embassy.

About this time, Ted got his assignment to Alaska. We decided in September that we would marry, even though it was going to be strange. I was sworn in as ambassador to the GDR in October. Ted and I were married on the second of January 1983, and went on a honeymoon, and he returned to Alaska, and I went to East Germany.

They rarely phoned each other, because calling "hurt too much."

We sent tapes back and forth. And after a while, we even stopped that. All you keep doing is taking a scab off. So we sent funny cards and newspaper clippings and letters. I would call occasionally, and he would. I really had to be in the pits to give him a call because I knew it was going to be worse after I hung up.

We knew it was going to be this way, and one of the reasons that we had sort of dilly-dallied over the years from '76, and never let it become anything except good friends and good colleagues was, I knew I wasn't going to give up my career, and he wasn't going to give up his, and we were moving in opposite circles. And I think we both had mentally dealt with that over the years as we realized that this friendship had more to it if we ever let it happen. So once we really started down the road to change the nature of this good friendship, why, that had all been sorted out.

Ridgway managed to see Deming in Alaska on a few occasions during her two years in East Germany, but Deming was able to visit her in East Germany only once, shortly before she left the post.

This time around, Ridgway did meet the president she would be representing abroad, Ronald Reagan.

It may have only been five minutes, but it did all of the things five minutes should do. It produced the friendly picture in front of the fireplace that allowed me to say, "When I saw the president, he expressed his views on what the relationship should be."

Ridgway had a keen understanding of not only the challenges of leading an embassy in an Iron Curtain country but the particular problems posed by proximity to West Berlin.

I stayed away from West Berlin, and I tried by example to encourage the substantive officers on the staff to stay away from West Berlin. With a closed society, much of what you do is sort of what I've always thought a [city] politician would do. You know your neighborhood, and you know it through the soles of your feet, and you can sniff it, and you feel it, and it's in the air, and it's in the restaurants, and it's in the shops, and it's on the trains—and if you go over to West Berlin you rupture that.

At one point I got the regional psychiatrist to come to visit. He was regional for Eastern Europe, and he [had] never [come] to East Berlin, and I got him up there. He said, "Well, you know you're not in the East." I said, "Look, I happen to think we have an unusual problem here. In Prague you can circle the wagons, and you have the high morale that comes from being inside those wagons. We don't circle the wagons because we have an opening at the rear, which is the West." He stayed about a week and said he was very sorry he hadn't come there sooner, and that he had not realized the erosion of the spirit that comes from going back and forth, so that you never make an adjustment one way or another.

[By never completing the adjustment], by the circle not being complete, having West Berlin, we lost the bonding process that helps so much at all the hardship posts around the world. I found we weren't able to do much about it with the families who had kids in school in West Berlin. They went back and forth all of the time. But those whose job it was to analyze East Germany we tried to encourage to live their lives in East Berlin and in East Germany so as not to disrupt the growth of a deeper appreciation of what it was all about.

In February 1985, Secretary George Shultz called Ridgway to feel her out about being assistant secretary for European and Canadian affairs. Ridgway was flattered and happy to take the position but did not foresee the difficulties she would have being confirmed.

I don't know the point at which everything went wrong. Just all of a sudden the nomination went up and sat, and sat, and sat, and I became part of what became "Free the State Department 29." Rick Burt [nominated as ambassador to West Germany] and I were paired together, and Sen. [Jesse] Helms [R-N.C.] didn't like either one of us, for somewhat different reasons, I guess. I flew back in June of '85. Ted was back here by that time. We went up to the Hill, and we had a perfectly normal hearing. Nobody appeared to oppose me, and Sen. [Claiborne] Pell [D-R.I.] made all the right noises again, and [Sen.] Nancy Kassebaum [R-Kans.]. There were some very good questions on general European policy and the like, but it was generally set aside that I was a known commodity and an experienced officer, and everybody was pleased to see me back and welcomed my taking up these issues. We heaved a sigh of relief, and we left.

We got word about an hour later that Senator Helms had notified the committee that he would not permit the questioning to close and he wished to see us that evening. So Ted and I and Rick and Gahl Burt went up that evening, to the old Senate Foreign Relations room. There was Helms and his staff, and then a number of other people turned up. [Sen.] Charles Mathias [R-Md.] turned up and [Sen. Edward] Ted Kennedy [D-Mass.] was there, [Sens.] John Kerry [D-Mass.], Claiborne Pell, Joe Biden [D-Del.], and I had a lot of help.

I went first, and Helms started in: "How can career officers serve for Carter and now for Reagan?" And then brought out a case that he was sure was going to finish things. That related to the asylum policy, and he wanted to know was it true that under my instructions a German family had been thrown out of the embassy and into the arms of the East German police? I said, "Yes." He then started to ask questions, "Did they go here, and did they take the family and. . . ?" I kept saying, "You know, Senator, I'd like to tell you how that story turned out, because I can tell from the line of your questioning that perhaps you don't know the ending of it." Well, he brooked no interruption whatsoever. I tried to stop him, to tell him, and finally he ended with sort of a great rhetorical flourish and asked, "And where are they today, Ambassador Ridgway?" I said, "In West Germany, Senator." And, of course, the other senators who were there laughed. I got a note afterwards from Joe Biden, saying, "You really stuck it to him." I hadn't intended to. I had tried to stop him. This was a very tragic case of a doctor who in great frustration did come into the embassy with his wife and children and threatened to kill them if we wouldn't let them in. He had surgical scissors and poisons and stuff like that, so we put him outside as a security threat. We had his name, we talked with the West Germans and the rest.

Helms at some point decided to accuse me of lying—that I had had no role in getting these people out, that they had been bought out by the West Germans. For all I know, that's true. I certainly do not know how they got from jail to West Germany. In my view, my own interventions and those of the secretary and those of other people certainly had their influence, but if the West Germans bought them out, to me it doesn't change the end of the story, which is that they're out.

A campaign on the right started out calling me a liar, and it had infected the consideration of the issue up on the Hill. So the weekend I came home, I came into the office to help the department finish culling the files for this case. That material was then made available in a rush on Monday morning to the senior committee leadership to read, to decide for themselves, had I lied. They were satisfied that I had not, so they brought the nomination onto the floor and I was voted in something like 89 to 9. The same nine, you know, the McClures, the Wallops, the Humphreys, Helms, Garn, Hatch. Nine people, and Rick got about the same vote. Of course, the campaign has continued. Very clever campaign. It's nicely done so that you can't sue. It will say in small print above a large headline, "Senate report alleges that . . ." and then the big headline, "Ridgway lies." But I can't do anything about it, so I just keep working, doing my job.

Ted was a wreck. I was annoyed, I was mad, but at this stage of the game, what can happen to me? I've got this wonderful husband that I don't get to see, I've got a career I can't go any farther in. What's to keep me from just saying, "I don't have to worry about this kind of stuff." It's dirty, it's ugly, it makes you angry, and you feel sullied by it, and you can't really defend yourself because they don't care if you defend yourself. That group isn't looking for the truth.

[The] job [itself] takes a terrible price. I've enjoyed being able to have as much influence as I have. I don't have time to feel satisfied about it. I just barely manage to keep moving one foot in front of the other. It's the top of the career, no woman has done it before. I think I'm doing it well, but I don't have time to assess it.

[Ted's] got his own exciting job. He was brought back from Alaska to establish the Coast Guard Intelligence Coordinating Center [and become] first commanding officer.

I come in at crazy hours with the secretary, and Ted doesn't like to have me take a taxi home, and, of course, the department rules don't permit you to be taken home. It's gotten to be almost a joke—he hates dirty tennis shoes and he wears these bright, white tennis shoes—it's almost gotten to be a family tradition on board the secretary's plane: no matter what time we arrive, if you look closely enough you will see this white pair of tennis shoes start to emerge from the shadows out at Andrews [Air Force Base]. Ted is out there, and it's driving rain, or it's 2:00 a.m.], and he's there.

Ridgway and her new boss had some "rocky moments" in their first months, which coincided with a shift in foreign policy between the United States and the Soviet Union.

Just one week after she was sworn in, she accompanied Shultz to Helsinki for his first meeting (31 July 1985) with the new Soviet foreign minister, Eduard Shevardnadze. That meeting, like the later one at the UN in New York on 1 October, was arranged so the two men could get acquainted, establish rapport, and define an agenda for the Reagan-Gorbachev summit meeting scheduled in November at Geneva.

Matters came to a head between Shultz and Ridgway at the New York meeting.

I was having problems with the way the department was organized, and getting ideas to him. He was having problems at my inability to get ideas to him in a timely fashion. We had a big blowup in New York. I had been criticized once too often about something not being on time when it had left me on time and had gotten all chewed up in the bureaucracy en route, and I was very upset about it, and so I asked to see him. I started in, and [a] phone call came just as I was getting to the point where I was going to start using four-letter words. When he put the phone down, he said, "You were saying." And I said, "I think I've decided not to put it quite that way." [*Laughs.*]

We went on, and that was when he understood I had been laboring under some real impediments that he wasn't aware had been there. One was the bureaucracy here, which was not responding to the uniqueness of the times. Here we had a breakthrough in U.S.-Soviet dialogue, and they were imposing the standard departmental machinery: 85 clearances and that kind of thing, and I couldn't reach him in a timely fashion. Well, I prefer to play by the rules, so I was going by the rules and, as a result, wasn't being responsive to what the secretary wanted. The second was that the moment the word gets out that the secretary [is] annoyed because Roz [doesn't] deliver on time, there is an institutional thing—it's not very attractive—it becomes more fun for the institution to watch you fail than to watch you succeed. It's better gossip if you fail, and I was well aware of this. When I talked to the secretary in New York in October, I just laid it all out, and he said, "You are entitled to reach me directly." He said it in front of his staff and that took care of it.

[Another problem] relates to [my] marriage. There were occasions when it's 14 hours into the day and I'd rather be home having dinner with Ted, and I still have briefing books to read and it's 9:00 at night. I was signing briefing papers to the secretary that I hadn't read on at least two occasions. The first, the secretary was amused. He said, "Roz, what does this mean?" Well, I hadn't read it, and I said, "I'm sorry, Mr. Secretary, I don't know." "Fine, don't you think you should?" "Yes, sir, I should."

The next time it happened, it was 5:45 a.m., and we had just gone up to New York, and there was a set of papers that I hadn't seen. We were meeting with Shevardnadze that morning, and we all knew [the secretary] would be up early, so I was up at 5:00 and showered and waiting. Sure enough, the phone rang. "Would you come upstairs? The secretary would like to go over some papers with you." So I went upstairs and he said, "Roz, there is a reference in here to 'UN Conference on Terrorism' in Milan and to the resolution, and it suggests that we urge the Soviets to follow that resolution. I have forgotten, what were the main ideas?" And I said, "Mr. Secretary, I don't know." That time wasn't so funny. You know, he may be a man that people think of as round, but he is not. His jaw straightened, and his eyes flashed, and he said, "Roz, this will not do."

This was a breakfast meeting we were having with Shevardnadze over at the UN mission. I met George Shultz at 7:00 in the morning at the elevator to go down. He said, "By the way, what's the weather outside? Is it clear?" I said, "Yes." Don't ask me why I said yes; I was so tired of saying no, I think. I said yes. I had no way of knowing what the weather was outside, and I thought, God, if it is raining, I'm finished. But we opened the elevator doors and the sun was streaming through the lobby, and I said, "Thank you, Lord!"

[Now] we're comfortable together. I think, friends and very fond of each other.

His instinct that there was a period of time required for making a team out of us was the correct one. The famous night of negotiating the joint statement [at the Geneva summit], when I was staring at an unacceptable Soviet position and I asked for a break, [I] went and called the secretary and said, "I would walk away from this." He said, "It's your call." I went back, and I said, "You can have your agreement, we will not proceed on the basis that you have outlined," and I was prepared to leave the table. I think if I had come back [to the department] the next weekend in July [and so] had missed the Helsinki meeting, we would have been not quite at the point where he could have said, "It's your call."

Given the high office she held in Shultz's State Department, Ridgway's many admirers hoped she would achieve the personal rank of career ambassador. Only Frances Willis, the first career woman to make ambassador, had been elevated to that high rank, and Willis's assignments had been much less important than Ridgway's. The number of career ambassadors is limited to a percentage of career ministers, and the single opening that occurred in this period went to Ridgway's friend, George Vest, in 1987. By the time more slots opened up, nemesis, in the guise of a change in administration, had overtaken Ridgway. George Bush became president and placed his friend James Baker as secretary of state. Once again, several high-ranking careerists were shunted aside.

Having survived summary treatment from Carter-Vance and Reagan-Haig,

Ridgway was pushed out by Bush-Baker, even though this time there was no change in political party. Paul Nitze, the former arms control negotiator, said on public television: "I think Jim Baker was unnecessarily unkind to people . . . doing the best job . . . like Roz Ridgway. . . . She did a great job and they really humiliated her. I thought it was outrageous."[5]

Nitze was not alone in his outrage. Constance Harvey, at age 84, had driven herself the 180 miles from Lexington, Virginia, to attend Foreign Service Day, always held the first Friday in May. There, for the first time, she saw and heard Rozanne Ridgway, whom she deemed by far the best speaker of the day. (James Baker's speech was "not much.") She thought it was a great loss Ridgway was leaving the service because she was "far and away the best."[6]

On 22 May 1989, the American Academy of Diplomacy gave Ridgway its Diplomatic Award for "exemplary performance under conditions of unusual hardship or stress," noting that her soundness of judgment at five Soviet summit conferences "made her a role model for American Foreign Service officers."[7]

Not long after, on 23 June 1989, Ridgway retired. Two hundred friends came to her retirement party to applaud her, and she received two awards: the department's highest accolade, the Distinguished Honor Award, and the Wilbur J. Carr Award, given to a career officer for special achievements as an assistant secretary."[8]

Now president of the Atlantic Council, her reputation continues to glow. On Foreign Service Day 1992, three years after Carol Laise had been so honored, Rozanne Ridgway was awarded the Director General's Cup. She was introduced as a "brilliant negotiator, a diplomat of uncommon skill and a superior strategist."[9] A fellow ambassador put it more simply: "When she walked in a room, there was authority."[10]

14

THREE-TIME AMBASSADOR
Melissa Foelsch Wells (1932–   )
Guinea-Bissau and Republic of Cape Verde
1976–1977
Mozambique 1987–1991
Zaire 1991–1993

To a rare degree, the life and career of Melissa Wells have combined high ideals with high adventure. She has elected to serve in places most people assiduously avoid, war-torn parts of the world where life comes down to daily survival. She has ventured beyond the duties of an ambassador to bring a special dimension to the job. When, for the third time, she was sworn in as ambassador, Under Secretary of State Lawrence Eagleburger said, "She puts a human face on diplomacy." [1]

Equally at home in bilateral and multilateral diplomacy, in some ways she is a throwback to that small band of intrepid, well-bred British and American women travelers who, in the last century, risked so much to explore beyond the boundaries of their cloistered Victorian lives. Like them, Wells encountered situations guaranteed to daunt all but the most courageous. Strongly independent and possessing great vitality and fortitude, she has coped with humor and sensitivity. At the same time, and without intention, she has blazed the trail for married women who want to combine raising a family with the heavy demands of a Foreign Service career.

She was born Meliza Foelsch in Estonia in 1932, the daughter of Kuno Georg Foelsch, a physicist, and Meliza Korjus, a professional singer, who came with her husband and child to Hollywood in the 1930s to star in MGM films. Meliza was raised in southern California and Mexico. After finishing two years at a Catholic women's college, she entered show business as a showgirl and synchro-

nized swimmer in a traveling aquacade troupe. She had been interested in the Foreign Service, and after the troupe went broke in Europe, she came to Washington determined to attend Georgetown University's School of Foreign Service. She worked her way as a secretary and was graduated cum laude in 1956. She took temporary work at the Bolivian embassy that summer, and the ambassador, anxious to retain her services, arranged for the embassy to pay for her to take a graduate Latin America area studies program.

Throughout her career she has done things that conventional wisdom said couldn't be done. Strikingly beautiful, she entered the Foreign Service by examination in 1958 and managed to get past the shoals of the oral exam and the inevitable question about her marriage plans with a joke about her six-foot height that disarmed the examiners. Within two years of entering, she married a fellow officer, Alfred Wells, but for reasons still unclear, she was never asked to resign.[2] She did not volunteer to leave.

The marriage crumbled, however, and her husband was transferred to London. Wells, with an infant dependent and against all precedent, was retained in the service and transferred to Trinidad. This assignment to a post suitable for a single-parent family showed a consideration for a woman officer's welfare well beyond the usual treatment of women by the Department of State in 1961. From Trinidad she went to Paris, from Paris to London, and there she and her ex-husband were reconciled. She again became pregnant and gave birth to their second son, becoming the first woman officer to have a baby at a post. Wells's experience provided the example that neither pregnancy nor giving birth (she took off three weeks) necessarily interfered with the running of an embassy section. Her husband retired from the Foreign Service to study architecture, which reduced their family housing and other allowances from his class 2 level to her class 5 level. Wells then discovered there were no family allowances for a woman officer. She fought that battle all the way up to the ambassador, who agreed with her that the ruling should be changed. It was.

Promoted to class 3 and with five years in the Departments of State and Commerce, she engineered a transfer for herself to Brazil as commercial counselor. There she learned to speak Portuguese, an important factor in her being selected to be the first U.S. ambassador to Guinea Bissau, a small former Portuguese colony in West Africa, and to Cape Verde, 300 miles offshore.

She opened both African posts under very difficult conditions; her first "office" at Cape Verde was a park bench. She loved the Cape Verde assignment, however, relishing the country's romantic association with the New England whaling fleets that stopped there when the United States was a new nation.

While she was at Bissau, Andrew Young, President Carter's new permanent representative to the United Nations, stopped by for a visit. Soon after his return to New York, he asked Wells to join his team as the delegate to ECOSOC [UN Economic and Social Council], that is, as one of five ambassadors serving under the permanent representative.

Three-time ambassador plenipotentiary Melissa Wells, 1993. Wells was ambassador to Guinea-Bissau and Cape Verde, to Mozambique, and to Zaire. *Courtesy of United Nations.*

I regard my experience at the UN as the only assignment I've ever had in trench warfare. [*Laughs.*] Somebody's always shooting at you.

In the atmosphere of the United Nations, the issues come up so fast, and they are so numerous, it's impossible to tackle all of them satisfactorily. They gain a momentum of their own. So much of what goes on—and I support the UN system fully—is signaling, which is valid and has a purpose, but you have to draw the line at some point. And I think that's one of the great problems today, that the public perceives the United Nations as just a big talking shop.

It's very intensive. In a bilateral relationship, I think it's easier to master your field in a certain amount of time. You make your contacts, you know what your goals are. You win some, you lose some. [With] multilateral [diplomacy], particularly on the UN side, you have to keep sight of where you're trying to go, and very often it's just such a free-for-all, and you try to maintain your dignity and discipline and keep on going.

The social schedule at the UN was frenetic, but Wells knew the pace was essential in that setting.

There just isn't enough time. We knew who our key contacts were, say, in the Western European group. We knew that we had to talk to the Group of 77.[3] We knew that there was this reception, that reception. So we'd say, "Are you going to this one? What time are you going to be there? Okay. You're going to that one next? All right. See you there. We'll continue there. In the meantime, will you talk to 77 on this one?" But you also had to coordinate with key delegations and your opposite number: "We're more or less on the same position. Would you sound out what his position is? Will you sound out what his position is?" "He didn't come to this reception." [*Laughs.*] You find yourself sailing into the room saying, "How are you doing? How are you doing? Oh, there you are. Yes. Here we go. I don't want to talk to you just now because I want to talk to him first about this."

Actually, some of this is fun when it gets to that stage, as the General Assembly [GA] is drawing to a close and the more difficult resolutions have been put to the back burner. Nobody wants to deal with the more controversial ones in the early stages of the GA, and then they all come up in bundles as the time is short. It's very hectic.

Languages always help you in trying to get to know someone. Very often I have found—I do have some language skills [French, German, Italian, Spanish, Portuguese]—that people almost prefer to speak English for some reason. Later on I may share the fact that I've lived in a country or have worked there and I speak a little of the language, and you start speaking in that language. It sort of builds up a little bond. Then we go back into

Melissa Wells at the United Nations, around 1978, as U.S. representative to the Economic and Social Council. Subsequently, Wells was lent by State to the UN for seven years, until her assignment as ambassador to Mozambique. *Courtesy of United Nations.*

English. Language skills certainly serve two purposes, and I think one of communication and appreciation, especially in terms of expressing what you're saying and understanding what they're saying exactly. The other, which is very important, too, is just the human touch.

Wells discussed the very different objectives of multilateral and bilateral diplomacy.

In a bilateral program, you are working with a government. You have policy objectives in that country. You are targeted on specific objectives. The end product in a bilateral relationship could be anything from a treaty to a ship visit to a trade agreement to a consular agreement, that sort of thing.

In multilateral work, you are not trying to get a trade agreement between two countries. You may be looking for an agreement on international standards. You are dealing with multiple partners. It's more complex because you're dealing with so many different players *and* you're dealing with a secretariat, which is very influential. They actually write the reports most of the time. So you have to cultivate contacts within the secretariat, and you have to cultivate the different delegations who are going to these meetings.

While at the U.S. mission to the United Nations, Wells was plagued by cysticercosis, a condition caused by a pork tapeworm infection she had picked up in Brazil. The parasites, or "beasties" as Wells calls them, lodged in her brain, where they caused a serious inflammation, resulting in "excruciating" headaches.

Before her severe headaches and seizures were diagnosed, however, Wells was in and out of hospitals, undergoing one test after another, for a year. The diagnosis was accompanied by the news that no cure was available, and the only treatment was a drug that had not yet been tried on humans.

I was at the mission to the UN, and after two and a half years, I said, "Look, I think I'm ready to change and move on." I was tired. I was burned out. Then I was having the health problems. I was looking for something but had the medical clearance problem. Then Bradford Morse, administrator of the UN Development Program, said, "Why don't you come work for us? Get a secondment. I have a great post for you."

I couldn't get a medical clearance to get out of State, I couldn't get a medical clearance to get into the UN. Then they come up with the worms in the brain that nobody has heard of, and there's no treatment for it. I thought, "Where do we go from here?" Then, thank God, this wonderful doctor, Dr. Benjamin Kean, was called in as a parasitologist by the State Department. He said, "Look, your trouble is that the last case of cysticercosis in Manhattan occurred in 1907. How do you feel about going overseas?"

I said, "Quite honestly, Doctor, I've been in and out of hospitals, and it's taken one year to find out what is wrong with me. If you don't let me go on with my career at this point, you are going to create problems in me. I must get on with my life." God bless him, he let me go. It was his say that allowed the State Department to let me go to the UN, [and] the UN took me. I lived through Uganda. I had partial seizure activity that I learned to live with. That's a totally different story in terms of how to deal with these things. I proved that I could do it, and my beasties and I got along.

She ended up in Uganda on a "secondment," a way of transferring from State to the UN whereby reemployment rights with State are retained. She remained in the UN for seven years.

I literally ended up taking the most difficult assignment. Uganda was offered immediately after [President Idi] Amin had left. At that point everybody expected Uganda would again fairly quickly return to becoming the pearl of Africa. Well, it didn't, and by the time I actually [went] there, it was a very difficult situation. I went there as res rep [resident representative, the senior UN official] and then became the special representative of the UN secretary-general, too.

The situation in Uganda after Amin's overthrow could not have been more dangerous. Wells described it as "true anarchy." The police had all been eliminated, leaving the Uganda Liberation Army and the Tanzanian Army, which spearheaded Amin's removal from power.

But then there was no institutional framework with which to support an army, you see. You have to feed it, house it, clothe it, pay it. What happened was that it degenerated into soldiers who had weapons just helping themselves, unfortunately, to the local population. You had certain areas, certain units who disciplined the soldiers, but actually there were very few. Even if you don't agree with the atrocious policies that somebody may be carrying out, [having a dictator] means that somebody is in charge, and at least you can go and talk to somebody if civilians are being murdered for transistor radios, for chickens, for wristwatches.

Given the existing conditions of lawlessness, it was not surprising that, more than once, she was in personal danger.

I was being driven home—which was in Entebbe—from Kampala. I was aware that a car was passing us. I was sort of looking off to the left. We drive on the left there, incidentally. It was passing us, but somehow it didn't seem to get on with the job of passing us, and that made me turn my head. I could see that the car was keeping up with us. There were three men in the car. The driver was on the other side. Two men were at the windows and had pistols. They were keeping up with us, and my first reaction was, "Oh, no! Here? Me?" I mean, I'd heard about this. It was always happening to someone else, not to you. They were saying, "Stop the car."

Of course, all this is split-second. George, the driver, still seemed unaware that this car was keeping up with us, and I said, "George, stop the car! Stop!" "What, Madam? What?" I said, "Stop the car!" Because they'll shoot you to get the car. By that time he realized that we were in trouble, and he started slowing down the car. Then the car pulled right in front of us, and as they got out of their car, I sort of went down on the floor, because I thought they would start shooting. I remember being down there, with my nose on the floor of the backseat, thinking, "Is this it? Is this the end? It's going to end *here*?" And then again—you see, I'm practical—I said, "I hope they kill me, because I don't want to lie here and suffer." The last thing you want is to need medical help under those circumstances.

There was no shooting, so I came up again, and by this time they were pulling George out of the car. A guy came up to me on this side. I had the window rolled up. He said, "Get out of the car! Get out of the car!" I remember looking at this revolver, because it was the first revolver I had seen in Uganda. I had been used to either AK-47s or Lee Enfield rifles, but I'd never seen this revolver. I thought, "Is that a real gun?" Because it was so small! Then I thought, "If he shoots, the glass is going to come into my face," which is a stupid thing to think about, because at this point, if you have a hole in your face, whether glass accompanies it or not is totally irrelevant. But this is what happens. Maybe it's vanity. I was not going to reach for anything, because two weeks before a Canadian priest had been killed on the same road. Apparently, as he got out of the car, he tried to reach for his briefcase. The thieves are not sure whether you're setting off the antitheft device which will impede their progress later on or whatever. "I can't get out of the car! I'm showing you my hands. I can't open the door!" It wasn't funny at that point.

He comes running around the side. Why I didn't open that door, I do not know. He came out this side, and he opened the door for madam, and I emerged with my hands up. "Hurry up! Hurry up!" George had been dragged across the road there. There was the other man in the driver's seat. So I got out, and then he jumped in. They turned around and got out of there.

I was left there on the side of the road, in the dark, and the first thing I thought was, "Where's George?" He'd been beaten up and was playing dead or wounded on the other side of the road. I got him up, and he was okay. He had a bad gash in his knee. I just put my arms around him and said, "George, we're alive!"

But then Wells discovered how difficult it was going to be to get a car to stop and help them. She began waving her full, pleated skirts at the passing cars "to make sure they knew this was a woman standing here." The headlights kept coming—and whizzing past—but no cars stopped. Wells kept waving her skirts to pantomime "Please stop the car!"

Then another set of headlights came. Suddenly I hear the brakes, "Eeeeeekkkkk!" It turned out to be somebody I knew. I said, "Please take us to the Tanzanian Army headquarters." I knew they had a radio [contact] with Kampala.

Once we were caught between two trucks carrying Ugandan soldiers. We were trying to pass, and we got caught in the gunfire. There was one time we were on the road trying to get to the border to go to Kenya, and we just turned a corner and there was a Tanzanian soldier, and he had the gun like this. "Stop!" And there was a man bleeding by the side of the road. We stopped the car. Then gunfire started. The soldier jumped into the front seat with his weapon, closed the door, and then shouted at the driver, and the driver immediately turned around and pulled away, and they were shooting at us. There had been an ambush there, and we just happened to arrive at that point, and he wanted to get out of there.

Incidents like these affected not only Wells but her family in Nairobi. She explained it to them in terms of taking responsibility: Someone had to be on the front line of relief operations, however dangerous it was.

Once I had seen bodies, dead bodies, from the slow violence of starvation, about which you can do something—you can't do all that much about the atrocities—there is no way that I can just turn my back and write a report and hope that somebody else will lead.

Every roadblock we encountered was a human negotiating situation. You can't just say, "Well, here I am. Here are my papers." No way. I mean, he can't read. He looks at the papers upside down, he pretends he's reading. [*Laughs.*] You get out, you give the Liberation handshake, you negotiate your way through in terms of human contact.

There were a couple of men I refused to take on trips because it was almost as if they had to prove something. They would jump out of the back of the car. I'd say, "Sit down!" The last thing you want is anybody . . . just sit there, they come to you. Don't start jumping around, because they think you're going to throw a grenade or something.

I think that women, because they are biologically mission-oriented, can withstand a lot of stress better than men in this kind of situation. I can say that, I've seen enough of it. On the whole, under a continuing stressful situation, I found that women react very, very well.

Wells has found it far easier to "take the initiative" in multilateral diplomacy than in bilateral.

Take the case of Uganda, where the initiative could only be taken by something like the UN. If it [is] related to a particular donor country, it gets bogged down.

Take something as sensitive as police training. By the time I had the gun in my face, I just went back to New York headquarters at the UN and said, "Look, you guys back here, you're fussing around [about] whether to do police training, and our human rights are being trampled on left and right over the simple lack of a police force!" I used to say, "If four out of five policemen disappeared off the streets of New York, I wish you the best of luck with your lifestyle!" So we made a case for it. I tried to get the U.S. government involved in this. I actually asked for kitchen equipment for the police training school. No way. They couldn't contribute. It was legislatively impossible for us. [Our group] started the program, and the Royal Canadian Mounted Police came down to teach, as trainers of police, and the program went on. It was very successful.

When the Uganda assignment was over, Wells transferred to Geneva to start the UN's Impact program, which develops programs on "avoidable disablement." In early 1985 "I had a whole new set of symptoms simply explode on me. Back to my doctors in New York."

By then, more was known about the drug Praziquantel. At the urging of her doctors, Wells took the highly experimental and risky treatment. She wanted to "go to the best" and arranged to receive the treatment at the National Institutes of Health (NIH) in Bethesda, Maryland.

NIH is a superb place! It's not a treatment hospital, it's a research hospital, and you're treated as a collaborator. You really are. It really makes you feel good about paying your taxes, I'll tell you! [*Laughs.*] I was at NIH for six or seven weeks last spring. Since then, it's been absolutely marvelous. I don't have headaches anymore. The conservative approach of the medical community is, "We won't know until you die to be absolutely sure as to what happened." But here I am. I have my clearance to go to Mozambique, and functionally I feel well.

Her seventh year of UN service was coming up for approval, and State was naturally interested in reviewing her secondment status.

We had talked a little earlier. My argument was, "I want to come back, but I want to go into a good job. I hear about all these senior people who are walking the halls and don't have anything to do. I love what I'm doing right now. How can I make sure that I will have a good job?" That's when it was agreed that my name would be submitted to the deputy secretary's committee for chiefs of mission. Again, I was delighted that this was going to happen, but I was very skeptical. I figured that this long out of the system, sure, everybody loves Melissa, but you've been out of sight, out of mind. All of a sudden there's new talent, and nobody knows you anymore, so to speak, in terms of your professional life. I figured, "All right. Let's give it a try." Then I remember I said, "I don't want to be just an ambassador. I want an interesting post!" [*Laughs.*]

So when the committee met, which was early January 1986, I had a call shortly thereafter to say that two names had been selected for Mozambique to be sent to the secretary. Then within another week or so, as I recall, the secretary decided on one name to forward to the White House for Mozambique, and that was my name.

Wells was "just stunned" as well as overwhelmed with "these wonderful emotions about having come into the State Department to begin with for the love of the service and all that." It was gratifying to have Mozambique come up for her a second time, because she had turned down the same assignment once before after Uganda, for the sake of her family.

Her confirmation hearing, however, ran aground on some unforeseen political shoals. Sen. Jesse Helms, at odds with the Department of State over U.S. policy toward Mozambique, held up Wells's nomination in an attempt to force State to extend recognition to Renamo (Mozambique National Resistance), a rebel group.

Secretary of State George Shultz supported Wells throughout the Helms campaign to derail her nomination. The standoff lasted until 9 September 1987— eleven months and two days, a new confirmation record. Wells was finally sworn in on 18 September 1987 in a ceremony at which Shultz spoke. Through it all, she kept both her nerve and her enthusiasm for the assignment.

Africa had long held a special fascination for her.

It's a combination of strange factors, everything from adventure stories that you hear when you're young, the films, the movies. As you grow up, you have this sense of [the] exotic, and you start learning more about it. It became quite clear that this enormous area of the world, all still under colonial administration at the time I'm talking about, was going to become important. There were indications already that colonial empires might not be around that long. It seemed to be the least developed area, which it certainly is. That appealed to me. People *still* don't understand that I'm dying to go to Mozambique. It's the challenge. It's the job. You know what's going on in Mozambique now. It's getting more exciting every day in terms of the scale of the job to be done. I love that.

[Mozambique is] part of this awareness that is going on in many parts of Africa that the model of planning that was adopted at independence just does not work. It *does not work*. It's demolished anything that existed.

[But] exciting things are going on in terms of sale of parastatal organizations, the assets. You don't hear about this. The fact that our AID program is directed toward the private sector because of legislation, because we are not to be dealing with a Marxist-Leninist government, creates a cramped situation in terms of flexibility, but is very exciting.

The challenge to go, to see this transition taking place within the much larger context of regional problems in southern Africa, and, of course, now the issue being apartheid in South Africa and our own sanctions, it's part of a very, very, very rich picture in terms of challenges.

The following segment of her oral history was recorded after her return from Mozambique, when once again she was awaiting Senate approval, this time on her nomination to be ambassador to Zaire.[4] She discussed her tour in Mozambique and how she became aware of the dissatisfaction of the local people with Frelimo

[National Front for the Liberation of Mozambique], the Marxist party in power. Wells had believed the Renamo rebels were "bandits" supported by South Africa, whose sole objective was to destabilize the government, and that they had little support among the populace.

I made it my business to travel a great deal, to visit the *campos dos deslocados*—these were the people who had been displaced, who are refugees within their own country. I talked to people in hospitals, to civilians. Those with amnesty obviously had been carrying weapons before, but essentially [I talked] to civilians, to try to piece together from them, number one, what happened to them? How was this attack? And two, what was their understanding of what this world is all about?

[I discovered] there was a strong internal component to the war that I had not been aware of and [that] was basically rooted in the mistakes that the Frelimo [leaders] had made when they came to power at the time of independence. Once I learned about these and raised them with the government, they began to respond and say, "Yes, we admit we made mistakes. We made mistakes."

Let me give you an example. Shortly after I arrived, I was, of course, making my calls, and I met with one of the leaders, what you would call the theoretician for the Frelimo party, [someone who could discuss] where they've been, where they're going. It was a bit of a stiff meeting at first, and he was definitely what one would call a hard-liner. As we started to talk, I said, "You know, I'd like to try out on you some of the questions that I had to answer for the Senate of the United States to be confirmed."

He reacted with amusement but quickly saw her point that the "language about Marxist-Leninist dogma" that Mozambiquans spoke, with no intention of implementing the dogma, colored others' perceptions of them. The point came up again later, after she and the theoretician had become good friends.

Before the Frelimo party congress in 1989, he put the question to me, saying, "Look, Melissa. If you could write it out, what would you like to see come out of this congress?" I came back immediately and said, "Remember the first time we met and I tried out those questions on you? Why do you need all these references in your charter to Marxism, Leninism, and all? You're not doing it. You're trying to privatize. The churches are open. Is this a monument that you need for sentimental reasons? This is your past. You're shooting yourself in the foot. It's time that you gave all this up."

Now, I cannot say that I'm personally responsible for this, because there was a general trend in this direction in any event, but I'm pleased to report that as a result of that congress, there were no further references to Marxism or Leninism in the party thinking.

Frelimo's mistakes turned many against it, but Wells could not understand why these unpopular actions had to be "counteracted in such violent fashion and with the use of terror against civilians." She was especially distressed by "children [being] abducted and trained to kill" by Renamo.

Shortly before the interview, public television had aired a documentary entitled "Diplomatic Profiles," which included a segment on Wells at her post in Mozambique. One sequence was of a mute little boy. Wells identified him as Frenisi and explained what had happened to him.

He went down to fetch water by the stream, as he did every day of his life. He came back to their hut, and there were men with guns surrounding it. Then they told him to set fire to the hut. They gave him a torch. Of course, the hut is what you call a *palhota*, a thatched roof and so forth, so that the thing went up in flames. Immediately the parents came running out, and then their heads were cut off. There are other gory parts to the whole thing.

When Frenisi came to us at the Lhanguene center, he just wouldn't speak to anybody. He would not participate in any of the activities. He'd be off in a corner, and then from time to time tears would pour from his eyes. I'd go there with ice cream and Coca-Colas and with Donald Duck cartoons, and I remember taking him and putting him on my lap, and he was like a little sack. I tried to cuddle him, but just no reaction whatsoever, except sometimes he cried.

Eventually the story came out via drawings. The reason he wasn't speaking was because he felt guilty. In his little six-year-old mind, *he* was the one who killed his parents because he set fire to the [hut]. I was there when they reenacted the psychodrama, which is where the other children who've all had brutal experiences as well, play different parts. Frenisi is sitting, watching. He watches a little boy playing his part, and they reenact the story. Frenisi sees that that there is nothing he could have done. Once we broke through the barrier, Frenisi spoke.

Wells's "modest estimate" was that 100,000 Mozambiquans had been killed in the preceding ten years. Her own contribution to dealing with the pain and trauma of so large-scale a tragedy was to talk the U.S. government into funding Lhanguene, a home for the conflict's youngest victims. The project started under the auspices of the U.S. Save the Children Federation and served as a training model for Save the Children U.K., Norway's Redd Barna, and other organizations.

The first priority was finding living quarters, and Wells arranged to convert a former student hostel.

We had to get it fit to live in, and Al [her husband] donated his services in terms of supervising the plumbing and making sure the toilets work and so forth.

But then the key thing was to bring the specialized talent from the States. [The documentary showed] the child combatants, I mean children abducted and trained to kill. What do you do with children who have been taught to bayonet and to kill? Do you just treat them like any other 12-year-old, or do you put them in prison, or do you "warehouse" them because they're unsafe for society?

At that stage there was not one trained psychologist or psychiatrist in all of Mozambique to develop a model in terms of training local people, to spot which child could possibly have what you call posttraumatic stress disorder, which is the key thing that we're looking for here.

Then in addition to that, we got into the question of reuniting the children with families, if you can find them. By the time I left Mozambique, we had reunited 2,000 children—2,000—in a country at war, where people can't read, where they have not ever seen a photograph of a loved one.

Early on, Wells visited Lahanguene at least once a week, usually every week-end.

I was overwhelmed with these children and their problems. While we were putting the project together, and then when the first team came, the child psychologist and psychiatric social worker, I was there for most of the interviews. I just wanted this thing to work. I gave a lot of my time because, quite honestly, you can't just handle it in a bureaucratic way. It wouldn't work. You see, we're used to emergency programs where we send food, we send medical supplies, tents, blankets, you name it. But "shrinks?" That's something else.

Children can be rehabilitated. Some of them are damaged for the rest of their lives, obviously. Children have been reunited. One of the ringleaders, who admitted in his interviews that he can remember killing six people, has gone back to live with his uncle. In his case, it was particularly sad because when they located the family, the family were not thrilled with bringing him back because they were afraid that they would get retribution from their neighbors, because he was involved in killing, you see. He'd been seen in attacks.

I've been in touch here in Washington to see what can be done in a more organized fashion for the "children of war." It's not just the Mozambique experience, it's the Uganda experience before that, where they had the *ki-dogos*—again, child soldiers. We know that it certainly went on in Cambodia. These are people who are alive, and they are the adults of tomorrow. They're carrying this stuff around in their heads, and we have to cope with it. We can't just lock them up. We can't just turn them loose either, turn them loose without talking to them, without trying to relieve them of guilt feelings, which is essentially what our program does. It has to be focused, done in a more organized fashion.

The peace talks have borne disappointing fruits thus far, but peace is never easy after a long war, and I'm still hopeful. We did achieve a more open political society. There's a new constitution. There is the commitment to political pluralism. Those are very important achievements. I'm glad that it happened on my watch, and I take some credit for it.

Her reception in Mozambique indicated that the 11-month delay in her confirmation probably—and ironically—worked in her favor by making her well known before her arrival in Mozambique.

I really, truly believe that everything happens for a purpose. There is no doubt in my mind that the delay in my confirmation made me a heroine by the time I arrived. I mean, this is like Joan of Arc! Children were being named after me! The first little Melissa was born the day that the Senate voted. The next Melissa was born the day that I presented credentials. I kept getting pictures about little Melissas up and down Mozambique. Then I really didn't answer them all. I wanted to discourage this, because there's just so many little dresses that I could buy. [*Laughs.*]

It turned me into a heroine and opened doors for me. I think I would have opened them eventually anyway, but, boy, did I get off to a running start! Now, please, please make it absolutely clear that I don't want to recommend this for any other ambassador, and once is more than enough. [*Laughs.*]

In 1989 the New Yorker *carried an article on Mozambique that discusses the "Melissa Wells factor" and says, "Mrs. Wells was widely known, and admired, by the time she arrived. And her performance* in situ *seemed only to increase her local popularity. She was Portuguese-speaking, experienced in Africa, knowledgeable about Mozambique, and endlessly energetic. . . . She is a serious reporter . . . asking hard questions and making detailed notes. And she is taken seriously by the Mozambiquan government."* [5]

15

THE ULTIMATE TANDEM
Jane Abell Coon (1929–   )
Bangladesh 1981–1984

Jane Abell Coon's career is a paradigm for the way women were treated by the Department of State in the postwar years. She was accepted into the ranks of professional diplomats without any great expectation of advancing to the highest rank, and she understood she would give up her career when she married Carleton Coon. During her years away from the service, the civil rights upheavals forced the Foreign Service to deal with the demands of women and minorities. As a consequence, she was invited to return at her former rank. Once back, her own efforts, coupled with White House pressure during the Carter years to advance women, shot her to the top.[1]

She had entered the Foreign Service via the Wriston program in 1956, having commenced government service in 1951 as an intern at the State Department. Early assignments enabled her to develop expertise in Southeast Asian affairs, and her career was progressing along very satisfactory lines when she left to marry a fellow Foreign Service officer. She both knew and accepted the consequences to her career, and for the next several years went with her new family to foreign assignments as a spouse rather than an officer. Only in hindsight did she recognize how demoralizing this change in status had been for her.

She reentered the service after nine years, still as a class 3 officer. (Her husband, who also had been a class 3 when she left the service, was by this time a class 1). She did not anticipate many promotions but hoped to be assigned interesting work, acknowledging that her choices would be limited by the demands of her husband's career. By an extraordinary combination of events, Jane Coon was quickly advanced to the rank of deputy assistant secretary of state and, within five years of her reentry into the service, became an ambassador. Her husband was also made an ambassador, and their posts, Bangladesh and Nepal, were close enough that they could see each other often. At a time when tandem couples were experimenting with different ways of handling dual careers, Jane and Carleton Coon became the Foreign Service role models—the "ultimate tandem." Their situation was very different from that of Carol Laise and Ellsworth Bunker. The Coons were both career officers and enjoyed none of the benefits that derive from being an intimate of a president.

Coon's career illustrates how the Foreign Service, without precedents to guide it, was groping for new protocols to meet the changing circumstances of women officers. For example, Jane, as U.S. ambassador, accompanied President Hussain Mohammad Ershad of Bangladesh on an official working visit to the United States, then almost immediately had to turn around and accompany the king and queen of Nepal on a state visit as the spouse of the U.S. ambassador. Her presence was considered necessary to provide female company for the queen, yet apparently no one thought it might be desirable for Carleton to go along on the Ershad visit to provide male company—or even, perhaps, reassurance to a foreign dignitary with no prior experience of the Western world.

Jane Abell was born in New Hampshire in 1929 and was raised with three older brothers in a small university town where her father was a professor. Her mother had been a Latin teacher, and all three brothers entered academia. She did not know exactly what she wanted to do but was sure she did not want to follow the family profession. Intensely curious about the world, she wanted, in a nebulous way, "something different."

By the time she was in her senior year at Wooster College in Ohio, and faced with "the awful specter of graduate school," she went along with a professor's suggestion that she take the federal Civil Service examination for junior professionals. "To my astonishment, I passed." She asked to go to the State Department, and in September 1951, "fresh out of college and green as grass," she embarked on her career. The intern program lasted nine months, at the end of which time she had to find a permanent slot for herself.

The summer of '52 was not a very good summer to get a job, but I managed to land one in the area office for South Asia for USIA. I spent a year there, but it was a terrible year because it was during the height of the McCarthy period. You felt that right down to my level. There were people losing their jobs. USIA was splitting off from the department. When the office I was in was being abolished, I eventually moved out with the file cabinets. Very demoralizing. So I had to find myself a job.

Eventually I found a job in the South Asia section of INR [Bureau of Intelligence and Research] and managed to keep my GS-7 [rating] in the process, which was very fortunate. That was a very lucky break, because I started working for a woman [who] was a splendid editor. I would produce my drafts on yellow pads. She edited them with a red pen or pencil. I would get them back and wonder if she had cut both wrists over them. [*Laughs.*]

It was a very useful experience for me. Like everybody else, I thought I could write, but I could produce a great passive verb. About the time I'd decided that I would take the Foreign Service exam, the Wriston thing came along. So I came in about '55 or '56 and stayed in INR, working by that time pretty much full-time on Pakistan.

Back in the fifties, you accepted the fact that you were a woman and therefore it was going to be more difficult to compete. I didn't particularly get upset by it. It was just part of the environment, and I hate to say I accepted it, but I didn't have any tremendous sense of injustice. I didn't have any great sense of anger over discrimination. In later years, talking it over with my husband, every male officer in his junior officer class came in with a fixed notion that they were going to shoot for the top, that becoming an ambassador was the name of the game. I don't literally ever remember during my first 16 years, *ever* dreaming that that could be possible.

I think probably I operated at two levels. There was always an expectation that there was a possibility of marrying and leaving the service, but I think there was also an equal expectation that this was a great and wonderful way to make a living. I think that young women now who come into the service find this absolutely inexplicable. Sometimes I find it inexplicable, too.

My predecessor's time was coming to an end in Karachi [Pakistan]. I worked to get myself in line as the candidate to succeed him in Karachi, and it seemed to be working. It was a logical onward assignment for me, and probably Karachi wasn't considered a plum by many, when you get right down to it. I thought it was the place I really wanted to go because I knew I could break in there.

I was assigned, [but then] the word came back that neither the ambassador nor the DCM nor the political counselor felt that it was a reasonable assignment—a woman could not do substantive work in Pakistan. Well, the prospects didn't look very good. I still don't know quite what happened. The assignment went up all the way to the assistant secretary, and he made the decision that I would go, but I went out with some trepidation, knowing that I wasn't wholly welcome in my new post of assignment.

I can still remember flying over endless desert, endless, endless desert, and finally somebody pointing out this small patch of white city on the edge of the sea and saying that was Karachi, surrounded by what looked to me like howling desert, thinking to myself, as my heart dropped, that I was going to spend the next two years of my life here.

The first things young political officers do are biographic reporting, descriptive reporting, and a certain amount of answering letters, a lot of just getting around and making contacts and trying to understand the local scene. I was there about six months when the consul general in Dhaka [East Pakistan] asked that someone be sent over on TDY [temporary duty] because his only political officer was leaving, and there was going to be a gap of about a month. Being the most junior and quite clearly the least productive member of the section at that point, they sent me off to Dhaka for three weeks. And that was very interesting. That was a lot of fun. I filled in as political officer. I made a lot of calls mostly by cycle rickshaw. Very, very useful, and, of course, it turned out to be of enormous use many years later, that I could say I'd been there in 1957. [As ambassador to Bangladesh, Coon would live in Dhaka.]

I was so curious and so excited about being at my first overseas post that I just plunged in and thoroughly enjoyed getting to know the country and the people. I felt, after I'd been there a couple of years, that as a woman, despite the resistance to my coming there, I had really, in many ways, a distinct advantage. I was in some ways a third sex as far as the Pakistanis were concerned. Their social mores really didn't apply to me. But at the same time I was a woman, and I could get into Pakistani families, which was virtually impossible for a man, so that I made a lot of very good friends.

I also had something of an advantage getting to know the very tiny handful of Pakistani professional women that existed then. In fact, there were about four of them, and we used to have lunch together about once a month. I learned an enormous amount about their problems as professional women in that society, and I learned a lot about the culture. I can still remember one lunch when one of the women—she must have been in her early thirties and had her doctorate from the University of Minnesota—came in and, almost blushingly, which was not her style, announced that she was being married. The instant reaction of all of the other women at the table was, "Have you met him?" I think I learned probably more at that post about the society and how it worked and how families functioned, and despite the fact that women were in purdah, there were frequently very strong women who wielded a great deal of power.[2] They were the ones that arranged the marriages, and they had an awful lot to do with issues of inheritance and land and property.

After two years in Karachi, I applied for Hindi language training on the grounds that if I got language training, it would be much more difficult for the department to consign me to other than political work. I did nine months at the Foreign Service Institute in '59–'60 on Hindi and was assigned to Bombay. The first year I was going to be consular officer, and then I would pick up from the political officer and replace him.

My assignment was made in January, and I wasn't going out until the following summer. I was told not to communicate with the post because the consul general, who was retiring in June, was unalterably opposed to women in the Foreign Service. He was very much old-school, and personnel said that it would be unwise to communicate with the post until absolutely the last minute before he was leaving. I went to a party to meet my new consul general, who was going out to replace this gentleman. My new consul general said, "Oh, I'm so glad to meet you, Jane. I had a letter from my predecessor, a long letter, three pages, explaining all of the reasons why a woman could not do consular work in Bombay, so I have been going through the department today to see if I could break your assignment."

So far he was unsuccessful. But this was literally *days* before I was supposed to leave for the post. He accepted the judgment of his predecessor that a woman couldn't do consular work. When I think of how many women are in consular work now!

I went out, but I went out again with that wonderful feeling that my boss thought I shouldn't be there. He knew nothing about consular work, and it was a one-person consular section, so I was on my own. It turned out to be really a piece of cake. I mean it was hard learning the job in terms of a one-person operation, but there was no problem in being a woman. Again, it turned out in some respects to be an asset.

What the old consul general had particularly emphasized that would be impossible for a woman to handle was shipping and seamen. In fact, it was probably easier for a woman to handle shipping and seamen than any other part of consular work. I very quickly discovered that most seamen had been raised at the knees of a strict mother, who had beaten into [their] head[s] that you don't swear in front of ladies. They'd come into my office, and I had arranged it so there wasn't a handy chair to sit in, so they would stand. They would start complaining about food on the ship, or working conditions. They'd say, "Ma'am, that go —— . . . uh, that da —— . . . uh, that—the captain is serving us absolute sh —— . . . ma'am, the food isn't good." [*Laughs.*] It would only take them five minutes before they were so absolutely paralyzed by their inability to communicate that it generally solved the problem.

I found that jail visits and that kind of thing were no problem. The Indians were extremely helpful. Usually an American sailor in jail was appreciative of anything you could do, like getting him put on a non-veg [nonvegetarian] diet schedule rather than a veg diet, and arrang[ing] to have some food sent in. As I say, it was probably an advantage being a woman.

I wouldn't trade that consular tour for anything, because I think you learn as much as a consular officer as you do in any other job in the service. You learn an awful lot about people.

During her second year in Bombay, Coon became a political officer. There she encountered a discriminatory housing situation.

The very energetic, rather aggressive PAO [public affairs officer], who was protecting some apartments [i.e., trying to save them for his own staff], worked out an arrangement where in the course of the year I would be moved six times. The consul general called me in to tell me about this arrangement, which, again, I'm perfectly certain would never have entered their heads with a male officer. At that point I put my foot down, and I said that was just an impossible situation because I needed to have my own apartment. If you're going to build up contacts, you can't move every two weeks.

I think probably that's the post where I made what reputation I got as a political officer. I made a breakthrough in terms of getting to know the chief minister of Maharashtra, whom no Westerner had gotten to know up until that time. In 1962, at almost the same time as the Cuban Missile Crisis, the Sino-Indian War occurred. As a result of the Sino-Indian War, Krishna Menon, who had become defense minister, was eased aside. To everyone's astonishment, the chief minister from Maharashtra was brought up to Delhi to be defense minister. This was an extremely crucial time in our relations, and I was the only person who knew him. That was a real break.

By the time she was transferred to Delhi in 1965, to be first secretary there, Coon had been promoted twice—in fact, she made class 3 when she was 35, which was very young.

In the course of my Delhi assignment, the India desk officer had come out, a man named Carleton Coon. The first time I met him I was up to my ears in a rather complicated arrangement between India, Nepal, and the United States. In the course of this effort, we undertook to provide some construction equipment to the Indians, [who] were going to use it to build a road that would go from the eastern to the western end of Nepal. I was very anxious to get a token shipment of four bulldozers and ten dump trucks. So I was introduced to Carleton Coon for the first time in the political counselor's office and turned on him roundly and said, "Where are my bull-dozers and my dump trucks?" [*Laughs.*] He was astonished because he had seen my name at the bottom of reports as J. S. Abell and didn't know I was a woman. He was married with a family, and I didn't think twice about the contact. I was assigned back to the States in February of '67, and I bought a small house on Capitol Hill. Meantime, I had seen Carl a couple of times professionally. Shortly thereafter his wife died of cancer.

In the following months Carl persuaded me that it would be wise to give up my little house on the Hill and become a Foreign Service spouse instead of a Foreign Service officer.

The marriage meant Coon also became stepmother to her husband's six children, ages four through sixteen. Her life of independence came to a halt.

I don't think I was aware of the business of giving up one's freedom. I wasn't quite clever enough to have figured that one out. Even after we were married, on several occasions I'd forget to tell Carl where I was going or when I was going to be home in the evening, and I discovered that you didn't do that. It took me a while to get used to.

Carl was assigned as DCM to Nepal, and going overseas made Jane more aware of what she had given up.

I was just absolutely swamped, when I look back on it. I think the last two years in Nepal I began to get very restless. Not recognizing it at the time, but in retrospect, I think I had periods of significant depression. It was a question of not having a job. When you have been in a professional situation and then are in a position where you are the spouse of the DCM, you have a change of identity, and your identity to a very large extent becomes a derivative identity. I think I had a hard time on the issue of a derivative identity.

I noticed it in social situations, and in my present job [dean of professional studies, Foreign Service Institute] I use it as a training device. At a cocktail party, when you would be introduced to a young male officer from another embassy, you would find, more often that not, he would be looking directly over your shoulder as he was introduced to you and shaking your hand, obviously looking for somebody interesting to talk to. I now act this out with junior officers. Suggest that this is not the way to get ahead.

The ambassador [Carol Laise] treated me as sort of half an officer, which I appreciated. She was very good about that, so that I was probably more on the inside than most spouses in a similar position. But it was still partly a derivative identity.

When we came back, someone from the department approached me on the subject of coming back into the Foreign Service. The window had been opened for women who had left during the period I left. I don't think I ever would have, on my own, applied. I'm not sure why. At that point I was thinking very faintly of going to law school, but this woman approached me and sent me all the papers and encouraged me to come in and talk. And we did, and I applied.

She was accepted with the understanding that her reentry would be delayed until Carl completed a tour in Morocco.

I came on duty roughly the end of September 1976. I was asked what areas I was interested in working in, and I was pretty out of touch by that time with the department. Nine years [away] is a long time. I don't remember what all I put down, but I did include OES, the Office of Oceans, Environment, and Science. I had some notion that this was going to be a brave new world for Foreign Service work, and I thought it was interesting. I didn't really anticipate a great deal of upward mobility after I came back. I was thinking in terms of adapting to Carl's onward assignments.

I was put into what was, as I look back on it, truly a dead-end job, in nonproliferation and nuclear export policy. I managed to shoehorn my way into a training course that was given by the Department of Energy on the nuclear fuel cycle. It is one of the best training courses in the U.S. government. Then, of course, the election was in November. Carter came in, and nonproliferation was a very hot issue. So this became a very busy and rather high-profile office. I dealt with, not the major nonproliferation issues, but a series of agreements on cooperation in the nuclear field with a variety of countries.

Late that spring of 1977, [the] principal deputy [assistant] in NEA [Near East and South Asian Affairs] asked me if I would be interested in the Pakistan country directorate, although I was vastly underranked for the job. It was normally a *one* job, class 1. And I said, "Yes, indeed!" I had South Asia experience, and I think NEA recognized that having someone that knew the nonproliferation game was useful, because that was virtually the only issue on our platter with Pakistan at that time. So they managed to swing the stretch assignment [taking a position rated higher than one's rank], and I came over as office director in summer of '77.

I think I was in well over my head but managed to stay afloat. This was at a period when [Secretary of State] Cyrus Vance was urging every bureau to have a woman as a deputy assistant secretary [DAS], and [they] approached me on moving up to the DAS job. I thought about it long and hard, and I told them I thought I would be much better off staying in PAB [the Pakistan-Afghanistan-Bangladesh country directorate], that I was not ready to move up. And I think I was right. You can't be out of the service for nine years without losing a lot of the key stepping-stones and the key experience that you need.

So I remained a second year in PAB and then was going to move over to the parallel country directorate, INS, the India-Nepal-Sri Lanka country directorate, when the DAS job opened up again, unexpectedly. [The assistant secretary] approached me again and said he thought I was ready. I wasn't sure, but I did take it.

It was an action-packed four years. It covered the first revolution in Afghanistan in '78, the very complex nuclear issues with Pakistan, which led to our cutting off aid to Pakistan, the execution of Zulfikar Ali Bhutto [deposed president of Pakistan]. And then, of course, from '79 to '81, there was the Iranian hostage thing, the evacuation of 950 dependents from NEA posts, [and] the Russian invasion of Afghanistan.

We had the whole gamut of foreign policy issues, plus the issues of terrorism and such things as the mob attack on the embassy [in Islamabad]. And of course, one of the most tragic events was Spike Dubs's assassination.[3] I arrived in Karachi on the fourteenth of February, where I was met with the news of Spike's assassination. I shortened my stay in Karachi, went directly up to Kabul, got there, I guess, two days after the assassination. I was there before the presidential plane arrived to take Spike back. I stayed on for about ten days, almost in the role of acting DCM to the chargé. That was a difficult period.

There's one other feature of that period, particularly '79 to '81. I was in the bureau as a DAS, and in '79 my husband, who had been in FSI as deputy director, came over to head up the Office of North African Affairs. So we were in—for NEA at any rate—an unprecedented situation where the wife was at the DAS level and the husband at the [lower] office director level. I give absolutely 100 percent marks to my husband for handling that magnificently.

Carl, who had *dearly* wanted to go back to Kathmandu as ambassador, was offered it, and NEA put me up for Bangladesh, and this seemed like the best of all possible worlds.

Coon had, in fact, considered another post at this time.

I knew that Dhaka was going to come open, and the other appropriate job in the subcontinent was DCM Delhi. That was coming open, too. I sat down with Nick Veliotes [then principal deputy assistant secretary for NEA] once, and I said, "Nick, I don't know. Maybe DCM Delhi would be the better of the two jobs. It's a huge mission. It's a big job. And who knows about Dhaka?" I can still remember Nick with his big cigar saying, "Jane, don't kid yourself. It's a lot more fun to have your own mission. It may be small, but it's your own." And I said, "Okay, Nick." So I was NEA's candidate. And for Bangladesh, when you get through the committee and are put to the White House, it's a pretty sure thing. You weren't likely to have too much political competition.

I was more nervous about it in many ways than Carl, in that here we were shooting for these two posts, and what if one of us didn't get it? Then what do we do? Because we were not anxious to have a long-distance marriage. So there was a certain amount of nervousness attached to it. Sometime in March, I think it was, I got the phone call. [President Reagan] asked me if I'd like to be ambassador to Bangladesh, and I said, "Sir, I'd be delighted." I can't remember quite what the circumstances were, but there were a whole lot of people in the kitchen. Somebody answered the phone and said, "Jane, it's the White House." I knew what it was, obviously. I grabbed the phone, tried to close the kitchen door, and came around and found myself sort of down on my hands and knees, with the telephone on the end of its wire, trying to sound composed and ambassadorial while there were half a dozen children screaming in the kitchen. [Laughs.]

Then you have to go about all the nitty-gritty of filling out a thousand forms. There was a tremendous time jam, as there is with every one of these ambassadorial posts—the hearing, then the confirmation by the Senate, then swearing-in. What Carl was backed up against was a Fourth of July reception, and he had to get there a week in advance in order to present his credentials to His Majesty, who only accepted the credentials of foreign ambassadors on Fridays. So we were really backed up there.[4]

God bless him, we were still a typical Foreign Service couple—he went out in June and left me to go out the end of July, and, of course, I had to get the house ready, the furniture into storage, and all of that. I swore I'd never do that again. So we became what a couple of junior officers who were a tandem couple said: "You know, you're known as the 'ultimate tandem.' " [Laughs.] I love being the "ultimate tandem."

Then we had a marvelous takeoff for his departure for Kathmandu. He was taking our two Lhasa Apsos with him. We got everything ready, the two dogs in their boxes, tickets, passports, the works, got into our two cars, with Carl and [me] in one car, and the children following with the dogs in the other car, headed for Dulles Airport. Got to Dulles: no children. They'd gotten off on the wrong exit. Well, we were in an absolute swivet. While we were there right in front of the Pan Am sign, I said, "You go on in and at least get your ticket through the tickets business."

He went in, and he came out looking pale. It was that wretched Pan Am flight that originates here at National and goes to JFK and then off. Well, we had not had the wit to look at our tickets, assuming international flights go from Dulles. About this moment [the children] came driving up, and with two cars, we took off for National and got there in about 20 minutes, just *barely* in time to make the flight. All of these connections were *crucial* to getting there in time to present his credentials. After all of these years in the Foreign Service, not to look at one's ticket! We felt like a couple of greenhorns.

Coon's own departure was no more relaxed. The unstable political situation in Bangladesh made it necessary for her to work at her DAS job up until the day of her departure for Dhaka. Her credentials ceremony took place five days afer her arrival.

My DCM told me I could have a rehearsal, but he didn't think it was necessary because it was a very set drill and all laid out in the protocol sheet. I decided that the better part of valor is to be prepared, so I said, no, I thought I'd go through with the rehearsal. I went over with one of the protocol people to the presidential palace. The presidential guard is lined up on the lawn. You're taken up on a little platform, and they play the national anthems, and then you walk down, review the guard, then go inside, where you're introduced to the president and the exchange of credentials takes place.

I walked up on the platform, and then I walked along the area where the guard would be standing. This is the monsoon season, and I had on medium heels, and with each step I sunk into the wet lawn and would have to go "errch" to extract myself, *each step of the way*. [*Laughs.*] I visualized myself *rooted* to the presidential lawn and never getting in to present my credentials. Which all goes to show that rehearsals have a function. So I wore my dress that I had very carefully selected,[5] and I did not wear the shoes that I was going to present the credentials in. I wore a pair of wedgie sandals that were not wholly appropriate to the dress, but at least didn't sink into the lawn.

The following day I made my first public entry into the diplomatic corps of Dhaka. It's a story I love to use on lessons of humility for us all. They were opening their first ceramics factory, a massive AID project and a very large factory. The diplomatic corps were all supposed to dance in attendance, so I went out, flag flying, and met my colleagues. This was my first official appearance. We sat outside the front gate of the factory and listened to a large number of speeches in Bengali, and I was really feeling pretty good, sitting there in the front row with the diplomats. The president finally got up and made his speech. He was handed the scissors, and he cut the ribbon, and he escorted the diplomats onto the floor of the factory. I had been rather

Ambassador to Bangladesh Jane Abell Coon, reviewing the honor guard at a ceremony to present her credentials, 11 August 1981. Because the ground was soggy, she was obliged to wear sandals with wedge heels to avoid sinking into the ground. *Courtesy of Jane A. Coon.*

unclear about what ceramic factories make. I had somehow thought that it was either petri dishes or those things on telephone poles. But it became quite apparent as the diplomatic corps marched perfectly straight-faced through what must have been three acres of toilet bowls and urinals.

Later, Coon learned that the U.S. government's decision to send a woman to a Moslem country had engendered curiosity and, among her colleagues in the Western European diplomatic corps, "considerable skepticism," though not among the Asians.

I think I can safely say that within a very few months, most of the people who were skeptical were coming around to me to consult on various aspects of the political situation. With the Bangladesh government, so far as I was able to ascertain, I did not sense any problems at all. The foreign minister was extremely gracious; the president, of course; the finance minister; other key members of the government accepted me as the American ambassador and it did not appear to be an issue.

240

You know, in the first year I was there, I was asked by several women's organizations to speak. I think maybe I spoke to one, but I consciously made a decision that it was important to be seen as the *American* ambassador and not the *woman* ambassador. So I did not take much of a role with women's organizations. I didn't make this decision lightly. I got together the professional women of the embassy, and we talked about it. They concurred that it was important that I be seen as the American ambassador and not a woman ambassador. My last year there, when I was well established, I did consciously accept invitations from women's groups.

I think I realized fairly early on the symbolic import for women of my being there. It was something that continued throughout my tour, and I found [it] in many ways quite touching. One of the first receptions given for me was a reception by the DCM for embassy staff, including the Foreign Service nationals and their wives. Many of the wives followed their husbands and were very shy. Repeatedly, throughout the evening, as I stood in the reception line, I would shake hands with Mr. So-and-so, and his wife then would take my hand and almost whisper in my ear, "We're so glad you're here." This became almost a pattern that many Bangladeshi women would repeat: "We're so glad you're here." "It's wonderful to have you here." "I'm glad the Americans sent you."

Because I had appeared so much on television at all these functions, my general recognition was very, very high. Just before I left Bangladesh, I was on a tour with the president, a helicopter tour of flooded areas in north Bengal. I was sitting under a tree, looking fairly disreputable, it being August and a very hot day, and I noticed two Bengali men standing there whispering to each other, and one of them finally came up and said, "Aren't you the American ambassador?" And this was a fairly distant corner.

Her first challenge in her new job was establishing a network of contacts in the Bangladesh government, which was still feeling the impact of President Ziaur Rahman's assassination. Her second, and virtually simultaneous, challenge was preparing for the stopover of Ambassador to the UN Jeane Kirkpatrick, who was visiting the various South Asian countries with which she would be dealing in the UN. The Bangladeshis were very excited about a visit from the first U.S. cabinet-level official in a long time.

We had to very quickly arrange her program, including the logistics. She stayed at the residence—and I had just barely moved in myself—with her husband and her security people.

I remember one lovely moment when the two of us were walking through the long vaulted corridor of the presidential palace to call on the president, and she turned to me and she said, "I'll bet this is the first time two women ambassadors have ever called on the president of Bangladesh." And I said, "I'll bet it is." That visit went very well.

Coon relished the relative freedom of heading up a post like Dhaka.

The beauty of being the ambassador to Bangladesh, and not the ambassador to a country where Washington is on your back all the time, is that you really have broad policy instructions, and you know perfectly well that probably no one much higher than a desk officer is reading most of your reporting. You make a lot of your own decisions, and if you want instructions from the department, you write your instructions, send them into the department, and ask them to send them back. Bangladesh may not loom large in American foreign policy, but it's a lot of fun being in a place like that.

The high point of her tour of duty came in October 1983 when Coon accompanied President Ershad during his first official working visit in Washington— indeed, his first visit outside the India subcontinent. She arrived a few days before Ershad did.

Sunday I checked into the department and moved into the Madison Hotel, where [Ershad] was going to be staying, and I had a suite. He was coming into New York Sunday evening. Just before I left for New York, I was informed that the marine barracks had been blown up in Beirut. I recognized that this was a most serious situation for us. I flew up to New York not having a very clear idea of what the impact would be on President Ershad's scheduled time with the president on Tuesday, two days later.

He came into New York, and I met him. The program went as scheduled in terms of his flying down to Washington Monday morning by American military aircraft, and then we were helicoptered into town, where he was greeted by the deputy secretary and the chief of protocol, and we went up by motorcade to the Madison. The rest of the day was largely a rest day. But the next morning in the Madison, I turned on my television set early, because

Ambassador Jane Coon in northern Bangladesh with President Ershad to view flood damage, July 1984. *Courtesy of Jane A. Coon.*

this was *the* day that we would have with the president, to hear the announcement of the American military action in Grenada. I called the State Department to ascertain whether or not there were going to be any changes in our program. There was no immediate answer.

I was supposed to be at the White House at 10:30 to participate in the briefing of the president. Eventually I was told to go ahead; they had no other instructions. We indeed went to the White House, and the president came out of a cabinet meeting on Grenada, came in, we had the briefing. He met with Ershad for about 45 minutes, as scheduled. We had the luncheon, followed by a brief photo op with the press. And I confess I was somewhat relieved.

After Washington we flew to Houston [and] Los Angeles. I left him there, [and] I returned to Washington, where I was going to change my spots entirely and turn into a spouse. Because His Majesty the King of Nepal was coming for a state visit, and my husband would be the ambassadorial figure. This was a great affair because it was a state visit and involved a state dinner. I once again met the president. I think there was a moment or two when he wondered [if he was seeing double].

For the Coons, as for Carol Laise and Ellsworth Bunker, maintaining their marriage involved careful planning.

The general pattern that we set was that I'd spend a few days one month up there, usually a long weekend. The following month he'd come down for a long weekend. So we'd see each other—I don't think we ever went more than six or seven weeks without seeing each other, and most of that time we saw each other at least every month.

I don't think an ambassador has a private life. You're kind of a public figure the whole time as long as you're in the country. Now, as soon as I got out of the country and got to Kathmandu, Carl might have been onstage, but I used to fight tooth and nail to have as few social events as possible and just to hole up together or go off on picnics or walks or what-not. Because that was as close as I could come to being a nonpublic figure.

Fortunately for the continuing success of their marriage, Carleton Coon had no problem with his wife's equal professional status.

I think he realized that I hadn't been altogether happy in a spousely condition, you know, not working, so I think he was delighted that I had my post and he had his post. It's not something we'd necessarily want to repeat, because I don't think we enjoyed being separated that much and that long.

Threats to her personal security did not faze Coon.

When I was out of the house, I was supposed to have a bodyguard with me provided by the Bangladeshis, a plainclothes police. There had been some threats, and there were when I was there—the Libyans and the North Koreans and the Iranians were all in Dhaka. [They] were always a trifle unpredictable. And the PLO. It was not that I was particularly concerned, but the host government preferred to have a bodyguard.

You never know how seriously to take these. There are a lot of crackpots out there, and you're not quite sure how seriously to take a crackpot, but the Islamic Jihad sent me a letter at one point, and I was not prepared to dismiss that as crackpot. So they beefed up security after that.

Whenever she traveled out of town, Coon was accompanied by "a jeep-full of Bangladeshi policemen with their pre–World War II rifles behind."

Every time I'd pull up at a guest house, there would be a guard of honor from the police, and I would have to review the guard of honor, which meant standing on a concrete block while they went through an exercise of banging their guns and putting them over their shoulders, whatever it is. Presenting arms, I guess it's called. At the crucial moment, I would say, "Dismiss," and they would all sort of march off. One feels like a *perfect fool* under these circumstances, but it is tolerable unless you have on-lookers—which happened on one occasion when two or three of my children were visiting and stood directly behind the policemen and made faces at me while I was reviewing the guard.

In reflecting on the period when she was chief of mission, Coon touched on the power that goes with the office.

There are a couple of things you have to remember: one is that [power] goes with the office and not you as a person, so you have to exercise a fair amount of care in not getting a swelled head. On the other hand, I think I would be less than honest if I didn't say that I just *thoroughly* enjoyed the job. There isn't a better job in the world. There you are, after all of these years in the bureaucracy, not having to *clear every blessed thing*. Being *in charge* of something.

There was another element that I was just thinking about. I suppose in any kind of Foreign Service work, there is a lot of variety in any given day, but as an ambassador you deal with an *unbelievable* amount of variety. Somebody asked me once what an ambassador did during a day, and I made a note of the incredible variety of things that came across my desk, and it was astonishing. I think you have an overview which nobody else has. I think that's one of the things career ambassadors have to learn, that theirs is an overview position. They're not a super-political officer or a super-econ officer. They are overseeing *all* of the work of the mission.

Sometimes I compare a chief of mission to an orchestra leader. Although each section of the orchestra—the brass, the violins, percussion, flutes, and what-not—are making their own contribution, I think it is the responsibility of the conductor—or the ambassador—to see that the sections play from the same score, that the mission is looking toward a common set of goals.

You also have to remember that an ambassador is there at a particular period. You can make a contribution in that piece of time but you're always building on what somebody else did.

We sustained what had been a good relationship with Bangladesh and perhaps improved it slightly. We made some genuine progress in development. It was a lot of fun to be there.

There were certainly many times when the violins and the wind instruments may have been a few beats apart. There may have been some dissonances in my orchestra. There was an occasional cello in the back row that needed a little more practice on his instrument, but I think for the most part we knew what we were about and did a reasonably good job. And for this I don't take the credit. I mean, the orchestra is what does it.

16

THE PRESIDENT'S ADVISER
Jeane Duane Jordan Kirkpatrick (1926–   )
United Nations 1981–1985

Jeane Kirkpatrick carried the Reagan revolution into the world arena. As U.S. permanent representative and ambassador plenipotentiary to the United Nations, her approach and political philosophy were as radically different from those of her predecessors as Reagan's were from Carter's. Her impact at the UN was immediate.[1]

How Reagan came to choose Kirkpatrick for such a highly visible post in his administration has become a legend. He read an article written by her and was so pleased with her views that he asked to meet her.[2] *The two hit it off, she became his foreign policy adviser during his 1980 campaign, and after the election she was chosen to be his permanent representative to the UN.*[3] *She also was made a member of the cabinet and a member of the National Security Council (NSC), but perhaps the most important appointment, from the standpoint of her effectiveness, was that to the National Security Planning Group (NSPG), the inner council of the NSC. She thereby became one of the handful of people actually responsible for formulating U.S. policy, occupying a position of great authority.*

These appointments gave her the most foreign policy clout any woman in the United States had ever had. Her relationship with Reagan—the fact that he liked her personally and granted her access to him whenever the need arose—gave her power that few men had. The UN permanent representative (perm rep) is technically under the assistant secretary for international organization affairs, two or three layers down from the secretary of state, but Jeane Kirkpatrick was able to bypass the bureaucracy and go directly to the president. "If I wanted to see the president, I could call up and get an appointment with the president. If I wanted half an hour, one on one, I could get half an hour, one on one." Thus she was also able to staff and run her mission her own way.

Having the president on her side enabled her to survive the hostility she encountered in the early days of her assignment. She had detractors everywhere

Jeane Kirkpatrick during her tenure as permanent U.S. representative to the United Nations, 1984. *Courtesy of U.S. Department of State.*

when she began, in the White House, in the State Department, and at the UN. The White House Republicans were leery of her because she was a registered Democrat whose husband had been very close to Hubert Humphrey. (She was, in fact, a neoconservative—liberal on domestic issues but as conservative on foreign policy as Reagan.) The Department of State's new chief, Alexander Haig, made little attempt to hide his disdain for her, and she upset careerists in the Foreign Service by bringing in her own people to fill most of the top jobs, shutting out from her inner circle those careerists who remained. At the UN, many of her colleagues were not happy with the selection of a woman, nor, at first, with her in particular. Fellow delegates said she lectured them rather than holding discussions. They accused her of being sharp-tongued and inflexible during nego-tiations.[4] She was criticized for her confrontational approach, as well as for her speaking style, her relative inaccessibility, and her top staff's lack of diplomatic and UN experience.[5] She was considered too pro-Israel and too pro-Latin America.

For several years before she took over, the United States had been on the receiving end of brickbats from the nonaligned Third World nations. By acting together, they could defeat measures the United States was pushing or pass spending bills for which the United States and the other major countries would have to pay. (Member nations are assessed on the basis of gross national product, and the United States customarily underwrote 25 percent of UN expenses.) Her immediate predecessors had followed a policy of forbearance and friendship in the face of hostility. In a dramatic reversal, Kirkpatrick asked why the United States should put up with such intransigence and "took down the 'kick me' sign." On her own initiative, she sent letters to nearly all of the delegates who had signed a one-sided anti-U.S. communiqué. In effect what she said was, "I noted what you did. You cannot hide behind a cloak of anonymity but will be held accountable for what you do." Some surprised delegates, accustomed to their anti-American behavior being ignored by the United States, replied, "We didn't know you cared," and promised to do better. The tone of hostility at the UN changed. From then on, those who wished to maintain friendly relations with the United States were much more careful of how they voted.[6]

Jeane Kirkpatrick had a rich background to prepare her for the UN position. Born in Duncan, Oklahoma, in 1926, she attended Stephens College in Missouri, then moved to New York to finish her B.A. at Barnard and M.A. at Columbia. As a French government fellow, she did further graduate work at the University of Paris's Institute de science politique. Her Ph.D. work was done at Columbia and included a dissertation on Peronist Argentina, an important early step in her career as a Latin America specialist. In 1955 she married Dr. Evron Kirkpatrick, a noted political scientist and guiding force in the Democratic party. Over the years, Kirkpatrick managed successfully to combine being a wife and mother of three sons with a career as an academician and prolific writer. At the time

Reagan selected her, she was a professor at Georgetown University and a resident scholar at the American Enterprise Institute for Public Policy Research.

Kirkpatrick's principal goal at the UN was "to represent the United States in the United Nations, which is more controversial than it sounds."

When I said that in response to questions, it was often suggested to me that the job of the U.S. permanent representative of the United Nations was more appropriately conceived as representing the United Nations to the United States. I stuck rather staunchly to my own conception, which happened also to be the president's.

Kirkpatrick was not prepared for the tremendous impact her arrival at the UN would make.

I had no notion what a shock my gender would be. Let me tell you how much the first woman I was. I was not only the first woman to head the U.S. mission to the United Nations. I was the first woman to ever represent a *major* power at the UN. I was the first woman to ever represent a *Western* government at the United Nations—Western broadly interpreted, [meaning] a European government, Eastern Europe or Western Europe. There had only been about three or four women to head missions at the United Nations before I got there. There had been a Guyanese, there had been a Sri Lankan, there had been a Liberian. That's about all. Such a *big* shock.

I didn't really know the extent to which the diplomatic corps of the world and the diplomatic profession are an exclusive male preserve. I also was the first woman to sit in the National Security Council on a regular basis, much less in what I sat in, which was the inner circle of the NSPG, of which I was a member in a not *ex-officio* but *personal* capacity. I didn't think there'd ever been a woman in those councils on a regular basis *at the table*.

I had grown accustomed to being the only woman in a lot of rooms that I was in. I was the first woman on the rank and tenure committee at the university, the first woman to be a senior scholar here at the American Enterprise Institute. But even so, I didn't think much about it. I didn't give much thought to it. And it turned out to be a bigger shock to my colleagues than I'd dreamed.

After my appointment, two other women were appointed by Western nations. The Belgians appointed Edmonde DeVer as permanent representative, where she has performed extremely well. She's a career officer, very highly regarded. The Swiss appointed a woman to head their mission. Now they're observers, but still they participate quite a lot. Nobody believes that those women would have been appointed if I hadn't been appointed.

I have no doubt that my appointment and survival of those first two years in fact opened doors for women in career foreign service positions in those two countries.

[It's] an extremely complicated, difficult, frustrating job, which is the big reason that the turnover is so rapid in it. You're dealing with 159 countries, and it's enormously complicated and difficult. They all want to see the permanent representative. If they're an ambassador, they want to see the permanent representative, in spite of the fact that you've got five other ambassadors there who are very competent. The demands are fantastic, so it's a very difficult job for anybody. I think there was also quite a lot of deep skepticism and concern about the Reagan administration. In the beginning, nobody knew what kind of people Reagan appointees were going to be. And on top of it, I was a woman. I think it was a problem—it just made me a little more strange than I already would have been as a Reagan appointee, or as a political appointee, because probably 80 percent of the UN perm reps are career officers. It's a high percentage.

I think with some of the Europeans, the Asians, at least as much as [with] the Africans and the Arabs, I sensed some sort of sex-related reticence—static, I would say. I think they just regarded me as a very odd creature. Now, since nobody ever gave me any training in how to be an ambassador, maybe I was a pretty odd creature. (*Laughs.*) This was maybe a little true, though I was, of course, very serious from the very beginning, and I worked prodigiously. And I did something else that most Americans haven't done, namely, I spoke a couple of languages [French and Spanish] well enough to do business in them, which is very important. I am told that I was the first U.S. perm rep who could actually function in other languages.

Once I established myself, demonstrated to my colleagues that I was serious and I did my work, and that I was businesslike, I think in fact that I probably profited as much from being a woman as I had ever suffered. I do believe that there are whole cultures in which men, like ambassadors and foreign ministers and even heads of state, may find it a little easier to deal with a woman than with another man. I think in macho cultures, like both Latin and Arab—and somebody said African—they're much less likely to regard a woman as a competitor. And I think woman are generally, including me, trained to be good listeners. I did an awful lot of listening and a lot of seeking of advice, and my colleagues liked that.

There's an interesting culture at the UN. It's an interesting mix of informality and highly stylized diplomatic communication. Everybody's on a first-name basis almost immediately, and I mean everybody, except the Vietnamese, the Khmer Rouge, the PLO, the people we don't speak to at all. My Soviet colleague and I were on a first-name basis from within the first two or three weeks I was there. On the other hand, everybody is very polite and relatively formal—I mean, formal in the conduct of business in a context of informal salutations. I think I adapted my own style of communication to that of my colleagues that I observed around me, especially the British, the French, and the Dutch. When I was with Latins, I talked like the Latins talk to each other—as "the ambassadors," you know.

I don't think I said many outrageous things. I will say this: maybe I was more outrageous than I realized. I developed very quickly a reputation for extraordinary and often shocking candor. Now, I never thought of myself as particularly candid. Nobody ever called me particularly candid before I went to the UN, so I think I must have been speaking in a way that made me seem shockingly frank.

Years before, Kirkpatrick had worked at the Department of State. She had left after a year because "I didn't want to work in a big organization." Now, as a seasoned observer of Latin American affairs, her impression of the department was negative.

I thought that the State Department had done an absolutely miserable job in Central America, if I may say so. I thought that because I started following U.S. policy toward Central America, particularly both El Salvador and Nicaragua, in about 1978, and I followed it unusually closely. I read all the hearings. I became convinced this part of the world was terribly important to us strategically, and the decisions we were making there were terribly important to us. I did very close analysis of predictions. When I say a "bad job," a "lousy job," I mean to say that the predictions that were made turned out to be not true. So I guess I had a poor opinion of the group. But I mainly attributed it to the Carter administration, frankly, rather than the Foreign Service.

I developed some views about what I took to be some biases—policy biases—in the Foreign Service, especially concerning the Middle East. I think I discerned those famous State Department Arabists rather early on. I became aware of this because we were continually dealing with attacks on Israel at the United Nations. It was the first issue I dealt with, and then obsessively through time we were dealing with complaints against Israel.

One of the crazy things about the job of perm rep is that you have to operate on many different levels. Any perm rep has to, in fact. I found that the NEA bureau was, in those days, out of step with the administration, by which I mean the secretary of state—with whom they should have been in step—and the national security adviser and the president and me. It was difficult. It was much harder than it should have been to get support and staffing to implement decisions made by the heads of government—the U.S. government.

Kirkpatrick herself hired the one member of the mission who didn't work out. The problem can be termed the "DCM syndrome"; it's one that, in Kirkpatrick's words, "the women political ambassadors have rather more frequently than others."

The first week that I went to New York, he literally proposed to me that perhaps I would like to take a trip around the world, observing missions and all that in order to learn something about the way the UN system works. He assumed I was not going to be interested in the running of the mission, he assumed I was not going to be interested in policy, he assumed I wasn't going to be interested in administration, and he assumed that it was going to be his job to do it all. And I felt very strongly that he systematically not only cut me out but cut me out and simultaneously took charge of the mission and the relationships in Washington and the process in a way that was going to be incompatible with my functioning.

I hate letting people go, firing people, I really hate it. In my life, generally, I hate it. I keep people a long time because I hate it so much, and I have fired very few people. He was the only person I ever let go at the UN the whole time I was there, out of a lot of people. But I concluded, and all the other [U.S.] ambassadors up there concluded, that we were not going to be able to function without getting rid of him.

For his replacement, she chose Kenneth Adelman, then a senior political analyst at the Stanford Research Institute in Arlington, Virginia. She didn't know him well, but she was determined to have an outsider, not another FSO. "It's a potentially very influential job, and I just didn't want somebody else trying to use the job to take over."

Having made the mistake I made with [the first deputy], I was simply scared to go back there twice. I didn't have the self-confidence, quite frankly.

That was really a pretty traumatic experience for me. I don't know how I survived those first months. Quite frankly, I'm a little surprised that I survived because there was so much I didn't know and so many ways to go wrong, and I was taking several of them, I think.

I had very good support from the White House. Now, I didn't have a completely free hand. There was a kind of mystique, too, of the administration in the very early days. Our most serious charge was that we were not to be taken over by the bureaucracy. This was really taken very seriously in the cabinet indoctrinations. I didn't go to any State Department indoctrinations, but I sure went to cabinet indoctrinations, and this was all taken very seriously.

Remember that I was a Democrat, and so I was regarded with a lot of suspicion actually by, for example, the "kitchen cabinet." They wanted me definitely to take some longtime Republican with me to the UN, and I chose Chuck [Charles] Lichenstein, [presidential assistant in the Nixon administration and deputy counsel in the Ford White House], who happens to be an old friend of ours as well as a longtime Republican. There was this great sigh of relief when I proposed Lichenstein.

I had some views about area competence, area culture, and language competence. I feel very deeply that that is one of our great strengths as a nation—our pluralism—and that we ought to utilize it. I had also talked to Don McHenry [her predecessor], and I'd studied where we were, and it was clear to me—and Don agreed, by the way—that there was a big opportunity with Latin America, and so I thought about José Sorzano [political scientist at Georgetown University]. [He] was very sophisticated and good. Every one of our ambassadors had major area responsibilities. It was terribly important to us, and this is something I would like to teach the department about multilateral diplomacy and staffing for it. It made a big difference in our effectiveness to have at the ambassadorial level somebody who was genuinely expert in every major area of the world, and at home in the language and culture. Every one of them had been assigned, as a serious part of their assignment, the development of close personal relations with people from their region, and following regional problems, in addition to whatever functional responsibilities they had in the mission.

Bill [FSO William] Sherman was our Asia specialist and did a lot with regard to all of the U.S. mission's activities concerning Asia, and then had the political [work]. I mean, we'd function like ward heelers, too. When it came time to try to round up votes, then Bill worked the Asian constituency. But he regularly followed those issues and cultivated those people. He was not just a nuts-and-bolts man, by any means. He supervised the administrative counselor, and he knew how the bureaucracy worked. He's the man who did that, and he kept that all oiled.

I took the Security Council, and I took the special relations with the ambassadors in the Security Council, plus running the mission, but I was the only one who didn't have a geographical area.

I tried very hard to allocate functions and responsibilities so that everybody was very clear about what they should do and what they were responsible for. I had a lot of confidence in them, and so it is a fact that I delegated a lot. At any given time, however, I stayed in touch with everybody.

I stayed in touch whenever there were problems. I stayed in touch from time to time with everything, but I did a lot of delegating, and I had confidence that the people who were in charge were doing it right. And they did, by and large. When I developed a concern about whether something was going right, then I focused very intensively on it until I became convinced that it was fixed, it was on track.

You know, sometimes it was asserted that I was inaccessible by my own mission. And sometimes I was inaccessible, because I spent quite a bit of time traveling back and forth to Washington. There are simply so many meetings, and especially the NSPG. The big thing that I participated in was the NSPG, which is really where it's been *at* in the Reagan administration and foreign policy, and much of the time it met relatively frequently. This was absolutely essential, I think, for our effective functioning. I really believe that my direct contacts in the top levels of the administration were absolutely essential to our effective functioning in New York. I don't think that it can work the other way either. It's just too complicated bureaucratically, and you get too involved with too many departments. You can't function simply through the departmental structure, through the geographical bureaus and IO [Bureau for International Organization Affairs], because it's at too low a level. There are a number of potentially quite delicate—politically delicate—issues for any president, any secretary of state. Delicate to the United States, with a lot of maybe different departmental perspectives in which the bureau and the assistant secretary may not really be wholly informed, or wholly in touch and wholly reflective. If you can't plug in at the top, then you're in very bad shape.

Being in the cabinet gave me access to authoritative decisions from the top level. You know the UN is unique in the fact that it confronts us and other countries with continuous decisions. We have to make choices, they have to be public, you have to vote yes or no. You can't fuzz the issue, because you have to act. We don't control this context in which we must act. It's terribly important to be able to get it right. And to be able to get it right, it is often necessary to be able to go right to the top and make really certain that you understand what the president and the secretary of state want out of this negotiation—and what they don't want. [Being in the cabinet also] gives one access to the ministers and even heads of states of other member states, and that's *very* important, since there is a constant stream of ministerial level visitors to the UN, and heads of states visitors. If you're a member of the cabinet, then you meet them—you develop relationships with them. You can call on those when you need their support. It makes a big difference for their ambassadors to know that you're on good terms with their foreign minister or even their head of state, and that you can call them if necessary. That's very useful in getting votes. I think it enhances the value of the permanent representative as a listening post for the U.S. government because it multiplies the number of ears that can give input on high-level views with foreign visitors.

With 159 countries represented when Kirkpatrick was there, the diplomatic social circuit at the UN could have overwhelmed her.

I didn't go to most of the national day [ceremonies]. I didn't because I just couldn't. I went to a few—just a few. I did a very great deal of socializing. The best way I know to tell you how much socializing I did is to tell you that when I was leaving, for the last two months I was there, I went to a dinner in my honor every night, and the last month I was there, I went to a luncheon *and* a dinner in my honor. And I left a good many people *without*, you know, having turned down their urging to let them have a dinner in my honor, because I didn't have time.

Kirkpatrick had a notable early success negotiating an agreement about the wording of a UN Security Council resolution against Israel. Unfortunately, the success was diminished by "snide comments" made by Alexander Haig, who claimed she had acted without authority.

On 7 June 1981, the Israeli air force bombed and destroyed Iraq's Osirak nuclear reactor, and Iraq demanded that the Security Council condemn Israel for its aggression. Because the reactor was believed to be capable of making atomic bombs that would present a threat to Israel's existence, Kirkpatrick adopted the argument that the Israeli acton could be considered self-defense.

Realizing that a vote against Israel was certain, she worked to change the operative wording of the resolution from "aggression" to "violation of the norms of international conduct," thereby obviating the call for sanctions against Israel. She met with the Iraqi foreign minister [Sadoun Hammadi] and got his agreement to the change in wording. Later, she joined her colleagues on the Security Council in a 15-0 vote against Israel.[7]

In his book, Haig makes no reference at all to Kirkpatrick. He suggests that his phone call to Hammadi turned the trick.[8] The president's 1981 report to Congress on the UN, however, states that during the course of nine Security Council meetings, "the United States worked with the delegation of Iraq to produce a broadly acceptable outcome of the issues."[9]

I was in absolutely continuous contact with Walt Stoessel, who was acting secretary of state, and Dick Allen [national security adviser]. I was in intermittent contact with Ed Meese [counselor to the president] and the president, but I was in touch with Walt Stoessel and Dick Allen two or three times a day. I mean, every time there was a question, I was in touch with them. I had a conversation with the president in advance of my first meeting with Hammadi, in which he made very clear what he hoped I could get, and there was perfect agreement.

This was a big, shocking traumatic experience for me, too. My life was very traumatic in those days, and things were happening to me I couldn't dream would happen to anybody. There was perfect understanding between the president and Ed Meese, who in those days was involved with all the issues, and Dick Allen, and Walt Stoessel, about what they wanted, and my job, I thought, was to try to do my very best to get [the agreement], and Al Haig was out in the Pacific.

I stayed in very close touch with them. Every time a new possibility developed, I was in touch with them, and I finally achieved exactly what they wanted. The president couldn't have been more pleased, and Walt couldn't have been more pleased. I must say, it never occurred to me that Alexander Haig wouldn't be pleased. We had tried to stay in touch with Haig, too, but we couldn't because the telephone connection was so bad. He was in Beijing and then, eventually, in Manila. We just had terrible connections, and the whole issue had sort of developed after he was gone, and we were under very heavy time pressures, and so we just had to proceed.

I was totally shocked when the stories appeared in the *Wall Street Journal* and the *New York Times*, saying Haig's aides said that Kirkpatrick hadn't followed instructions. First he said I'd done unauthorized things, and then he said he did it really—that I shouldn't have gotten that agreement, but that he really got it, neither of which was true. I did what I was supposed to, and I did follow instructions, and he didn't do it.

As a matter of fact, this is an interesting thing, this is a sex thing, I think: Hammadi—the Iraqi foreign minister, who is thought around the UN to be one of the meanest, sourest people any place—I think this is a man for whom being a woman probably helped me. I think he was a little nicer with me than his reputation led me to believe that he was with anybody. And I was probably a little nicer to him than an American male diplomat might have been.

He had a real dislike for Haig—Hammadi did—and he expressed that several times in the course of those negotiations. Then the last day, when we had finished—we had got an agreement, it had already been announced—and about ten minutes later, Alexander Haig called Hammadi, feeling that he could, perhaps, help out in closing the deal, and Hammadi didn't even tell him that we had reached an agreement. He didn't tell him anything because he didn't like Alexander Haig. He just didn't respond to anything that Haig said to him, basically. This left Haig with the impression that the situation wasn't closed, and therefore, when he heard that there was an agreement, he thought he had done it. But anyway, it was very bad.

I learned from journalists on the plane, much to my shock, that Alexander Haig had asked them to put the story out that appeared in the *New York Times* and the *Wall Street Journal*, and it was a fabrication. The president called me in France. (I left the day after this happened.) The president called me to tell me how badly he felt about it and how pleased he was with my performance. Haig called me, too, to apologize and say he had nothing to do with it. He would get to the bottom of it and somebody would pay. This was all lies. That was sort of an incredible experience.

Another event in which Kirkpatrick was heavily involved was the attempted takeover of the Falkland Islands by Argentina. A critic wondered in print if her "pursuit of the ideas advanced in 'Dictatorships and Double Standards' bore some responsibility for Argentina's invasion." He speculated that her known sympathy for Latin American regimes may have led the generals to believe the United States would take their position, not the British one. Haig was "furious" with her for holding meetings with Argentina's foreign minister and UN perm rep (she was trying to bring an end to the fighting) "and accused her of being 'mentally and emotionally incapable of thinking clearly on this issue.'"[10]

Roger Fontaine [NSC staff assistant] and I had lunch with the Argentine ambassador, visiting somebody not long before the Falklands issue. They had made some sort of move on the Beagle Channel, and we made a big point to communicate the fact that our government would never understand if they used force on the Beagle Channel.

Nobody ever mentioned the Falkland Islands, because in the extremes of our minds it never occurred to anybody that they would do such a thing. By the way, Peter Carrington [British foreign secretary] says the same thing about himself and the British. The fact is that it was so inconceivable to us that we didn't even hear what later we clearly recognized, in hindsight, had been sort of clues. We missed them. We missed the clues because it seemed so inconceivable. Who knows what the Argentineans thought? They had no reason to believe that the United States would in any way condone such an action, no reason at all. I can't conceive of why they would imagine that we would take a less serious attitude toward the Falklands than toward the Beagle Channel, which we talked to them a lot about. Unless they thought that our omission was significant, which is an interesting question.

The disagreement between Haig and me was actually not even really about the Falklands. By that time, Alexander Haig really didn't like me at all, and I don't even know why, frankly. I don't know why he disliked me as much as he did, except that a friend said that he had been powerfully prejudiced against me before he'd even met me. He said to my friend, "I don't know how anybody expects I will work with that bitch."

There was a kind of disagreement between us, but no more disagreement than there was between [Secretary of Defense Caspar] Cap Weinberger and I, who have been fast, good colleagues. My position on the Falklands was that we ought to remain neutral. I very strongly supported Haig's mediation efforts. I carefully avoided any contact with the Argentineans of an informal sort from the time of the beginning of those mediation efforts until the end of them, and I never had any contact at all, except sort of the minimal necessary to do with the Security Council business at the UN. And I had lots of people with me. I had learned a few basic self-protective practices by that time. That did not prevent Haig from spreading some sort of rumor that I was somehow sabotaging his negotiations. He says in his book that he heard this from the British. That's a very odd thing. But then, who knows?

Kirkpatrick discussed her relationships with the representatives from the major countries—Japan, the NATO countries—and others as well.

My relationships with the Security Council were particularly close—the Security Council ambassadors. I worked most closely of all with the British and the French throughout my time there, but I also had good relations— reasonably good relations—even with the Chinese. Eventually I developed a reasonably cordial relationship with the Soviet ambassador—not a close one, but a cordial one. He had a luncheon in my honor when I left, for example, invited all the NATO and the ANZUS [Australia and New Zealand] ambassadors, which was nice. Nobody had done that for a U.S. ambassador in many years—in living memory—at the UN. I'm trying to think who else I was particularly close to. Oh, several of the Latins, the Central Americans, the Costa Rican ambassador, for example, one of the Colombian ambassadors. Some of the Asians we worked very closely with, and I came to be on really quite personal terms with the Thai and the Singaporan and the Malaysian. Of all the other NATO ambassadors, besides the British and the French, I was probably closest to the Dutch and the Belgians.

I had some friends among the Africans, too. I've helped promote some foreign ministers in Africa today, so to speak. They were permanent representatives whom we developed particularly good relations with and helped them in Washington, and helped them win promotions at home, as a matter of fact. The current secretary-general of the OAU [Organization of African Unity] and former foreign minister of Niger, [Idé] Oumarou, was a very good friend of mine. I was able to work with the francophone Africans especially, because of being comfortable in French.

Since most of them are not comfortable in English, this is very important. French is more important, by far, for dealing with the francophone Africans than [for] dealing with [the] French and the Belgians, most of whom speak English.

In the last analysis, Kirkpatrick found the UN to be ineffective—but important nonetheless.

It's ineffective in relationship to its central responsibility, which is peaceful resolution of conflict and peacekeeping and peacemaking. Some of the independent agencies of the UN are quite effective—UNHCR [High Commissioner for Refugees], UNICEF [United Nations Children's Fund], WHO [World Health Organization], but generally speaking, the UN is quite ineffective. It is a seriously bloated, overblown, international bureaucracy with a lot of the worst aspects of many national bureaucracies combined. The budget is basically out of control, and so is personnel.

There are a lot of nice people there whom I enjoyed knowing and working with, and whom I not only respect but like. I don't advocate United States withdrawal from the UN because I think it's too important to many small, poor Third World countries. I don't think it's objectively important to them, but it's subjectively. I think what's most important to the Third World countries is that there be a place in which they can meet people, a lot of arenas, you know, in which different kinds of problems are discussed and in which they can speak, just get a hearing. We need, therefore, to be very energetic and realistic about defending ourselves, and helping that body focus on more constructive enterprises.

Jeane Kirkpatrick was longer at the UN than any permanent representative since Adlai Stevenson who was there from 1961 to 1965. She outlasted Alexander Haig by nearly three years and could have stayed longer had she so wished. Her tenure was long enough to ensure two major accomplishments: redressing the situation that existed between the United States and the unaligned nations, and exercising much tighter fiscal control over the U.S. contribution by inserting in every resolution a provision that if the resolution increased the budget of the UN, the United States would diminish its contribution by that amount.[11]

Her influence at the United Nations was profound. As for the UN's influence on her, her friend and colleague, William Sherman, said she ranked being permanent representative as one of the three important experiences in her life. The other two were passing her Ph.D. oral exam and being a mother.

17

HER EXCELLENCY, THE AMBASSADOR OF THE UNITED STATES OF AMERICA

The State Department's Office of Equal Employment Opportunity no longer prepares lists of women ambassadors. Since more than 76 have been appointed, the office sees no need to track the number of those who have achieved the rank of ambassador plenipotentiary. The pioneering women succeeded, despite all the impediments put in their way, and performed so creditably that the old arguments have been put to rest. At least officially, women as ambassadors have arrived. And yet they are a long way from achieving parity with men, and their numbers do not reflect the female percentage of the American population.[1]

This study of 44 women ambassadors, illustrated by these selections from 15 of their oral histories, has provided answers to the four main areas of the investigation: (1) What did the first women ambassadors have in common, and were there differences between career and noncareer ambassadors? (2) How well have women functioned as chiefs of missions? (3) What were the disadvantages or advantages to being a woman in a male institution? (4) Have any of our women ambassadors had a real influence on U.S. foreign policy? A fifth question should be added: What are the prospects for top women diplomats in future years?

SIMILARITIES AMONG WOMEN
AMBASSADORS

While the interviews provided no standard portrait of a woman chief of mission, some striking similarities among the subjects were noted. Almost all the women had above-average educations. From an early age, all evinced great curiosity about the world and a desire to explore it. They were women of high energy, the majority being risk takers who dared to explore new situations and look for their own answers. A trait that surfaced again and again is what the military calls the "gusto factor": these ambassadors *loved* their jobs and rated being ambassador at or near the top of their lifetime experiences. They brought strong ideals to the task, along with great pride in the ethic of service to country and a firm belief in the democratic principle. Additionally, all were workers, capable of long and sustained effort, and nearly all had a strong sense of self-worth, although they tended to downplay their own achievements and give credit to team efforts.

The vast majority of these women were above average in height. Most were charismatic and physically attractive. Nearly all were good at sports, enjoyed physical activity, and when young were called tomboys. Most were early—and voracious—readers. They appear to have been special children whose parents and teachers took a great deal of interest in them, gave them extra attention, and made efforts to provide educational opportunities that more often than not included some years at an all-female preparatory school or college. They were idealistic, pragmatic, and ardently patriotic. Their preferred management style was collegial, not hierarchical.

They shared one other characteristic that deserves special mention—courage. Constance Harvey risked her life acting as a clandestine courier for Allied interests in Vichy France. Melissa Wells willingly accepted a posting to a country in the grip of total anarchy, where mob rule was the law. The dangers faced by Foreign Service personnel are immediately obvious to anyone entering the lobby of the Department of State. There on the walls is an ever-expanding list of Foreign Service personnel lost abroad through disease, wars, terrorist attacks, and random shootings. Diplomats have been held hostage by fanatics, and five ambassadors have been murdered by terrorists.

But other forms of courage are evident in these pages: Clare Boothe Luce did not flinch before heavy public and private criticism of her fight against the Communist unions in Italy. Rozanne Ridgway stood up to Soviet pressure at summit negotiating tables. Mary Olmsted risked her career to fight for women's rights in the Department of State. Anne Cox Chambers defied the perceived values of her Georgia friends and associates to back, on principle, an unknown peanut farmer running for governor. Jeane Kirkpatrick dared to confront the prevailing anti–United States attitude at the UN and took controversial and unpopular steps to ensure respect for her country.

The majority of these women pioneers would be considered remarkable according to the standards of any age, including our own. What is astonishing is that many of them achieved at high levels when society was still opposed to their efforts. This is not to say all were equally successful; there were very few like Rozanne Ridgway, consummate diplomats who are good at all aspects of the business. Others capitalized on their own experiences. Anne Armstrong, a first-class politician, made a very effective ambassador to Great Britain by concentrating on her representational skills. Mari-Luci Jaramillo tapped into her Latin American roots and Spanish-language fluency to enter deeply into the political and social life of Honduras. Mabel Smythe Haith, a recognized expert on African affairs, arrived at Cameroon exceptionally well prepared for political and cultural reporting and establishing rapport with her hosts.

Differences between Career and Noncareer Women

Of the marked differences between the ambassadors from within the career service and those appointed from other professions, one of the most striking was in their marital statistics.

Of the 17 careerists, only four ever married, compared with 26 of 27 noncareer women who married. Moreover, three of the four career marriages did not take place until the women's careers were well established and they were near or over 40 years old. On the other hand, the four career marriages were relatively enduring (only one was interrupted by divorce), whereas there were numerous divorces for the married noncareerists.

Marital Status of First 44 U.S. Women Ambassadors

	Total	Married	Divorced at Some Time
Career	17	4	1
Noncareer	27	26	12
Total	44	30	13

Marital Status of First 44 U.S. Women Ambassadors While Ambassador

	Married	Never Married	Divorced	Widowed
Career	4	13	0	0
Noncareer	13	1	7	6
Total	17	14	7	6

From the evidence, it is clear careerists paid a price in their personal lives. Entire careers were premised on the assumption that a private life ranked below "the good of the service." While none appeared to harbor regrets for the choices they made, it should be noted that their male colleagues were never required to decide between a career in diplomacy and marriage and family. With so few marriages among them, children were a concern for only two careerists, Jane Coon, who raised stepchildren, and Melissa Wells, who had two of her own. Many noncareer ambassadors were mothers, but their child-rearing years were usually long past by the time they reached high office, and children therefore did not play a large part in their lives while they were ambassadors. It is of interest that noncareerists, more frequently than careerists, adopted a maternal attitude toward their staff members. Chambers and Farkas are good examples of noncareerists who regarded themselves as being personally responsible for their staff's well-being.

Husbands have been a protocol problem for host countries. A husband has no official duties such as custom has long decreed for the wives of ambassadors. He does not have to pay calls, nor is there any standardized protocol ranking for him (wives take their husband's rank).[2] A husband has been free to do pretty much as he wishes, provided his pursuits do not present his wife with a conflict-of-interest dilemma, but a husband who stays with his wife in the country has to have enough self-confidence to accept the secondary role. Most husbands have pursued their own careers, frequently in nearby countries, and have often been separated from their wives for extended periods. The fact is that diplomatic life is very stressful on marriages.

A major advantage enjoyed by several noncareer ambassadors over their career counterparts stands out: the ability to get the personal attention of the president or other White House principals. Jeane Kirkpatrick had access to President Reagan whenever she needed it. Mari-Luci Jaramillo was close to several senior White House staff members, through whom she was able to see President Carter. Anne Cox Chambers could call Jody Powell when she needed help. Anne Armstrong, herself a former power in the White House, had many high-level contacts. Clare Boothe Luce was close socially as well as politically to President Eisenhower and John Foster Dulles. In contrast, of the careerists, only Carol Laise was similarly situated, with access to President Johnson through her husband, Ellsworth Bunker, one of Johnson's close advisers.

While careerists do not have the advantage of close ties to the White House, they are often more welcome in some of the smaller countries frequently used by presidents to "pay off" political supporters. Indeed, some countries have requested a career woman in preference to a noncareer man, as when the Dutch informally asked for Margaret Tibbetts when it was announced that she was to become an ambassador. Professionalism was more important to them than the sex of the ambassador.

Noncareer women experienced much more difficulty with their deputies (who were always career) than did the trained diplomats. (Although one or two of them also reported instances of clashes with their second-in-command.) Armstrong, Chambers, Farkas, Kirkpatrick, Luce, all had problems at first. Armstrong and Luce were able to work through the difficulties, but the other three started over with persons they selected. The majority of noncareer ambassadors, and especially those who had worked in politics, began their duties with negative, even hostile, ideas about Foreign Service personnel. But after interacting with the professionals, most, though not all, experienced a complete turnabout in attitude.

Of the three parts of an ambassador's job—reporting, negotiating, and representation—the careerists generally excelled at reporting and negotiating and were less concerned with representational activities. Many of them objected to what Margaret Tibbetts calls the "catering" aspect. They saw representation as but one part of the job and questioned the value of certain practices, such as frequent consorting with the diplomatic corps or the country's social elite. On the other hand, noncareerists were more likely to view representation, [furthering public relations and establishing a friendly relationship with the host country's principals and power brokers] as their principal objective and primary role. Clare Boothe Luce, an exception among the noncareerists, was good at all three responsibilities. A whiz at representation, she proved an imaginative negotiator and a competent political reporter. With a light touch, she once effectively explained a complicated political problem *in verse*.

SUCCESS OR FAILURE AS CHIEFS OF MISSION

These women ambassadors made it clear they did not try to adapt their behavior to diplomacy's masculine standards but, on the contrary, brought their own individual strengths to their work. They ran their missions in their own ways but at the same time observed the proprieties demanded of women.

Their approaches were as varied as the women themselves and depended in large measure on what each saw as her chief responsibility. Some, like Armstrong and Chambers, wanted to improve already good relations with a host country. Farkas saw her mission in part as encouraging trade with the United States. Jaramillo's goal was to help a country transform itself into a democracy. Luce focused primarily on containing communism and reducing its influence in Italy. Tibbetts, Ridgway, and Kirkpatrick believed their objective was to further the interests of the United States and did not regard furthering relations between countries as the desideratum.

Luck always plays a part in the success of a mission. Anne Armstrong happened to follow two U.S. ambassadors who were not especially popular. With her good looks, attractive husband, public-speaking ability, and enthusiasm, she could do no wrong in the eyes of the British public. Conversely, Ruth Farkas, in addition to the problems associated with her Nixon campaign contribution, had the bad luck to follow a man regarded as the most popular American ambassador to Luxembourg in decades, and her efforts in that country were inevitably somewhat eclipsed.

It must be said that not all 44 female appointments proved to be good choices. A couple were, to put it kindly, ineffective, but their presence did no actual harm because strong deputies covered the missions and embarrassment was pretty much contained within the State Department. Fortunately, the few instances (not included in this book) where personal conduct was not impeccable occurred in countries where people were either broad-minded regarding the behavior of Western women, or sophisticated. No woman was declared persona non grata and asked to leave, nor were any recalled. Certainly none had the dubious distinction shared by several male ambassadors of actually setting back relations between the United States and a host country. All in all, these women performed to a high standard.

DISADVANTAGES TO BEING A WOMAN IN A MALE PROFESSION

Throughout the early decades covered by these testimonies, women, like children, were considered best if seen but not heard. Hostility against them in the workplace ran deep, being chief of a diplomatic mission was considered unwomanly, and women who took on a man's work were deeply resented.

George Vest recounted the first time he ran into this attitude: "I joined the Foreign Service in 1947. I was vice consul in Bermuda. The boat came in, and Mrs. Ruth Bryan Owen Rohde (the first woman chief of mission) called, as was the custom in those days, to pay a courtesy call on the consul general. It says something about the old attitudes that when I brought to his attention that Mrs. Rohde had come in to pay her respects, he felt free to say he was too busy and would I please see her? Because she was a woman. He was an extreme case. But, nevertheless, it was an illustration of attitudes which were still very widely prevalent."[3]

Some of the earliest women ambassadors ran into misogyny in the host country. Elbridge Durbrow, Luce's deputy, reported that before her arrival his Italian contacts at the Foreign Office asked: "Why make us a third-class power by sending a lady to a Latin country?"[4]

Women who asserted themselves were subject to verbal attacks that, more often than not, were of a sexual nature. "Bitch" was a common pejorative. (Alexander Haig used it for Jeane Kirkpatrick.) In cartoons of Luce, breasts were always emphasized. What better way to denigrate a woman than to depict her with droopy breasts? Jokes about her name ("Loose" for "Luce") were legion, although her husband, with the same name, never suffered sexual slurs (although he frequently offended people). Women had to develop tough hides to survive the calumny leveled against them—by other women as well as men—and were then often accused of being "hard-boiled" or "unladylike." Kirkpatrick was called "tough" and "unfeminine" when she debated. William Sherman, discussing the negative views held by men at the UN about Kirkpatrick, gave this explanation: "She is an intelligent woman ready to debate any issue with a great deal of intellectual brilliance. Once she had made up her mind on a policy, she was steadfast in maintaining it."[5] A third method of attack, the loose rumor, was used against Carol Laise, who was accused of being a spy. The Indian press called her a "Mata Hari," a derogatory name connoting untrustworthiness and illicit sexual behavior, both of which were false. Spy rumors about her were recycled again and again.

It is astounding how often men, in discussing these ambassadors, made a point of praising their "femininity." Although many referred to Carol Laise as the "Iron Lady" or "America's Margaret Thatcher," sooner or later assurances would come that she had "kept her femininity." Rozanne Ridgway was said to be a marvel for many reasons, and one of these was that "she never lost her femininity." Clare Boothe Luce, renowned for her delicate beauty, often had recourse to her "femininity." In 1941, Walt Rostow says, "I was assistant to OSS's representative on the joint intelligence committee, and Clare came back from China, and she was going to come and talk to the intelligence committee [as a correspondent for *Vogue* magazine]. There was a rather stuffy ambassador and general and admiral. This lady was late, and she was very late, and they were getting restive. The ambassador felt the honor of the State Department was at stake. And finally she comes in, and she was young and a good-looking woman—a very good-looking woman—and she batted her eyes at them and apologized and said, 'You know, I was just talking to [a high official in the Pentagon], and he kept me. I'm so sorry.' And she settled down, and she talked. Quite intelligent. She got them in hand pretty well."[6]

When Luce did not "bat her eyes," however, but instead refused concessions, she was not described as "forthright" or "decisive" or "strong," or with any of the adjectives commonly used to describe an assertive man's behavior; she was said to be "hard as nails" and called a "steel butterfly."[7]

All of the women had encountered some discrimination, whatever profession they had followed, but surprisingly few seemed to worry about it. They accepted the fact of discrimination as a condition of the times and carried on without too much grumbling. Mary Olmsted was the only one who really took up arms against a male chauvinist system.

From the beginning, the Foreign Service did not make proper use of women's talents. It is clear from Constance Harvey's testimony that she was hindered in her career development and was never given the mentoring her male colleagues enjoyed. Opportunities to learn were denied her, as when she was not allowed to go on a temporary duty assignment. Years later, Jane Coon was *chosen* to go on temporary duty, and it proved of great help in developing her expertise. Although Coon still encountered prejudice—her first two assignments overseas were nearly quashed by senior officers, and she was discriminated against in the matter of housing—she was quick to point out that her male colleagues were very helpful to her. Her experience was a marked contrast to Harvey's of 20 years before.

A young university woman commented after reading these testimonies, "The women don't seem to be as angry about the way they were treated as young women would be now." She was also astonished that "they didn't give themselves enough credit and played down the fact they were good." Most career women of this period were, in fact, taught to be modest and had low expectations. They never anticipated becoming ambassadors, and several of their oral histories reflect their wonderment at having reached high rank, coupled with gratitude for being so handsomely rewarded for what were, in fact, their own extraordinary efforts.

The question arises, however, of why they didn't make more of an effort to help lower-ranking women. Some undoubtedly felt opposition to male rule would only antagonize the hierarchy and only time could bring about changes. Others had a different reason. When Carol Laise was director general, she was said to have "agonized" over whether or not to choose women for certain positions.[8] She believed the needs of the service should govern all choices, that competency was the criterion. She was seldom convinced a woman was the best of the candidates and feared that advancing a weak candidate would in the long run hurt the women's cause.[9] While this approach, shared by Margaret Tibbetts and other Foreign Service women, has validity, it overlooks a vital point: women's ratings were based on evaluations made subjectively and nearly always by men. "The needs of the service" was the argument used to slow the advancement of women. It created a catch-22 situation: because of the way women were treated, there was no large pool of mid- or upper-level women, and the dearth of high-ranking women proved that women weren't as able as men.

Nevertheless, the lack of an early high-level mandate for affirmative action may have been a blessing, since those in the department who wanted to set aside countries for women only did not prevail. By insisting that all FSOs be available for duty anywhere, the service avoided categorizing—and thus devaluing—specific posts. Those in the women's movement, struggling against these and other limiting concepts, knew that true reform would result only from the recruitment of large numbers of highly qualified women along with changes in assignment policies to allow women the experience necessary for advancement. A glance at the most recent recruiting figures offers proof that the women's movement made a difference: 38 percent of the 676 entering officers for 1990–93 were women,[10] and at the other end of the spectrum, about one-third of the candidates on the 1993 list of nominations for promotion to the senior Foreign Service schedule were women.[11]

Women did not have to fight the battle of equal pay in the Foreign Service since, from the beginning, their salaries were the same as men's. Constance Harvey claims that no one ever focused on the salaries of women in the early days because there were so few to pay; by the time affirmative action brought in larger numbers of women, it was too late to change their pay scale.

Unlike married male ambassadors who have had their wives to run the residence, entertain, and maintain community relations, the women have had to be their own "wives." The earliest incumbents devised ways to cope, often with the help of a sister or a friend. In recent years the department has authorized hiring assistants, but this practice deprives the embassy of an officer position, which Ridgway, for one, refused to give up. Some husbands, including Heriberto Jaramillo and Tobin Armstrong, helped by assuming representational functions. Carol Laise and Jane Coon, both married to serving ambassadors, found themselves overseeing their husbands' residences from time to time. Coon was also called upon to fill the wife's role during an official visit when her husband escorted the king and queen of Nepal around the United States. This occurred shortly after she, *alone*, had accompanied the president of Bangladesh on his working visit to Washington. It is clear that in taking on positions held by men, women diplomats have not managed to free themselves from *women's work*.

One perceived disadvantage for women, the lack of respect from the host government and people, proved to be a nonissue once a woman was at the post. All American women ambassadors have been accorded the deference and respect appropriate to their position. The power of the United States ensures that the sex of an ambassador is irrelevant.

The Positive Side of Being a Woman Ambassador

It came as a surprise that these ambassadors believed that, despite the disadvantages cited, being women afforded them advantages, principally in allowing them to speak bluntly to male officials, especially in the developing nations, without offending them. Because they were female, their words were not perceived as threats. In Mary Olmsted's opinion, a woman representing the gigantic might of the United States is less likely than a man to "insist on being a big wheel" and is therefore accepted as a nonthreatening, sympathetic presence and a source of support. It may even be that when leaders of a fledgling, formerly colonial country are suddenly thrust onto the world stage, they find the presence of a woman ambassador from the United States to be reassuring.

Constance Harvey reported being consulted by Arab officials about how to open an Algerian mission when she was consul general at Strasbourg. She believes it was easier for them to seek her assistance because the elements of competition and losing face were not considerations, as they would have been with a man. Conversely, Nancy Ostrander pointed out that a woman is freer to ask a man for advice or information than a man would be, once again because the question of face-saving does not arise.

These women ambassadors reported that their sex, far from diminishing the value of U.S. representation, *added* an important dimension, for just as women politicians in the United States have been perceived by the general public as more honest and more genuinely concerned about such issues as worker safety, public health, and education, so women ambassadors have been viewed as more caring, more interested, more approachable, more believable. It is not uncommon for a woman ambassador to be fondly remembered by the people years after she has left a country.

The idea of a woman in a position of such power, with authority over all the males in her mission, often made host country officials stop and think. Several women ambassadors from America had a direct impact on local attitudes and were responsible, by their very presence, for the appointment of women to positions no woman had ever before held in the host country. Mary Olmsted was told that the men in power finally agreed that if an important country like the United States sent a woman as a representative, Papua New Guinea should also name women to high positions. Jane Coon's arrival brightened the lives of countless Bangladeshi women, as did Mari-Luci Jaramillo's in Honduras. And in Cameroon, it was a remarkable coincidence that six months after Mabel Smythe's arrival, women's membership in the National Assembly reached an unprecedented high of 10 percent.

Women had yet another advantage in that they could go where men could not and mix freely with the female population, better enabling them to understand the customs and mores of the local culture. Consulting with local women has helped in the search for solutions to problems such as overpopulation, subjugation of women, and exploitation of children. It is in these areas, indeed, in all matters of human rights, that women have made strong contributions. A prime example is Melissa Wells's work salvaging the hopeless lives of the children of war in Mozambique.

INFLUENCE OF WOMEN AMBASSADORS
ON U.S. FOREIGN POLICY

Ambassadors are sent to a country to *implement* foreign policy that has been decided upon by the president and his advisers. A glance at history, however, will show that in the past many envoys, selected from among the most influential citizens and often close friends of the president, did indeed make policy while serving as envoys. Presidents chose persons they could trust to make proper decisions, and conversely, the ambassador could be sure his decisions would be endorsed by the chief executive. This necessary, and effective, way of doing business before the days of instant communications characterized the relationship between Clare Boothe Luce and the Eisenhower-Dulles team. She actually did influence U.S. policy in Italy, especially policy on the containment of communism and the settlement of Trieste. Carol Laise had significant input into U.S.-Indian affairs before she became ambassador, particularly U.S. policy toward Chinese incursions on India's borders. She set forth the issues to be discussed by Eisenhower on his trip to India and so controlled the president's agenda. She also was part of the Harriman mission on Kashmir.

Some women were able to influence policy during their assignments at the Department of State: Margaret Tibbetts had a hand in negotiating military base and atomic weapons agreements, and Rozanne Ridgway was chief negotiator on Secretary of State Shultz's policy team at all the Reagan-Gorbachev summits. Only one woman of the 44, however, has been part of a White House inner circle. Jeane Kirkpatrick, as a member of that select band helping to promulgate overall foreign policy, has had the most impact of any woman in the field of U.S. diplomacy.

A great deal of latitude is possible for ambassadors to countries not considered important to U.S. interests. Coon, in Bangladesh, wrote her own instructions and then carried them out. Cataclysmic events elsewhere often mean the ambassador has to wing it, as Ostrander did during the coup in Suriname.

Since the majority of women ambassadors, however, have served in small countries, few have been in a position to influence general lines of foreign policy. If it is true, as many have said, that several of these women had the qualities to be major players, this is cause for regret. According to corridor judgments, Tibbetts might well have been the first woman assistant secretary for European and Canadian affairs, the job Ridgway later got, and Ridgway could have handled the higher positions of under secretary or even secretary of state, two positions no woman has yet filled.

THE FUTURE FOR WOMEN IN DIPLOMACY

In a 1985 interview, Carol Laise said women could rise in the service, without serious problems, to almost the most senior levels. She explained that, at that point, when so much responsibility and pressure is involved, men want no extra distractions and, needing to be 100 percent confident about their deputies or assistants, will usually pick someone they know very well. The chances of this being a woman, given the small number in the higher ranks, are not great. She added that a woman's presence inhibits some men who feel a need to "clean up their act," while others feel constrained to change their operating style. As an example, she offered Henry Kissinger, whose method of dealing with subordinates was to "beat on them." "Henry," she said, "is very uncomfortable beating on a woman."

But relations between the sexes are gradually taking on greater flexibility and respect, particularly at overseas postings, where more men have had to rely on the judgment of women superiors. No longer can sex be used as a bar to being assigned difficult or dangerous missions. Melissa Wells acquitted herself well under some of the most difficult conditions in the world and showed as much strength and determination as any man. Ridgway and others have proved that women can successfully negotiate with the toughest opponents. But—and it is a big but—women must be given a fair chance at jobs that will position them to play influential roles.

One by one, and grudgingly, the geographic areas are falling to women. For nearly 30 years, all assignments of women chiefs of mission were to posts in Europe; then in 1961 the first woman ambassador was sent outside that area, to Ceylon (now Sri Lanka). The Caribbean was broached in 1969, Africa in 1972, Pacifica in 1975, Central America in 1977, and the Arab world in 1988. The traditional reasons used to exclude women from these regions proved to be smokescreens for discrimination, but there are still many areas of the world that have never had an American woman ambassador. A disproportionate number go to Third World countries, or to what Rozanne Ridgway calls "hyphenated islands."

The future for women in the field of foreign relations is unpredictable. The Clinton administration is committed to advancing the status of women, and Hillary Rodham Clinton is using her great influence to convince the country it cannot afford to waste the talents of half its people. In 1992, the "Year of the Woman," a significant number of women were elected to the U.S. House of Representatives, and the number of women senators went from two to seven. There is now a second woman on the Supreme Court.

As of 30 June 1993, about 10 percent of U.S. chiefs of mission are women, and of this 10 percent the great majority (75 percent) are careerists. These figures contrast sharply with the ones in this study. Of the first 44 women, only 37 percent were careerists. (It is significant that for men ambassadors during the same period, the figures for careerists was 65–75 percent.) The pool of viable women career candidates was so small that presidents were obliged to search elsewhere for suitable nominees.

When Mary Olmsted began her work on behalf of women 20 years ago, women comprised only 4.8 percent of the Foreign Service officer corps.[12] Today the figure is 23 percent.[13] There should be no dearth of solid candidates for high rank in the future, provided women officers are given career opportunities equal to those given men. However, old discriminatory practices continue to hold women back. A continuing class action suit brought by women officers protests personnel practices that keep them in consular assignments and therefore out of specialties that would help their chances for advancement.[14]

Another complaint is that supervisors tend to rate men by achievements but stress personality traits when rating women. Commenting on the annual evaluating process, Richard Moose, the new under secretary for management, writes, "Critics believe that the culture of the department, *particularly the Foreign Service's culture* [italics added] may be abetting . . . discrimination . . ."[15]

Adding to the difficulties are looming austerity measures necessitated by the crippling national debt. This will probably mean severe reductions in the number of positions in the senior ranks and will affect men as well as women. Cutbacks will mean fewer chances for promotions and therefore fewer chances of rising to ambassador.

Given all these impediments, although the last 60 years have seen enormous changes in the status of women in the United States, and although the department management's stated goal is to achieve a Foreign Service that better reflects the nation's demographics, it is unrealistic to expect women to head half of America's embassies any day soon. But at least, and thanks in large measure to these pioneers, today there are far fewer prejudices against women ambassadors.

Appendix A First 44 Women Chiefs of Mission by Administration

Ambassador	Country	Date	Rank
Franklin Roosevelt (1933–45)			
1. Ruth Bryan Owen	Denmark	1933–36	EE/MP
2. Florence Jeffrey Harriman	Norway	1937–40	EE/MP
Harry Truman (1945–52)			
3. Perle Mesta	Luxembourg	1949–53	EE/MP
4. **Eugenie Anderson**	Denmark	1949–53	AE/P (first)
Dwight Eisenhower (1953–60)			
5. **Clare Boothe Luce**[b]	Italy	1953–56	AE/P
6. Frances E. Willis (career)	Switzerland	1953–57	AE/P
	Norway	1957–61	(first career)
John F. Kennedy (1961–63)			
Frances E. Willis	Ceylon	1961–64	AE/P
Eugenie Anderson	Bulgaria	1962–64	EE/MP
Lyndon Johnson (1963–68)			
7. Katherine E. White	Denmark	1964–68	AE/P
8. **Margaret Joy Tibbetts**[b] (career)	Norway	1964–69	AE/P
9. Patricia Roberts Harris	Luxembourg	1965–67	AE/P
10. **Caroline Clendening Laise**[b] (career)	Nepal	1966–73	AE/P
Richard Nixon and Gerald Ford (1969–76)			
11. **Eileen Donovan** (career)	Barbados	1969–74	AE/P
12. **Betty Crites Dillon**	ICAO (Montreal)[c]	1971–77	EE/MP
13. **Jean Mary Wilkowski** (career)	Zambia	1972–76	AE/MP
14. **Ruth Lewis Farkas**[b]	Luxembourg	1973–76	AE/P

15. Nancy Rawls (career)	Togo	1974–76	AE/P
16. **Shirley Temple Black**	Ghana	1974–76	AE/P
17. **Mary Seymour Olmsted**[b] (career)	Papua New Guinea	1975–79	AE/P
	Solomon Islands[c]	1978–79	AE/P
18. **Anne Legendre Armstrong**[b]	United Kingdom	1976–77	AE/P
19. Marquita Maytag	Nepal	1976–77	AE/P
20. **Rosemary L. Ginn**	Luxembourg	1976–77	AE/P
21. **Patricia M. Byrne** (career)	Mali[c]	1976–79	AE/P
Jimmy Carter (1977–80)			
22. **Melissa Foelsch Wells**[b] (career)	Guinea-Bissau and Cape Verde	1976–77	AE/P
23. **Anne Cox Chambers**[b]	Belgium	1977–81	AE/P
24. **Mabel Murphy Smythe**[b]	Cameroon and Equatorial Guinea	1977–80	AE/P
25. **Rozanne Lejeanne Ridgway**[b] (career)	Finland	1977–80	AE/P
26. **Mari-Luci Jaramillo**[b]	Honduras	1977–80	AE/P
27. **Nancy Ostrander**[b] (career)	Suriname	1978–80	AE/P
28. **Geri M. Joseph**	The Netherlands	1978–81	AE/P
29. **Marilyn P. Johnson** (career)	Togo	1978–81	AE/P
30. **Joan M. Clark** (career)	Malta	1979–81	AE/P
31. **Sally A. Shelton** (Colby)	Barbados, Grenada, Dominica, Saint Lucia, Antigua, St. Christopher-Nevis-Aguilla, St. Vincent	1979–81	AE/P
32. **Anne Clark Martindell**	New Zealand and Western Samoa	1979–81	AE/P
Nancy Rawls	Ivory Coast[c]	1979–83	AE/P
33. Anne Forrester (Holloway)	Mali	1979–81	AE/P
Patricia M. Byrne	Burma[c]	1979–83	AE/P
34. **Barbara Newell**	UNESCO (Paris)	1979–81	AE/P
35. **Frances Cook** (career)	Burundi[c]	1980–83	AE/P
36. Barbara M. Watson	Malaysia	1980–81	AE/P
37. **Theresa Healy** (career)	Sierre Leone[c]	1980–83	AE/P
Ronald Reagan (1981–88)			

38. **Jeane Jordan Kirkpatrick**[b]	United Nations	1981–85	AE/P
39. **Jane Abell Coon**[b] (career)	Bangladesh	1981–84	AE/P
40. **Faith K. Whittlesey**	Switzerland	1981–83	AE/P
41. **M. Virginia Shafer** (career)	Papua New Guinea and Solomon Islands	1981–84	AE/P
42. **Jean S. Gerard**	UNESCO (Paris)	1981–84	AE/P
Rozanne L. Ridgway	German Dem. Rep	1983–85	AE/P
43. **Helene A. von Damm**	Austria	1983–85	AE/P
44. **Millicent Fenwick**	FAO (Rome)	1983–87	AE/P
Faith K. Whittlesey	Switzerland	1985–88	AE/P
Jean S. Gerard	Luxembourg[c]	1985–90	AE/P
Melissa Wells	Mozambique[c]	1987–91	AE/P
George Bush (1989–92)[d]			
Shirley Temple Black	Czechoslovakia	1989–92	AE/P
Frances Cook	Cameroon	1989–92	AE/P
Melissa Wells	Zaire	1991–93	AE/P

Women ambassadors interviewed are in boldface.
[b]Oral history in book.
[c]Service continued under succeeding president.
[d]Bush appointed 25 women AE/Ps, 15 of them career.
A forty-fifth woman, **Sharon E. Ahmad**, was appointed to Gambia in 1982 but for health reasons never served there.

Appendix B Approximate Officer Rank Comparison, U.S. Military and U.S. Diplomatic Services

Navy	Army Air Force Marines	Foreign Service Officers		
		FS Act 1946	Amendments 1955–56	FS Act 1980
Ensign	2d Lt.		0–8	0–6
		0–6		
Lt. j.g.	1st Lt.		0–7	0–5
Lt.	Capt.	0–5	0–6	0–4
Lt. Cdr.	Maj.		0–5	0–3
		0–4		
Cdr.	Lt. Col.		0–4	0–2
Capt.	Col.	0–3	0–3	0–1
Flag Rank				
Rear Adm. (lower half)	Brig. Gen.	0–2	0–2	OCa
Rear Adm.	Maj. Gen.	0–1	0–1	MCb
Vice Adm.	Lt. Gen.		Career Minister	
Adm.	Gen.	NA	Career Ambassador	

aCounselor
bMinister Counselor

Notes and References

Chapter 1

1. Harold Nicholson, *Diplomacy*, 3d ed. (London: Oxford University Press, 1963), 252.

2. An ambassador must bear heavy burdens and responsibilities, yet a simple oath of 71 words transforms an ordinary citizen into the president's personal representative and embodiment of a mighty nation: "I do solemnly swear that I will support and defend the Constitution of the United States against all enemies foreign and domestic, that I will bear true faith and allegiance to the same, that I take this obligation freely and without any mental reservation or purpose of evasion, that I will well and faithfully discharge the duties of the office on which I am about to enter, so help me God."

3. William Barnes and John Heath Morgan, *The Foreign Service of the United States* (Washington, D.C.: Department of State, 1961), 146, 47.

4. She was finally allowed to serve overseas in 1925: she was sent to the legation at Bern, despite the opposition of the American minister to Switzerland. From Bern, she was transferred to the legation in Panama and resigned from the service in 1927. Homer L. Calkin, *Women in the Department of State: Their Role in American Foreign Affairs* (Washington, D.C.: Department of State, 1978), 73–78.

5. Ibid., 68–71.

6. Ibid.

Chapter 2

1. Constance Ray Harvey, interviews with author, Lexington, Va., 11 and 12 June 1988.

2. Any Foreign Service employee who married a citizen of another country had to tender his or her resignation, which was rarely declined.

3. Calkin, *Women*, 81–84.

4. The consular and diplomatic services, although joined, have their own separate

titles. Officers serving at embassies may carry titles of both services, but at consulates they use only consular titles. Harvey entered the service "unclassified," a beginning rank for entering career officers that is no longer used. Noncareer vice consuls and consuls, usually specialists, were under a separate personnel system and were not advanced into positions of leadership in embassies.

5. These are diplomatic titles, not to be confused with clerical workers.

6. As a career officer, Harvey's name would be on the official social list wherever she was stationed. Noncareer vice consuls would not be invited to elite parties.

7. After France fell in 1940, Germany occupied the northern part of the country and the U.S. embassy shifted to Vichy, which became the capital of the southern part. The United States maintained the embassy and consulates elsewhere in the south until the American invasion of French North Africa in November 1942. All U.S. personnel were interned by the Germans at that time. Because local (i.e., non-American) employees of the embassy and consulates did not have diplomatic status, many were imprisoned and some died in concentration camps.

8. The SS Gripsholm was a neutral flagship used by the Red Cross to transport exchanged diplomats, prisoners, and others. It sailed decked out with lights so it could be easily identified by warships.

Chapter 3

1. Clare Boothe Luce, interview with author, Washington, D.C., 19 June 1986.

2. Stephen Shadegg, Clare Boothe Luce (New York: Simon & Schuster, 1970), 253.

3. Career Ambassador Robert Murphy at that time was assistant secretary of state for UN affairs. In his book Diplomat among Warriors (New York: Doubleday & Co., 1964), Murphy says Tito's Communist government was facing an enormous wheat crop shortfall (470–71). Since, under capitalism, Yugoslavia had exported surplus wheat, this staggering failure of the collective farm system would have had serious propaganda consequences had it become public knowledge. As a result of secret negotiations carried out by Murphy, the United States provided 400,000 tons of wheat. This was certainly one factor in the settlement of the Trieste problem, about which Murphy says Luce "had worked . . . intelligently and successfully for months." John Gunther, in Inside Europe Today (New York: Harper & Brothers, 1961), states "that it was generally understood that the Marshal would be invited to visit the United States after the settlement" (349). If such a promise was made, it was not kept.

4. Luce's deputy, Elbridge Durbrow, credits Luce with telling the press it was "open diplomacy secretly arrived at," a play on Woodrow Wilson's phrase "open covenants of peace openly arrived at." Durbrow interview with author, Washington, D.C., 28 May 1986.

5. A. Robert Smith, The Tiger in the Senate (Garden City, N.Y.: Doubleday & Co., 1962), 48–53.

6. Wayne Morse had been sharply criticized in Time when he switched his

allegiance from the Republican to the Democratic party after the election of 1954. Ralph G. Martin, *Henry and Clare* (New York: G. P. Putnam's Sons, 1991), 350.

7. There is some confusion about how long Cabot served in Brazil. Shadegg says "only a little over a year," while Martin says six months. According to State's listing of ambassadors, Cabot remained for two years. *Principal Officers of State and United States Chiefs of Mission, 1978–1986* (Washington, D.C.: Department of State, undated), 27.

Chapter 4

1. William J. Crockett, Department of State, memo to Kenneth O'Donnell, White House, 4 March 1964, central files, Johnson Library Archives, Austin, Tex. This and another signed photograph from the president would go with her and be prominently displayed. Their importance in the eyes of the Norwegians would be immense. The closer to the president an ambassador seems, the more powerful she or he is believed to be.

2. Margaret Joy Tibbetts, interview with author, Bethel, Maine, 28 May 1985.

3. George Vest, interview with author, Washington, D.C., 12 February 1987.

4. Hélène K. Sargeant, "Oral History of Margaret Tibbetts," Women in Federal Government Series (Cambridge, Mass.: Schlesinger Library, Radcliffe College), 1982.

5. The government in question was North Vietnam.

6. Sargeant, "Margaret Tibbetts."

7. Nicholas von Hoffman, *Citizen Cohn* (New York: Bantam, 1988), 144–54.

8. Senator McCarthy, in his crusade against Communists in the government, claimed that the Department of State was the haven for many, and his followers took drastic measures to discover and root them out.

9. Katie Louchheim, Lyndon Johnson's acting assistant secretary of state for education and cultural affairs, was responsible for placing women in high positions.

Chapter 5

1. Caroline Clendening Laise, interviews with author, Washington, D.C., 29 April, 8 and 9 May, 13 and 18 June, and 17 July 1985. These interviews were commissioned by and are part of the Women in Federal Government Series, Schlesinger Library, Radcliffe College.

2. Dr. Dorothy Robins-Mowry, research associate, Wilson Center, interview with author, Washington, D.C., 6 June 1986.

3. Bishop Melvin E. Wheatley, Jr., interview with author, Bethesda, Md., 24 April 1993.

4. Alger Hiss, an assistant secretary of state, was accused of being a Communist

spy by the journalist Whittaker Chambers and subsequently tried and convicted of perjury in 1950. He always maintained his innocence.

5. A prestigious yearlong course of study for senior officers given at the Foreign Service Institute.

6. William Moyers to John Macy and William Crockett (State), 19 March 1966; James Falcon to Macy, 23 March 1966; Louis Schwartz to Macy, 29 March 1966; all White House memos in Macy Files, Johnson Library Archives.

7. Ellsworth Bunker to Pres. Lyndon Johnson, 2 December 1966, central files, Johnson Library Archives.

8. Jane Abell Coon, eulogy for Carol Laise, Washington National Cathedral, 17 September 1991. (Laise died on 25 July 1991).

Chapter 6

1. Ruth Lewis Farkas, interviews with author, New York, N.Y., 22, 24, and 25 October 1985.

2. These scandals began in the fall of 1974, when Gerald Ford nominated Peter Flanigan, formerly on Nixon's staff, to be ambassador to Spain. There was immediate opposition in the Senate because Flanigan had worked with Maurice Stans, Nixon's fund-raiser, and was considered by some to be guilty of helping to "sell embassies." Newspaper accounts always included mention of the Farkas contribution as an illustration. More damaging to Farkas, because more prolonged, was the fight over the New Hampshire Senate seat between John A. Durkin and Cong. Louis C. Wyman. Wyman had acted as an intermediary between the powerful men in Nixon's White House and the Farkases. Throughout the ten months it took to decide the New Hampshire election, which had to be rerun, newspaper accounts reiterated Wyman's role in the "Farkas Fracas." These accounts were reprinted in the Luxembourg newspapers, much to the embarrassment of the U.S. embassy staff and its ambassador.

The more relevant of the many newspaper accounts appeared in the *Washington Post* (15 and 24 March and 8 June 1973, 18 July and 24 September 1974), the *Washington Star* (13 April 1973), and the *New York Times* (14 July 1975).

3. John Hollingsworth (Foreign Service officer), interview with author, Alexandria, Va., 15 October 1985; Fred Galanto (Foreign Service officer), telephone interview with author, 27 September 1985; Peter Tarnoff (former Foreign Service officer), interview with author, New York, 15 April 1989; Allister Farkas (grandson), interview with author, Washington, D.C., 21 March 1987.

4. In August 1974 Herbert Kalmbach, Nixon's personal attorney, testified before the House Judiciary Committee that he had met Farkas at an August 1971 luncheon arranged by Wyman, at which the possibility of her having an ambassadorship was raised (*Washington Post*, 27 August 1974). Farkas testified before a federal grand jury that Wyman "had 'tricked' and 'seduced' her and her husband into the contribution, leading them to believe it was legal." (*Washington Post*, 7 April 1975).

Farkas, with her solid educational and professional background, was an appropriate candidate to be an ambassador and was under consideration by the Nixon White

House as early as 1971, as evidenced by a 5 August 1971 memo from the president's own secretary, Rosemary Woods, to Peter Flanigan. Curiously, she was again proposed for Costa Rica. Later, Jamaica was suggested, but the third proposal, Luxembourg, was the ultimate choice for her.

A lengthy search in the Nixon presidential archive for documentation about Farkas's appointment proved more than a little frustrating because every file requested that might bear on the subject was blocked by Nixon's lawyers. On the final day of an exhausting search, the Peter Flanigan files turned up. Among them were copies of several documents, all marked "original to White House Counsel." This handful, possibly overlooked by the lawyers, were enough to convince me that whatever the Farkases' intention might have been, the Nixon people's was very clear: they looked on the appointment as a quid pro quo for a gift (Cong. Louis C. Wyman to Peter Flanigan; 1 March and 5 April 1972; telcon memo for Flanigan, 21 March 1972; Fred Malek to Flanigan, 16 June 1972; unidentified White House notes, 17 June 1972. Congressman Wyman noted that the president was down in the polls in New York City and believed an announcement of Farkas's appointment just before the election "would mean in New York City between two or three hundred thousand Jewish votes" because Farkas was "very well liked and respected" (Cong. Louis C. Wyman, memo of conversation, given to Peter Flanigan, 27 September 1972).

5. David Humphrey of the Lyndon B. Johnson Library kindly looked through several of the unopened files and, although he found evidence that Farkas had been recommended for different positions, discovered nothing that specifically linked her to Costa Rica. He said, "It doesn't prove there was no such action, only that proof is not in the places you would expect to find it. Her vita is impressive. There are very substantial entries on it." Telephone conversation with author, 3 March 1994.

6. The day of the Senate hearing, 13 March 1973, the *Washington Star* featured a story on the Farkases' campaign contribution and Ruth Farkas's appointment to Luxembourg. It is to that story she refers.

7. The record shows that the remark was made by Sen. George Aiken (R-Vt.).

8. This part of the oral history provides a fascinating insight into the way subsequent events can alter memory. Farkas took such a public pounding over the next three years that it must have colored her recollection of the Senate hearing. The transcript reveals that all the senators, including Percy, Aiken, and Gale McGee (D-Wyo.), were very impressed with her credentials. Percy said he felt sure the whole thing was "nothing more than your demonstrated generosity." The hearing was brief, and the remarks to Farkas were both polite and complimentary. But the question of possible wrongdoing had been publicly raised, and Farkas and her family felt humiliated.

9. Tarnoff interview.

Chapter 7

1. Mary Seymour Olmsted, interviews with author, Washington, D.C., 25 June and 3, 11, 18, and 26 July 1985.

2. Foreign Service Officer Charles W. Thomas committed suicide allegedly because of despondency after being dropped from the service. The Foreign Service term for involuntary retirement is "selection-out."

3. Mary S. Olmsted, "To Open a Post" (unpublished).

Chapter 8

1. This and other comments by Ronald Spiers, then under secretary for management and formerly deputy chief of mission to Anne Armstrong, were from an interview with the author, Department of State, Washington, D.C., 3 April 1987.

Dean Elspeth Rostow, a historian, writer, and lecturer on foreign affairs who studied at Cambridge University and has remained close to the British scene, said in an interview with the author on 27 October 1989 at Austin, Texas, "Generally she gets good marks. There are some who have said that she was as effective an ambassador as we've had."

2. Anne Legendre Armstrong, interviews with author, Washington, D.C., 7 October 1987, and 9 May 1988.

3. Esther Stineman, *American Political Woman: Contemporary and Historical Profiles* (Littleton, Colo.: Libraries Unlimited, 1980), 7.

4. Donnie Radcliffe, "Diplomatic Names and Nicknames," *Washington Post*, 20 February 1976.

5. David S. Broder ("Another Trouble-Shooter Named Anne," *Washington Post*, 28 May 1978) wrote: "When Armstrong came to the Nixon White House . . . she did her damndest to open the windows and let in a little of the fresh air of controversy that was even then blowing around the president. But six months after Watergate, the 'bunker mentality' was far too entrenched for her to change, and she watched unhappily as Nixon's support dwindled."

6. Quoted by Elizabeth Mehren and Betty Cuniberti, "Women Vice-Presidential Candidates May Be Just the Ticket," *Los Angeles Times*, 6 November 1983.

7. Until the reformations of the 1980s, there were four classes of missions, class 1 being the highest and commanding a higher ambassadorial salary and representational allowance and more lavish housing, official cars, and so on. Today there are no classes, each embassy being allotted the resources necessary to carry out its assigned mission. The only difference is that ambassadors to posts that were class 1 or 2 are paid at the salary of an under secretary, while those to former class 3 or 4 posts are paid at the salary of an assistant secretary.

8. Radcliffe, "Diplomatic Names": "That evening, at a dinner in Armstrong's honor given by the British ambassador to the United States, among the 'top echelon' guests was Clare Boothe Luce, who told the forty guests that 'women have been skilled in diplomacy for thousands of years by you male chauvinist pigs. Women have been taught to listen and an ambassador needs to do that. They've been taught to use gentle words . . . to learn how to get what they want in the interest of their family. Diplomacy is a feminine art.' "

9. Judy Harbough, interview with author, Washington, D.C., 18 May 1988.

10. Mondale had been sworn in as vice president. He went to London after the inauguration, on 27 January 1977. He stayed one night.

11. Judy Harbough says Foreign Minister Anthony Crossland made a point of turning toward Armstrong and publicly praising her in front of Mondale and his staff.

12. Albert Eisele, Mondale's press secretary, is quoted in the *New York Times*, 29 January 1977, as saying the dinner for 31 at the prime minister's official residence "was not quite a working session and was somewhat bacchanalian." The tenor of his remarks was, at the very least, undiplomatic. Harbough says that Armstrong was "specifically and pointedly excluded from the dinner" but later was called by Mondale from his plane and asked to "bail him out" and soothe the hurt British feelings. She said the whole episode was a "mess" and caused an "uproar with the British."

Chapter 9

1. She was Mabel Murphy Smythe during her service as an ambassador.

2. Mabel Murphy Smythe Haith, interviews with author, Washington, D.C., 27 May, 10 and 18 June, 21 and 23 October 1986, and 14 April 1988.

3. The family history can be documented for more than 300 years. Haith has copies of papers from her great-grandfather, including an affidavit certifying he was a free man, that reads: "The genealogy that Andrew Dibble, a free person of color . . . is the son of Mindah, the daughter of Beck who was the daughter of Catherine Cleveland."

Chapter 10

1. Anne Cox Chambers, interviews with author, New York, N.Y., 23 October and 1 November 1985, and Atlanta, Ga., 11 November 1986.

2. Elizabeth (Liz) Carpenter, interview with author, Austin, Tex., 27 October 1989.

3. Tim Towell, Chamber's political officer, who watched all this happening, commented on the insensitivity of the deputy who was so authoritative. His remarks could apply as well to any other careerist who treats a noncareer ambassador with less than total respect: "He just didn't get the political reality of life here. He was a pro, but he didn't understand the basic reality that whatever she looked like, whatever he thought, this is the president's ambassador and that's it. You help your ambassador, you give them advice. There's a way of doing it so it comes out right for the nation." Interview with author, Washington, D.C., 5 June 1986.

4. Ibid.

5. Refers to the controversy over the U.S. proposal to upgrade, reduce in number, and change the disposition of the NATO tactical nuclear weapons. Europeans feared

the proposal represented an American intention to desert them. *New York Times*, 21 February 1977.

6. Amedou Ould Abdallah, interview with author, United Nations, New York, N.Y., 14 April 1987.

Chapter 11

1. Mari-Luci Jaramillo, interview with author, Albuquerque, N.M., 21 February 1987.

2. Clare Boothe Luce, appointed to Brazil in 1959, resigned without serving.

3. Fernando Rondon, interview with author, Washington, D.C., 18 May 1987.

4. [Anonymous, at the FSO's request], interview with author, Department of State, Washington, D.C., 3 June 1986.

5. Ibid.

6. Torres was director of the White House Office of Hispanic Affairs. Valdes was White House chief of protocol.

Chapter 12

1. Nancy Ostrander, interviews with author, Washington, D.C., 14, 21, and 28 May, 11 June, 16 July, 12 August, and 9 September 1986.

2. At Jonestown, Guyana, on 18 November 1978, several hundred members of an American religious cult, mostly U.S. citizens, committed mass suicide at their jungle headquarters. The cult was led by the Rev. Jim Jones.

3. Sergeant Doe led a successful insurrection in Liberia on 12 April 1980, at which time he brutally murdered the senior officials of the deposed regime.

4. On 27 February 1980 a radical group in Bogota seized Ascencio and 80 other guests who were attending a reception at the Dominican embassy. Ascencio was held hostage for two months.

Chapter 13

1. Rozanne Lejeanne Ridgway, interviews with author, Washington, D.C., 18 March, 21 April, 29 May, and 24 June 1987, and 29 June 1989.

2. Theodore Sellin (FSO), interview with author, Washington, D.C., 24 July 1985.

3. Jane Coon (dean of professional studies, Foreign Service Institute), interview with author, Washington, D.C., 5 February 1985.

4. Vest interview.

5. Paul Nitze, speaking on "The MacNeil/Lehrer Newshour," 26 October 1989, WNET, New York.

6. Constance Harvey, telephone interview with author, 8 May 1989.

7. "Honors and Awards," *State* (Department of State newsletter), no. 324 (July 1989): 14.

8. It is ironic that Wilbur J. Carr was a major figure in the attempt in the early 1920s to keep women out of the Foreign Service officer corps. As director of the consular service, he proposed that women be added to the list of those who could not be certified to take the Foreign Service exams. Calkin, *Women*, 70.

9. "Foreign Service Day," *State* (Department of State newsletter), no. 356 (June 1992): 4.

10. Richard Bogosian, telephone interview with author, 10 July 1990.

Chapter 14

1. Melissa Foelsch Wells, interviews with author, Washington, D.C., 17 October 1986, 27 February 1987, and 18 April 1991.

2. Elinor Constable, also an FSO who married, challenged the system in 1958. Constable questioned the legality of being asked to resign, demanding to be shown the written rule. She was right, there was no rule; the entire practice rested only on custom. Constable believes her challenge may have protected Wells from being asked to resign. Although Constable left the service, she had proved there were no legal grounds for the custom. (She worked outside the service, reentered in the 1970s, and rose to become an ambassador and then an assistant secretary.) Elinor Constable, interviews with author, Washington, D.C., 2 April and 3 September 1986.

3. A caucus of developing countries that meets on economic issues.

4. This would be her third time out as AE/P. The only other woman to have had three AE/P tours was Frances Willis.

5. William Finnegan, "A Reporter at Large," *New Yorker* (29 May 1989): 81, 82.

Chapter 15

1. Jane Abell Coon, interviews with author, Washington, D.C., 3 July 1985, 4 November 1986, and 6 and 12 February, 26 March, 9 April, and 9 July 1987.

2. Purdah is the Hindu practice of secluding women.

3. Adolph Dubs, U.S. ambassador to Afghanistan, was seized as a hostage by opposition extremists in February 1979 and held in a hotel room. The government forces, with Soviet advisers, went in to rescue him. Although American embassy officials who were present insisted they hold their fire, they blazed their way in, killing Dubs. The Americans charged that Dubs had been assassinated.

4. Dorothy Robins-Mowry, then a senior USIA official, attended Carleton Coon's swearing-in. She recounted that Jane "rushed in late because she had been up on the Hill testifying for her own ambassadorship. You could just see her face glow, and throughout the whole rest of the proceedings she was really the most supportive, housewifely type. It was interesting to observe this, knowing she had just been up on the Hill for herself." Interview with author, Washington, D.C., 4 June 1986.

5. Moslem rules for female modesty require that women cover their shoulders, back, and upper arms. Because green is the Bangladeshi color, Coon had chosen a white and green cotton dress, with long sleeves and a high neck.

Chapter 16

1. Jeane Duane Jordan Kirkpatrick, interview with author, Washington, D.C., 28 May 1987.

2. "Dictatorships and Double Standards," *Commentary* (November 1979). Kirkpatrick's thesis was that there are two kinds of dictators, authoritarian ones, such as the shah of Iran, with whom the United States could work, and totalitarian ones, such as Castro and the other Communist dictators, with whom it can't. Her political philosophy governed her actions at the UN.

3. Robins-Mowry claimed that Kirkpatrick had hoped to be head of USIA in the new administration. Interview with author, Washington, D.C., 19 February 1987.

4. Linda Fasulo, *Representing America* (New York: Frederick A. Praeger, 1984), 284.

5. Seymour Maxwell Finger, "The Reagan-Kirkpatrick Policies and the United Nations," *Foreign Affairs* (Winter 1983–84): 457.

6. William Sherman (FSO, former deputy representative to the Security Council), interview with author, Washington, D.C., 4 February 1986.

7. Allan Gerson, *The Kirkpatrick Mission* (New York: Free Press, 1991), 14–16. Nicholas Veliotes wrote: "The key factor was intensive negotiations in New York between Amb. Kirkpatrick and Iraqi Foreign Minister Hammadi." Assistant Secretary Veliotes, memo to Under Secretary James Buckley, 20 June 1981.

8. Alexander Haig, Jr., *Caveat* (New York: Macmillan, 1984), 184.

9. *United States Participation in the UN* (Washington, D.C.: U.S. Government Printing Office, 1983), 6.

10. Finger, "Reagan-Kirkpatrick," 453.

11. Sherman interview.

Chapter 17

1. The ten years since the period covered by this book have seen some slow improvement in the role of women. A 1993 book about women's efforts to gain

positions of prominence in the departments of State and Defense offers conclusions based on interviews conducted after 1990 that are nearly identical, so far as the State Department is concerned, to the ones that came out of this study. The authors consider women's progress as "agonizingly" slow and observe that "by no means are women treated equally or equitably at State or are their views given equal hearing." Nancy E. McGlen and Meredith Reid Sarkees, *Women in Foreign Policy* (New York and London: Routledge, 1993), 305.

These opinions must be tempered somewhat, in view of the very recent positive efforts by State management to reduce discriminatory practices against women.

2. Eugenie Anderson, the fourth woman U.S. envoy, was the first to be accompanied by a husband. (The first three were widows.) During her 1949–53 tour, the Danes gave John Anderson the title of "distinguished foreign visitor," which had no real status. Eventually, Eugenie Anderson complained, and the Danes accorded him the rank of minister for protocol purposes. Jan Musty and Lila Johnson, "Oral History of Eugenie Anderson," Minnesota Historical Society, St. Paul, Minn.

Patricia Harris insisted on a formal ruling from the Department of State protocol office. Eventually word came that the U.S. position was that the husband would take the rank of the wife, but that the host country must make its own decision. This is known informally as the "Harris ruling." Steve Goodell, "Oral History of Patricia Harris," Lyndon B. Johnson Library, Austin, Tex.

3. Vest interview.

4. Durbrow interview.

5. Sherman interview.

6. Walt Rostow (special assistant to Presidents Kennedy and Johnson), interview with author, Austin, Tex., 26 October 1989.

7. Durbrow did not believe she used her femininity overtly in Rome but said it would have been difficult for a gallant Italian to say no to a beautiful woman. Durbrow interview.

8. Robins-Mowry, interview, 4 June 1986.

9. Stephanie Kinney (FSO), interview with author, Washington, D.C., 24 June 1986.

10. Donna Gigliotti (director general's office, Department of State), telephone interview with author, 11 August 1993.

11. In 1993, 23 of 70 (32.8 percent) officers promoted from FS-01 to officer counselor (FE-OC) were women; 8 of 24 (33 percent) promoted from FE-OC to minister counselor (FE-MC) were women; one man only was promoted from FE-MC to career minister FE-CM); and no one was nominated for the rank of career ambassador (FE-CA). "1993 Nominations for Promotion within and into the Senior Foreign Service Schedule" State (Department of State newsletter) special bulletin (September 1993).

12. Calkin, *Women*, 127.

13. Bureau of Personnel library, Department of State, 20 August 1993.

14. Women Foreign Service officers accuse State of violating antidiscrimination rulings of 1989. "Clippings," *Foreign Service Journal* (August 1993): 7.

15. "Message on Foreign Service Personnel Reform from Under Secretary Moose" (department notice) (Washington, D.C.: Department of State, 23 December 1993), 5.

Selected Bibliography

Books

Acheson, Dean. *Present at the Creation*. New York: W. W. Norton, 1969.

Adams, Sherman. *Firsthand Report*. New York: Popular Library, 1962.

Alsop, Susan Mary. *Yankees at the Court: The First Americans in Paris*. Garden City, N.Y.: Doubleday, 1982.

———. *The Congress Dances: Vienna 1814–1815*. New York: Simon & Schuster/ Pocket Books, 1985.

American Assembly. *The Representation of the United States Abroad*. Final Report of the Ninth American Assembly. New York: American Assembly, Columbia University, 1956.

Arkhurst, Frederick S., ed. *U.S. Policy toward Africa*. New York: Frederick A. Praeger, 1975.

Bacchus, William I. *Staffing for Foreign Affairs*. Princeton: Princeton University Press, 1983.

Baldrige, Letitia. *Roman Candle*. Boston: Houghton Mifflin, 1956.

———. *Of Diamonds and Diplomacy*. New York: Ballantine, 1968.

Ball, George W. *Diplomacy for a Crowded World*. Boston: Little, Brown, 1976.

———. *The Past Has Another Pattern*. New York: W. W. Norton, 1982.

Barber, James David, and Barbara Kellerman, eds. *Women Leaders in American Politics*. Englewood Cliffs, N.J.: Prentice-Hall, 1986.

Barnes, William, and John Heath Morgan. *The Foreign Service of the United States*. Washington, D.C.: Department of State, 1961.

Bernstein, Carl, and Bob Woodward. *All the President's Men*. New York: Simon & Schuster, 1974.

Binnendijk, Hans, ed. *National Negotiating Styles*. Washington, D.C.: Foreign Service Institute, Department of State, 1987.

Biswas, Jayasred. *U.S.-Bangladesh Relations*. Calcutta: Minerva Associates, 1984.

Boothe, Clare. *Europe in the Spring*. New York: Alfred A. Knopf, 1940.

Bowles, Chester. *Ambassador's Report*. New York: Harper & Brothers, 1954.

Briggs, Ellis. *Anatomy of Diplomacy*. New York: David McKay, 1968.

Brinkley, David. *Washington Goes to War*. New York: Alfred A. Knopf, 1988.

Brownmiller, Susan. *Femininity*. New York: Fawcett Colombine, 1984.

Brownstein, Ronald, and Nina Easton. *Reagan's Ruling Class*. Washington, D.C.: Presidential Accountability Group, 1982.

Buckley, William F., Jr. *United Nations Journey: A Delegate's Odyssey*. Garden City, N.Y.: Anchor, 1979.

Busk, Sir Douglas. *The Craft of Diplomacy*. New York: Frederick A. Praeger, 1967.

Cable, Mary. *Top Drawer: American High Society from the Gilded Age to the Roaring Twenties*. New York: Atheneum, 1984.

Calkins, Homer L. *Women in the Department of State: Their Role in American Foreign Affairs*. Washington, D.C.: Department of State, 1978.

Campbell, John Franklin. *The Foreign Affairs Fudge Factory*. New York: Basic Books, 1971.

Casdorph, Paul D. *Let the Good Times Roll*. New York: Paragon House, 1989.

Chamberlin, Hope. *A Minority of Members: Women in the U.S. Congress*. New York: Frederick A. Praeger, 1973.

Childs, Marquis. *Witness to Power*. New York: McGraw-Hill, 1975.

Colby, William. *Honorable Men: My Life in the CIA*. New York: Simon & Schuster, 1978.

Cole, Taylor, ed. *European Political Systems*. 2d ed., rev. New York: Alfred A. Knopf, 1961.

Crapol, Edward P., ed. *Women and American Foreign Policy*. Westport, Conn.: Greenwood Press, 1987.

Dash, Samuel. *Chief Counsel*. New York: Random House, 1976.

Diebel, Terry L. *Presidents, Public Opinion, and Power*. Headline Series No. 280. New York: Foreign Policy Association, 1987.

Edwards, India. *Pulling No Punches: Memoirs of a Woman in Politics*. New York: G. L. Putnam, 1977.

Eisenhower, Dwight D. *Mandate for Change 1953–1956*. New York: Signet, 1965.

Elder, Robert E. *Overseas Representation and Service for Federal Domestic Agencies*. Foreign Affairs Personnel Study, vol. 2. Washington, D.C.: Carnegie Endowment for International Peace, 1965.

Elson, Robert T. *The World of Time, Inc.* New York: Signet, 1965.

Essai, Brian. *Papua and New Guinea*. Melbourne, Aust.: Oxford Press, 1961.

Fasulo, Linda M. *Representing America: Experiences of U.S. Diplomats at the UN*. New York: Frederick A. Praeger, 1984.

Fausto-Sterling, Anne. *Myths of Gender*. New York: Basic Books, 1985.

Finger, Seymour Maxwell. *American Ambassadors at the UN*. New York: Holmes & Meier, 1988.

Finnegan, William. *A Complicated War: The Harrowing of Mozambique*. Berkeley and Los Angeles: University of California Press, 1993.

Foster, John W. *A Century of American Diplomacy*. Boston: Houghton Mifflin, 1900.

Fried, Richard M. *Nightmare in Red*. New York: Oxford University Press, 1990.

Friedan, Betty. *The Feminine Mystique*. Twentieth anniversary edition. New York: Dell, 1983.

Galbraith, Evan. *Ambassador in Paris: The Reagan Years*. Washington, D.C.: Regnery Books, 1987.

Galbraith, Kenneth. *Ambassador's Journal*. Boston: Houghton Mifflin, 1969.

Gerson, Allan. *The Kirkpatrick Mission*. New York: Free Press, 1991.

Goldman, Eric F. *The Crucial Decade*. New York: Random House, Vintage, 1960.

———. *The Tragedy of Lyndon Johnson*. New York: Dell/Laurel, 1974.

Green, Constance McLaughlin. *Washington: Capital City, 1879–1950*. Princeton: Princeton University Press, 1963.

Gunther, John. *Inside Europe Today*. New York: Harper, 1961.

Haig, Alexander M., Jr. *Caveat: Realism, Reagan, and Foreign Policy*. New York: Macmillan, 1984.

Hamilton, Lord Frederic. *The Vanished Pomps of Yesterday*. Garden City, N.Y.: Doubleday/Doran, 1934.

Harr, John E. *The Anatomy of the Foreign Service: A Statistical Profile*. Foreign Affairs Personnel Study, vol. 4. Washington, D.C.: Carnegie Endowment for International Peace, 1965.

———. *The Development of Careers in the Foreign Service*. Foreign Affairs Personnel Study, vol. 3. Washington, D.C.: Carnegie Endowment for International Peace, 1965.

Harriman, Mrs. J. Borden (Florence Jaffrey). *From Pinafores to Politics*. New York: Henry Holt, 1923.

Harriman, Florence Jaffray (Mrs. J. Borden). *Mission to the North*. Philadelphia: J. B. Lippincott, 1941.

Hartman, Robert. *Palace Politics: An Insider's Account of the Ford Years*. New York: McGraw-Hill, 1980.

Hastings, Peter. *New Guinea: Problems and Prospects*. Port Moresby, Papua New Guinea: Cheshire Publishing, 1973.

Hatch, Alden. *Ambassador Extraordinary: Clare Boothe Luce*. New York: Holt, Rinehart, 1966.

Haugen, Barbara, ed. *Women: A Documentary of Progress during the Administration of Jimmy Carter (1977–1981)*. Washington, D.C.: White House, 1981.

Heald, Tim. *Old Boy Network*. New York: Ticknor & Field, 1984.

Hersh, Seymour M. *The Price of Power: Kissinger in the Nixon White House*. New York: Summit Books, 1983.

Herz, Martin F., ed. *Consular Dimensions of Diplomacy*. Lanham, Md.: University Press of America, 1982.

————. *The Modern Ambassador: The Challenge and the Search*. Washington, D.C.: Institute for the Study of Diplomacy, Georgetown University, 1983.

————. *215 Days in the Life of an American Ambassador*. Washington, D.C.: School of Foreign Service, Georgetown University, 1981.

Hughes, Emmet John. *Ordeal of Power*. New York: Dell, 1964.

Hughes, H. Stuart. *The United States and Italy*. Rev. ed. Cambridge: Harvard University Press, 1965.

Hymowitz, Carol, and Michaele Weisman. *A History of Women in America*. New York: Bantam, 1978.

Isaacson, Walter, and Evan Thomas. *The Wise Men*. New York: Simon & Schuster/ Touchstone, 1988.

Jaworski, Leon. *The Right and the Power: The Prosecution of Watergate*. New York: Simon & Schuster/Pocket, 1977.

Johnson, Haynes. *Sleepwalking through History*. New York: Doubleday/Anchor, 1992.

————. *In the Absence of Power*. New York: Viking Press, 1980.

Johnson, Paul. *Modern Society*. New York: Harper & Row/Colophone, 1985.

Jones, Arthur G. *The Evaluation of Personnel Systems for U.S. Foreign Affairs*. Foreign Affairs Personnel Study, vol. 1. Washington, D.C.: Carnegie Endowment for International Peace, 1965.

Kagan, Norman. *Political History of Post-War Italy*. New York: Frederick A. Praeger, 1966.

Kaplan, Robert D. *The Arabists: The Romance of an American Elite*. New York: Macmillan, 1993.

Kennan, George F. *American Diplomacy, 1900–1950*. Chicago: University of Chicago Press, 1951.

————. *Memoirs 1925–1950*. New York: Bantam, 1967.

————. *Memoirs 1950–1963*. New York: Pantheon Books, 1972.

Kirkpatrick, Jeane J. *Dictatorships and Double Standards*. New York: Simon & Schuster, 1982.

————, ed. *Political Women*. New York: Basic Books, 1974.

Kobler, John. *Luce: His Time, Life, and Fortune*. Garden City, N.Y.: Doubleday, 1968.

Krock, Arthur. *Memoirs*. New York: Popular Library, 1968.

Lamb, David. *The Africans*. New York: Vintage Books, 1987.

Latham, Earl. *The Communist Controversy in Washington*. New York: Atheneum, 1969.

Lenz, Elinor, and Barbara Myerhoff. *The Femininization of America*. Los Angeles: Jeremy P. Tarcher, 1985.

Mak, Dayton, and Charles Stuart Kennedy. *American Ambassadors in a Troubled World: Interviews with Senior Diplomats*. Westport, Conn.: Greenwood Press, 1992.

Manchester, William. *The Glory and the Dream*. Boston: Little, Brown, 1974.

Mandelbaum, Michael, and Strobe Talbot. *Reagan and Gorbachev*. New York: Random House/Vintage, 1987.

Mankiewicz, Frank. *United States v. Richard M. Nixon: The Final Crisis*. New York: Ballantine, 1975.

Martin, Judith. *Common Courtesy: In Which Miss Manners Solves the Problem That Baffled Mr. Jefferson*. New York: Atheneum, 1985.

Mattox, Henry E. *Twilight of Amateur Diplomacy*. Kent, Ohio: Kent State University Press, 1989.

McCamy, James L. *Conduct of the New Diplomacy*. New York: Harper & Row, 1964.

———. *The Administration of American Foreign Affairs*. New York: Alfred A. Knopf, 1950.

McCulloch, David. *Truman*. New York: Simon & Schuster, 1992.

McGhee, George C., ed. *Diplomacy for the Future*. Lanham, Md.: University Press of America, 1987.

McGlen, Nancy E., and Meredith Reid Sarkees. *Women in Foreign Policy*. New York: Routledge, 1993.

Michaels, Marguerite. *Showing the Flag: A Report from Inside a U.S. Embassy*. New York: Simon & Schuster, 1982.

Miller, Merle. *Lyndon: An Oral Biography*. New York: Ballantine, 1980.

Morgan, William D., and Charles Stuart Kennedy. *The U.S. Consul at Work*. Westport, Conn.: Greenwood Press, 1991.

Moynihan, Daniel Patrick. *A Dangerous Place*. Boston: Little, Brown, 1975–78.

Murphy, Robert. *Diplomat among Warriors*. 1964. Reprint. New York: Pyramid Books, 1965.

Myers, Isabel Briggs, and Peter B. Myers. *Gifts Differing*. Palo Alto, Calif.: Consulting Psychologists Press, 1980.

Nash, Gerald D. *The Great Depression and World War II*. New York: St. Martin's Press, 1979.

Neustadt, Richard E. *Presidential Power*. New York: New American Library/Signet, 1964.

Newsom, David D. *Diplomacy and the American Democracy*. Bloomington: Indiana University Press, 1988.

Nicolson, Sir Harold. *The Evolution of Diplomacy*. New York: Collier Books, 1954.

———. *Diplomacy*. 3d ed. London: Oxford University Press, 1962.

Olmsted, Mary, et al., eds. *Women at State: An Inquiry into the Status of Women in the United States Department of State*. Washington, D.C.: Women's Research and Education Institute, 1984.

Plischke, Elmer. *Conduct of American Diplomacy*. 2d ed. Princeton, N.J.: D. Van Nostrand, 1961.

Raymond, John, ed. *Queen Victoria's Early Letters*. Rev. ed. New York: Macmillan, 1963.

Rector, Robert, and Michael Sanera, eds. *Steering the Elephant*. New York: Universe Books, 1987.

Reedy, George. *The Twilight of the Presidency*. New York: New American Library/Mentor, 1971.

Reston, James. *Deadline*. New York: Random House, 1991.

Rostow, W. W. *The United States in the World Arena*. New York: Harper & Brothers, 1960.

———. *View from the Seventh Floor*. New York: Harper & Row, 1969.

Rubin, Barry. *Secrets of State*. New York: Oxford University Press, 1985.

Rusk, Dean. *As I Saw It*. New York: Penguin Books, 1990.

Sanford, Linda Tschirhart, and Mary Ellen Donovan. *Women and Self-Esteem*. New York: Penguin Books, 1984.

Schoenbaum, Thomas J. *Waging Peace and War*. New York: Simon & Schuster, 1988.

Schoenbrun, David. *Triumph in Paris: The Exploits of Benjamin Franklin*. New York: Harper & Row, 1976.

Schulz, Donald E., and Douglas H. Graham, eds. *Revolution and Counterrevolution in Central America and the Caribbean*. Boulder, Colo.: Westview Press, 1984.

Schulzinger, Robert E. *The Making of the Diplomatic Mind*. Middletown, Conn: Wesleyan University Press, 1975.

Shadegg, Stephen. *Clare Boothe Luce*. New York: Simon & Schuster, 1970.

Sheed, Wilfred. *Clare Boothe Luce*. New York: E. P. Dutton, 1982.

Sherwood, Robert E. *Roosevelt and Hopkins*. Vols. 1 and 2. 1948. Reprint. New York: Bantam Books, 1950.

Shultz, George P. *Turmoil and Triumph: My Years as Secretary of State*. New York: Charles Scribner's Sons, 1993.

Simpson, Colin. *Katmandu*. New Delhi: Vikas Publishing, 1976.

Simpson, Smith. *Anatomy of the State Department*. Boston: Beacon Press, 1967.

Smith, A. Robert. *The Tiger in the Senate: A Biography of Senator Wayne Morse*. Garden City, N.Y.: Doubleday, 1962.

Spaulding, E. Wilder. *Ambassadors Ordinary and Extraordinary*. Washington, D.C.: Public Affairs Press, 1961.

Speakes, Larry, with Robert Pack. *Speaking Out*. New York: Charles Scribner's Sons, 1988.

Steigman, Andrew L. *The Foreign Service of the United States: First Line of Defense.* Boulder, Colo.: Westview Press, 1985.

Stineman, Esther. *American Political Women.* Littleton, Colo.: Libraries Unlimited, 1980.

Stone, I. F. *In a Time of Torment.* New York: Random House, 1967.

———. *Polemics and Prophecies, 1967–1970.* New York: Vintage, 1972.

Sullivan, Mark. *Our Times: The Turn of the Century.* New York: Charles Scribner, 1926.

Sulzberger, C. L. *A Long Row of Candles.* Toronto: Macmillan, 1969.

Susman, Warren I. *Culture and History: The Transformation of American Society in the Twentieth Century.* New York: Pantheon Books, 1984.

Swanberg, W. A. *Luce and His Empire.* New York: Dell, 1972.

Symington, James W. *The Stately Game.* New York: Macmillan, 1971.

Thayer, Charles W. *Diplomat.* New York: Harper & Brothers, 1959.

Thompson, Margery, ed. *As Others See Us: United States Diplomacy Viewed from Abroad.* Washington, D.C.: Institute for the Study of Diplomacy, Georgetown University, 1987.

Toqueville, Alexis de. *Democracy in America.* Phillips Bradley ed., vol 2. New York: Vintage Books, 1945.

Trevelyan, Humphrey. *Diplomatic Channels.* Boston: Gambit, 1973.

Truman, Harry S. *Years of Trial and Hope 1946–1952.* New York: Signet, 1956.

United Nations. *Basic Facts about the United Nations.* New York: United Nations Publications, 1987.

U.S. Congress. House of Representatives. Subcommittee on International Operations, Committee on Foreign Affairs. *Investigation of the U.S. Ambassador to Switzerland.* 100th Cong. 1st sess. 1987.

U.S. Department of State. *The Ambassador and the Problems of Coordination.* Prepared by the Historical Office for the Subcommittee on National Security, Staffing, and Operations of the Senate Government Operations Committee. Washington, D.C.: U.S. Government Printing Office, 13 September 1963.

———. *Diplomatic Social Usage.* Washington, D.C.: Foreign Service Institute, 1984.

———. *Foreign Relations of the United States, 1952–1954.* Vol. 8, section on *Trieste.*

———. *The Foreign Service Act of 1946* Public law 79–724, as amended to December 1968. Washington, D.C.: Department of State, 1968.

———. *The Foreign Service Act of 1980* Public law 95–4657, as amended to June 1984. Washington, D.C.: Department of State, 1984.

———. *Message on Foreign Service Personnel from Under Secretary Moose.* Department notice (office of origin: M), 23 December 1993. Washington, D.C.: Department of State, 1993.

———. *Principal Officers of the Department of State and United States Chiefs of Mission, 1778–1986.* Washington, D.C.: Department of State, c. 1987.

———. *"This Worked for Me . . .": Mission Chiefs Pool Useful Ideas and Techniques.* Washington, D.C.: Department of State, 1964.

———. *United States Participation in the UN.* Report by the President to the Congress for the Year 1981. Department of State Publication no. 9340. Washington, D.C.: Department of State, 1983.

Von Damm, Helene. *At Reagan's Side.* New York: Doubleday, 1989.

Von Hoffman, Nicholas. *Citizen Cohn.* New York: Bantam, 1988.

Washington Post, Staff of the. *The Fall of a President.* New York: Dell, 1974.

White, Theodore H. *In Search of History.* New York: Harper & Row, 1978.

———. *The Making of the President 1968.* New York: Simon & Schuster/Pocket, 1970.

Wicker, Tom. *JFK and LBJ: Influence of Personality upon Politics.* New York: William Morrow, 1968.

Willis, David K. *The State Department.* Boston: Christian Science Publishing Society, 1968.

Wilson, George Grafton. *Handbook of International Law.* 3d ed. St. Paul, Minn.: West Publishing, 1939.

Winks, Robin W. *Cloak and Gown: Scholars in the Secret War 1939–1961.* New York: William Morrow, 1987.

Articles

Acheson, Dean. "The Eclipse of the State Department." *Foreign Affairs* 49, no. 4 (1971): 593–606.

Bell, Coral. "From Carter to Reagan." *Foreign Affairs* 63, no. 3 (1985): 490–510.

Bernier, Rosamond. "A Very Special Eye." *House and Garden* (April 1986): 127–32, 232–36.

Eyre, David W. "Clare, The Honolulu Years." *Honolulu* (December 1987): 80–83, 122–28.

Finger, Seymour Maxwell. "Jeane Kirkpatrick at the United Nations." *Foreign Affairs* 62, no. 2 (1983): 436–57.

Finnegan, William. "A Reporter at Large, The Emergency—II." *New Yorker* (29 May 1989): 69–96.

Furgurson, Ernest B. "Ambassador Helms." *Common Cause* (March-April 1987): 16–21.

Gelb, Leslie H., and Anthony Lake. "Four More Years: Diplomacy Restored?" *Foreign Affairs* 63, no. 3 (1985): 465–89.

Geyelin, Philip. "Reagan Crisis: Dreaming Impossible Dreams." *Foreign Affairs* 65, no. 3 (1987): 447–57.

Herzog, Chaim. "UN at Work: The Benin Affair." *Foreign Policy* 29 (Winter 1977–78): 140–59.

Hoffman, Stanley. "The Hell of Good Intentions." *Foreign Policy* 29 (Winter 1977–78): 3–26.

Hyland, William G., Jr. "Reagan-Gorbachev III." *Foreign Affairs* 66, no. 1 (1987): 7–21.

Johansen, Robert C. "The Reagan Administration and the UN: The Costs of Unilateralism." *World Policy Journal* 3, no. 4 (1986): 601–39.

Johnson, U. Alexis. "Caught in the Nutcracker." *Foreign Service Journal* (September 1984): 28–36.

Kennan, George F. "Morality and Foreign Policy." *Foreign Affairs* 64, no. 2 (1985): 205–18.

Kirkpatrick, Jeane J. "Anti-Communist Insurgency and American Policy." *National Interest* 1 (1985): 91–96.

Lazear, Edward P., et al. "Women in the Labor Market." Symposium. *Journal of Economic Perspectives* 3, no. 1 (Winter 1989): 3–75.

Luce, Clare Boothe. "Politics into Religion and Vice Versa." Excerpted transcription of address to National Press Club, Washington, D.C., 24 October 1984. *Human Life Review* 11, nos. 1 and 2 (Winter-Spring 1985): 190–96.

Morris, Sylvia Jukes. "In Search of Clare Boothe Luce." *New York Times Magazine* (31 January 1988): 23–27, 33.

Pringle, Robert. "Creeping Irrelevance at Foggy Bottom." *Foreign Policy* 29 (Winter 1977–78): 128–39.

Purcell, Susan Kaufman. "War and Debt." *Foreign Affairs* 61, no. 3 (1983): 660–74.

Riding, Alan. "The Central American Quagmire." *Foreign Affairs* 61, no. 3 (1983): 641–59.

Rubin, Barry. "Constant and Changing." *Foreign Service Journal* (November 1984): 26–31.

Schlesinger, Arthur, Jr. "Foreign Policy and the American Character." *Foreign Affairs* 62, no. 1 (1983): 1–16.

Schlesinger, James. "Reykjavik and Revelations: A Turn of the Tide?" *Foreign Affairs* 65, no. 3 (1986): 426–46.

Silberman, Laurence H. "Toward Presidential Control of the State Department." *Foreign Affairs* 57, no. 4 (1979): 872–93.

Yost, Charles W. "The Instrument of American Foreign Policy." *Foreign Affairs* 50, no. 1 (1971): 59–68.

Archives

Washington Post, New York Times, Foreign Service Journal (1983–93), and *State* (1983–93) files.

Relevant National Archives files

Files at the Franklin D. Roosevelt, Harry S. Truman, Dwight D. Eisenhower, Lyndon B. Johnson, and Gerald R. Ford presidential libraries. (Richard M. Nixon's papers were at a repository in Alexandria, Virginia).

U.S. Department of State documents obtained under the Freedom of Information Act: selected cables and other diplomatic correspondence between the department and Central and West African embassies (April-May 1976), Paramaribo, Suriname (February-March 1980), Rome, Italy (September 1953–February 1954), and embassies in Honduras and El Salvador (1969).

Miscellaneous

Alison Palmer et al. v. George P. Shultz. Proceedings. Civil action no. 76–1439. U.S. District Court for the District of Columbia.

Goodell, Steve. Oral History of Patricia Roberts Harris, 19 May 1969. Johnson Library Archives, Austin, Tex.

Joyce, Jean. "Oral History of Mary Olmsted." 1974. Women's Action Organization Series. Cambridge, Mass.: Schlesinger Library, Radcliffe College.

Kirkpatrick, Jeane J. Interview on "Meet the Press." Verbatim text. Department of State cable to secretary, 6 June 1982.

———. Interview on "This Week with David Brinkley." 22 February 1987.

Musty, Jan and Lila Johnson. "Oral History of Eugenie Anderson." 1971. St. Paul: Minnesota Historical Society.

Nitze, Paul. "Conversation: Paul Nitze." "Macneil/Lehrer Newshour," 26 October 1989. Transcript, Overland Park, Kans.: Strictly Business.

Olmsted, Mary. "To Open a Post." Unpublished manuscript in author's possession.

Ridgway, Rozanne. Interview on "This Week with David Brinkley." 17 September 1987.

Sargeant, Hélène K. "Oral History of Margaret Tibbetts." 1982. Women in Federal Government Series. Cambridge, Mass.: Schlesinger Library, Radcliffe College.

Wells, Melissa. Featured in PBS documentary "Profiles in Diplomacy," 17 April 1991.

Index

Entries describing career history are ordered chronologically and appear in italics. Photographs appear in bold. Entries in which the last name of interviewees are capitalized (as in OSTRANDER, Nancy) refer to their testimony; lower case references (as in Ostrander, Nancy) refer to instances in which others mention the individual.

305

Australia, 92, 102; high commissioner, 103

Baker, James, 209, 210
Baldridge, Letitia (Tish), 43
Bangladesh: floods, 241; Moslem dress codes, 292n8; unstable political situation, 239, 241
Barnes, Harry G., Jr., 70
Basel, Switzerland, 20, 26
Beagle Channel, 258, 259
Beaudoin, King of Belgium, 140, 147
Belgium: American companies, 145; language issues, 53; male chauvinism, 143
Bell, Griffin, 138
Bennett, Tapley, 140, 142–43
Bern, Switzerland, 18, 20, 23
Bhutto, Zulficar Ali, 237
Biden, Sen. Joseph, 206
Biographic Register, 18
Blair, Margaretta, 135
Board of Examiners, 92
Bonn, Germany, 27
Bougainville, Solomon Islands: Secessionist movement, 101–2
Bracken, Katherine, **48**
Brazil, 41, 42
Bruce, Evangeline, 111
Bunker, Carol Laise. *See* Laise, Caroline Clendening
Bunker, Ellsworth, 33, 61, 66, 70, 267
Bunker Mrs. Ellsworth. *See* Bunker, Harriet, and Laise, Caroline Clendening
Bunker, Harriet, 66
Burke, John, 184
Burt, Richard, 206
Bush, George, 209
Butz, Earl L., 113

Cabot, John, 42, 285n7
Callaghan, James, 117
Cameroon, 128; AID farm training centers, 128–29; importance of UN vote to U.S., 130–31
Cape Verde: association with New England whaling fleets, 212
Career/non-career: definition of, 4
Carnegie Peace foundation, 38
Carpenter, Elizabeth (Liz), 141
Carr, Wilbur J., 291n8; Wilbur J. Carr Award, 210
Carrington, Peter, 258

Carter, Amy, 138
Carter, Chip, 138
Carter Jimmy, 4, 117, 137, 138, 139, 143, 144, 145, 148, 151, 161, 196, 266
Carter, Rosalynn, 138
Cassidy, Tom, 25, 26
Castro, Melgar, 160
Chambers, Anne Cox, 4, **149**, 265, 266, 267, 268; and Belgian male chauvinism, 143; praise for, 146, 148
CHAMBERS, Anne Cox: *background and education, 135–36; father's influence on, 137; marriage of and life as young matron, 136–37; membership on boards, 137; second marriage, 137; working for gubernatorial candidate Jimmy Carter, 138; the Carters as neighbors, 138; campaigning for Carter for president, 138; nominated ambassador to Belgium, 139; ambassadors' course, 139; objection by AFSA to nomination, 139; antagonism of FSOs, 140; advice of Dean Rusk, 140; advantage of shooting ability as a plus, 141; renovating residence, 141–42; problems with DCM on arrival, 142–43; visit of king and queen to U.S., 143–44; missile problem, 144; King Baudoin's approval of Carter's policies, 144; working with American business community, 144–45; friendships with Belgian officials, 145; faux pas over Carter's greeting, 145–46; cordial relations with Chinese ambassador, 147; landing rights for SABENA, 147; receives Ordre de la Couronne, 148; on respect for Foreign Service people, 146; on rewards of being an ambassador, 148*
Chambers, Robert, 137
Chambers, Whittaker, 285n4
Chancery: definition of, 11
China, 50; incursions into India, 67
CHISLU (Italian Christian labor union), 38
Christopher, Warren, 155–56
Churchill, Winston S., 37
CIA, 25, 37, 101, 185
Clark, William, 202, 203
Cleveland, Grover, 7
Clinton, Hillary Rodham, 275
Clinton, William, 275
Cohn, Roy, 57
Commerce, Department of, 52, 90
Committee on Foreign Relations, U.S. Senate, 6

The Author

Ann Miller Morin, a writer and lecturer now living in Maryland, has been at work on this oral history project since 1984. Her expertise in the field of diplomatic life stems from her own experiences. During her husband's 31 years as a Foreign Service officer, she and her family lived in the Far East, Africa, Europe, and the Near East. A professional educator, her career was determined by her husband's assignments and included teaching in five countries. She was principal of the American schools in Baghdad and Algiers.

This is her second major study related to the U.S. Foreign Service. The first, a master's thesis, explored the social and educational problems of Foreign Service children.